True Education Reader

Book Seven

TRUE EDUCATION READER SERIES

BOOK SEVEN

BY

MARION ERNEST CADY

So they read in the Book in the law of God distinctly, and gave the sense, and caused them to understand the reading.—*Bible.*

Second Edition
(*Revised*)

www.TEACHServices.com • (800) 367-1844

World rights reserved. This book or any portion thereof may not be copied or reproduced in any form or manner whatever, except as provided by law, without the written permission of the publisher, except by a reviewer who may quote brief passages in a review.

The author assumes full responsibility for the accuracy of all facts and quotations as cited in this book. The opinions expressed in this book are the author's personal views and interpretations, and do not necessarily reflect those of the publisher.

This book is provided with the understanding that the publisher is not engaged in giving spiritual, legal, medical, or other professional advice. If authoritative advice is needed, the reader should seek the counsel of a competent professional.

Copyright © 2015 TEACH Services, Inc.
ISBN-13: 978-1-57258-350-4 (Paperback)
Library of Congress Control Number: 2005928403

PREFACE

The "True Education Reader Series" consists of seven books designed for use in the corresponding first seven grades, or years, of school work. Book Seven will also be found suitable for advanced reading in intermediate and higher schools.

These books have been prepared in response to an earnest request of many teachers for a complete series of school readers entirely free from myths, fairy tales, and all that tends to undermine faith in the sacred Word, and to unfit the pupil for the highest service. Educators and thinking people generally recognize the alarming tendency in the world to-day toward a lack of faith in God and His Word. This is but the natural result of much of the teaching of the present age. Many school readers abound with that which is false and unreal, and this can not but unfit the mind to meet the realities of life or to appreciate sober truth. To help stem this tide toward the artificial and the skeptical, the subject-matter in the True Education Readers is drawn entirely from the true and beautiful in life, in nature, and in revelation. The authors have recognized that "truth is stranger than fiction," fact more wonderful than fancy, and that the imagination of the child can therefore be best aroused, interested, and developed in the realm of truth and fact.

Those who have the highest appreciation of language regard the Bible as the great fountain head of all that is pure, and true, and beautiful, and for this reason many choice selections have been taken from this Book. A variety of other reading is provided in the form of poetry, nature lessons, biography, etc., which will familiarize the pupil with the various styles of composition, and afford drill in the various modes of expression. Special attention is called to the selections embodying lessons of morality, and manners—a phase of education too much neglected. It is sincerely believed that these lessons will be found helpful in the development of right character. In the preparation and selection of articles, care has been exercised that both in thought and in language the reading should keep pace with the developing powers of the child's mind, and that they should be of such a nature as to create and foster a taste for the best in literature.

A special feature of Books One to Six of this series is that they provide in a simple and natural way all the work in English needed for the first six grades, except the supplementary reading. It is an undisputed fact that English is the most important yet the most neglected branch of learning, or at least the one most inefficiently taught. To read and speak and write and spell the English language correctly is a rare accomplishment. And no wonder. When, as is often the case, the study of language or grammar is separated from language itself, or at the best is based upon a study of disconnected sentences or paragraphs, many pupils find it scarcely more than the study of an almost meaningless list of rules, definitions, and technicalities, a task in which they take little interest, for which they see no reason, and from which they derive little if any benefit. When, however, the subject is presented in connection with an interesting reading lesson, attention being given to the expression and the meaning of thought, it becomes to the pupil a vital thing, full of interest and value, for he learns the language, together with such technicalities as are necessary, as he needs to *know* and *use* it.

The study of closely related subjects,—such as reading, language, composition, and spelling,—in their natural setting, tends to reduce the confusion produced in the mind of the pupil by a large number of separate subjects pursued independently of one another, and insures more efficient work. This truth is recognized by the authors of Baker and Carpenter's Readers, and in the preface of these readers it has been well expressed in the following words:—

"The plan of teaching English that gives the pupil *the habit of observing* the facts of language *as he reads,* must be the best guarantee of his permanent hold upon it and his continued growth in it. This idea, indeed, is not new. Books upon composition draw largely upon literature for their exercises, and reading books introduce—though timidly and incompletely—lessons in the study of language."

The True Education Readers make the relation of reading, spelling, language, and composition close and vital, and are a working out of the idea toward which both readers and language books have been tending during the past decade or more.

Not only is the unifying of certain related lines of study a means of facilitating and strengthening the progress of the pupil, but it is a solution of the problem of how to simplify the overcrowded curriculum. It is an economy of time, energy, and money.

In choosing the selections for Book Seven the following tests have been applied:

1. Does the selection present only clean, wholesome instruction?
2. Does it have proper diction?
3. Is it properly graded?
4. Is it entertaining as well as instructive, so that it will create a taste for the good in literature?

The varied character of the selections chosen for Book Seven gives the pupil a broad view of the field of knowledge, and provides a high standard which it is believed will aid him in determining what is profitable reading.

In the first six books of this series the pupil has had much drill in the formation and use of words, in expression, accentuation, emphasis, and articulation. He has also had carefully graded lessons in language and composition. In Book Seven no special effort is made to continue the lessons in composition, as, at this stage, the pupil is expected to use separate text-books in grammar and composition. Special attention is given to developing the power of good expression. To this end, lessons on expression are distributed throughout the reader, and with these are given abundant examples for practice which illustrate the principles presented. The power of good expression can not be acquired without a thorough knowledge and mastery of the organs of voice, and of the sound elements entering into the structure of the English language. The lessons on expression are therefore preceded by instruction in Vocal Physiology, Vocal Articulation, Vocal Symbols, and Vocal Pronunciation.

Students using this book are of sufficient age and education to have an introduction to the study of the elementary principles in rhetoric and literature. Accordingly, a few lessons are given in Figures of Speech. The student is required to point out and classify these figures as they occur in the reading lessons; also to explain their use and value in the connection in which they are used.

For much of the material on Vocalization, the author is indebted to Row, Peterson and Co., of Wabash Ave., Chicago, Ill., for valuable matter taken from Salisbury's "Phonology and Orthoepy," also to Mrs. E. G. White for permission to use extracts from her writings. The poems by J. G. Whittier and H. W. Longfellow are used by permission of, and by special arrangement with, Houghton, Mifflin, and Co., publishers of their works. The poems by Bryant are used by permission of D. Appleton and Co. "The Bells," by E. A. Poe, is used by permission of Thomas Y. Crowell and Co.

The lessons on Figures of Speech are adapted from William's "Composition and Rhetoric" published by D. C. Heath and Company.

M. E. CADY.

College Place, Washington, Jan. 1, 1908.

SUGGESTIONS TO THE TEACHER

"Give attendance to reading."

In perhaps no other subject is the student generally so deficient as in reading and the closely related subject, spelling. A thorough knowledge of these subjects places him on vantage ground in his pursuit of knowledge. Through them he has power, not only to acquire knowledge, but to impart to others what he has gained.

The following are a few of the suggestions that the author has found helpful in teaching reading:—

1. Adopt the motto, "Not how much, but how well." Place a premium on *quality*, rather than on quantity. One paragraph or stanza well read, is better than a dozen stumbled through.

2. Have your pupils take position before reading. A marksman takes position before firing. Reading can not be properly done with the body in a relaxed condition. A pupil should not be allowed to stand on one foot; to lean on a fellow pupil; to sway the body back and forth; or to take any attitude that indicates listlessness, laziness, or indifference. On the contrary, his position should indicate that body, mind, and soul are united in the endeavor to give the fullest and truest expression to the reading.

3. Impress on the pupil the great value of the vocal instrument and acquaint him with its delicate structure and proper use. This can be done in teaching the lessons on "Vocal Physiology."

4. Do not allow the pupil to read either in a low, monotonous tone or in a "sing-song" tone of voice. Do not stand near him while he is reading, as this will encourage the habit of reading in a low tone. The reading should be loud enough to be heard in any part of the room. Read and practice Isaiah 40:9 in harmony with its sentiment.

5. Teach thoroughly the sound elements of the English language and the symbols used to indicate these sounds as developed in the lessons on "Vocal Sounds" and "Vocal Symbols."

6. Give special attention to the articulation drills. Good reading is not possible when this work is neglected. Read the first clause

of Nehemiah 8:8, and note in the last clause the results that came from the effort put forth to read distinctly.

7. When the above suggestions have been successfully carried out, the student is prepared to take up the study of Vocal Expression. True expression is the last round in the reading ladder. It is the goal attained, for without *ex*pression the reader can make no *im*pression. What one does not feel he can not express, and therefore can not make others feel. Many teachers as well as pupils are incased in a shell of formality, and their reading is formal, lifeless, mechanical, destitute of feeling, expressionless. This shell of formality should be broken, and life, animation, feeling, full and free expression should take possession of all the reading classes. A careful and thorough study of the lessons on "Vocal Expression" will, without doubt, bring such desirable results. Let the pupil, as soon as he is able, apply the principles of expression to each new selection as he reads it.

8. After the pupil has become acquainted with the various figures of speech from the examples given, have him point out and indicate the value of these figures as they occur in the lessons.

It is believed that a knowledge of the more common figures of speech will add interest to the reading, and will prepare the pupil to appreciate his future study of rhetoric and literature.

9. Do not neglect the exercises following each reading selection, as they are a part of the required preparation of every lesson. The pupil will not neglect the preparation of this part of the lesson if the teacher is faithful in requiring recitation upon it. Introduce also supplementary reading, as this will give variety, and often aid in giving a more comprehensive knowledge of the subject matter in the reader.

10. Finally, be enthusiastic. Enthusiasm is contagious. Read "with the spirit . . . and with the understanding also." Lead the way. Be an example to your flock in the matter of good reading as well as in other good things.

M. E. C.

CONTENTS

PROSE SELECTIONS

SUBJECT	AUTHOR	PAGE
THE GOOD READER	Anonymous	17
THE SCRIPTURES AND THE SAVIOUR	Rousseau	24
THE GREAT EARTHQUAKE	Uriah Smith	29
THE BOBOLINK	Irving	33
CHARLES II. AND WILLIAM PENN	Anonymous	41
WILLIAM PENN'S TREATY WITH THE AMERICAN INDIANS	Edinburgh Review	44
THE STEAMBOAT TRIAL	Abbott	52
THE BIBLE AS AN EDUCATOR	Mrs. E. G. White	56
COURAGE TO DO RIGHT	Anonymous	61
CHARACTER OF THE PURITAN FATHERS	Greenwood	71
THE SEA AND ITS USES	Selected	81
THE TALENT OF SPEECH	Mrs. E. G. White	85
DANIEL IN A HEATHEN SCHOOL	Daniel 1	94
THE STARS	Uriah Smith	99
DECISIVE INTEGRITY	Wirt	102
THE TOWN PUMP	Nathaniel Hawthorne	107
THE LIVING WATER	The Bible	111
THE FUTURE INHERITANCE	Mrs. E. G. White	120
INFLUENCE	Mrs. E. G. White	128
TEACHING IN PARABLES—PART I.	Mrs. E. G. White	135
TEACHING IN PARABLES—PART II.	Mrs. E. G. White	139
WORK	Thomas Carlyle	157
THE DAWN	Edward Everett	168
THE BIBLE THE BEST OF CLASSICS	Grimke	178
THE DARKENING OF THE SUN AND MOON	Thoughts on Daniel and the Revelation	180
THE FALLING OF THE STARS	Thoughts on Daniel and the Revelation	183

SUBJECT	AUTHOR	PAGE
THE ATMOSPHERE	Selected	189
THE CREATION	Mrs. E. G. White	191
SOURCE AND AIM OF TRUE EDUCATION	Mrs. E. G. White	196
THE EDEN SCHOOL	Mrs. E. G. White	204
GOD SEES NOT AS MAN SEES	Mrs. E. G. White	218
IMMENSITY OF GOD'S WORKS	Joseph Addison	227
THE SKY	Ruskin	236
PATERNAL INSTRUCTION	Law	243
A KNOWLEDGE OF GOD	Mrs. E. G. White	246
CONVERSATION	Sir Matthew Hale	254
THE SEASONS	Monthly Anthology	263
DEPORTMENT	Mrs. E. G. White	268
THE CHARMS OF THE MOUNTAINS	William Howitt	288
THE TRUE DIGNITY OF LABOR	William Howitt	304
A HUMAN BEING WITH NOTHING TO DO	Selected	308
TIME	Mrs. E. G. White	316
PAUL'S DEFENSE BEFORE KING AGRIPPA	Bible (Acts 26)	321
DAILY PRAYER—MORNING	Channing	326
DAILY PRAYER—EVENING	Channing	330
THE HAPPINESS OF ANIMALS A PROOF OF DIVINE BENEVOLENCE	Parley	333
THE INSTABILITY OF TEMPORAL THINGS	Greenwood	339
ON THE PLEASURE OF ACQUIRING KNOWLEDGE	Alison	343
AUTUMN	Alison	349
ON THE USE AND ABUSE OF AMUSEMENTS	Alison	356
THE MUTUAL RELATION BETWEEN SLEEP AND NIGHT	Paley	364
THE ADVANTAGES OF A TASTE FOR NATURAL HISTORY	Wood	367
THE BLIND PREACHER	William Wirt	390

POETRY SELECTIONS

SUBJECT	AUTHOR	PAGE
JEHOVAH REIGNETH	Psalm 95	37
THE WINGED WORSHIPERS	Charles Sprague	48
ODE TO A WATERFOWL	William Cullen Bryant	63
THE SHIELD OF OMNIPOTENCE	Psalm 91	67
THE GOODLY LAND	Isaiah 35	76
MAN THE LIFEBOAT	Selected	92
THE BELLS	Edgar Allen Poe	115
THE HEAVENLY COUNTRY	Anonymous	127
THE BRIGHT SIDE	Selected	131
GOD'S FIRST TEMPLES	William Cullen Bryant	145
WORSHIP OR SERVICE?	Caroline A. Mason	150
THE COUNCIL OF HORSES	John Gay (adapted)	151
THE HORSE IN BATTLE	Bible (Job 39:19-25)	154
THE DESTRUCTION OF SENNACHERIB	Lord Byron	164
LANDING OF THE PILGRIM FATHERS	Felicia D. Hemans	165
TRUST IN GOD AND DO THE RIGHT	Selected	170
THE TOWN CHILD AND THE COUNTRY CHILD	Allen Cunningham	171
THE NORTHERN LIGHTS	John Greenleaf Whittier	175
THE WATER MILL	D. C. McCallum	187
NATURE WORSHIPS GOD	John Greenleaf Whittier	208
PSALMS OF PRAISE	Bible (Psalms 148, 149, 150)	214
THE LABORER	William D. Gallagher	222
FAITH, HOPE, AND LOVE	"Children of the Lord's Supper," translated from the Swedish by Longfellow	233
INSCRIPTION FOR THE ENTRANCE INTO A WOOD	William Cullen Bryant	240
GOD	Derzhavin	250
CLEAR THE WAY	Charles Mackay	258
THE BURIAL OF MOSES	Cecil Frances Alexander	259
MIDNIGHT	William B. Tappan	262
LOAVES AND FISHES	L. H. Sigourney	266
THE RAINBOW	Baldwin's London Magazine	277

SUBJECT	AUTHOR	PAGE
LITTLE HAL	Selected	280
THE MORE EXCELLENT WAY	1 Corinthians 13, A. R. V.	286
THE MOUNTAINS	Howard T. Lee	294
THE LAUNCHING OF THE SHIP	H. W. Longfellow	297
A VIRTUOUS WOMAN	Solomon	302
LABOR	Frances S. Osgood	309
THANATOPSIS	Bryant	311
THE LOVING-KINDNESS OF JEHOVAH	Selections from the Psalms	315
APOSTROPHE TO THE OCEAN	Byron	324
HE CARETH	Selected	332
THE VANITY OF HUMAN PRIDE	William Knox	336
"ALL THINGS ARE OF GOD"	Moore	342
CHRIST IS RISEN	C. M. Snow	345
APOSTROPHE TO THE SUN	J. G. Percival	353
THE PLANETARY SYSTEM	Mangnall	362
WHILE WE MAY	Selected	366
FROM "THE DESERTED VILLAGE"	Goldsmith	369
"BLESSED ARE THEY THAT MOURN"	Bryant	375
A SUMMER MORNING	Thomson	376
GOD'S DOMINION AND MAN'S DEPENDENCE	Psalms 24 and 90	379
GOD IS EVERYWHERE	Anonymous	381
WORK AWAY	Selected	383
ABSALOM	N. P. Willis	386

VOCALIZATION AND EXPRESSION

VOCAL PHYSIOLOGY
    I. The Vocal Organs 21
    II. The Breathing Process 27
    III. Vocalization 39
    IV. The Organs of Speech and Hearing 50
SOUND
    I. Kinds of Sound 59
    II. Classification of Oral Elements 65
    III. Quality of Oral Sounds 69

	SUBJECT	AUTHOR	PAGE
IV.	Description of English Sounds		78
V.	Description of English Sounds		90
VI.	Description of English Sounds		96
VII.	Description of English Sounds		105
VIII.	Description of English Sounds		112
IX.	Table of English Sounds		118

VOCAL SYMBOLS 124
VOCAL ARTICULATION 132
VOCAL PRONUNCIATION
   I. Syllabication 143
  II. Accentuation 155
 III. Words Commonly Mispronounced 162
EXPRESSION .... *Adapted from the National Fourth Reader* 195
   I. Emphasis 202
  II. Slur 206
 III. Inflection .... *Adapted from the National Fourth Reader* 210
 IV. Modulation
    1. Pitch 217
    2. Force .... *Adapted from the National Fourth Reader* 221
    3. Quality .... *Adapted from the National Fourth Reader* 224
    4. Rate .... *Adapted from the National Fourth Reader* 229
  V. Monotone 235
 VI. Personation 239
FIGURES OF SPEECH .... *Adapted from William's "Composition and Rhetoric."*
   I. Figures Based on Resemblance 273
  II. Figures Based on the Law of Association 283
 III. Figures Based on Contrast 295
 IV. General Exercises on Figures 300

THE SCRIPTURES AND THE SAVIOUR

HOFMANN 1824—

BOOK SEVEN

THE GOOD READER

"How readest thou?"

1. It is related of Frederick the Great, king of Prussia, that, as he was seated one day in his private apartment, a written petition was brought to him with the request that it should be immediately read. The king had just returned from hunting, and the glare of the sun, or some other cause, had so affected his eyesight that he found it difficult to make out a single word of the manuscript.

2. His private secretary happened to be absent, and the soldier who brought the petition could not read. There was a page, or favorite boy servant, in attendance in the corridor, and upon him the king called. The page was a son of one of the noblemen of the court, but proved to be a very poor reader.

3. In the first place, he did not articulate distinctly. He huddled his words together in the utterance as if they were syllables of one long word which he must get through with as speedily as possible. His pronunciation was bad, and he did not modulate his voice so as to bring out the meaning of what he read. Every sentence was uttered with a dismal monotony of voice, as if it did not differ in any respect from that which preceded it.

4. "Stop!" said the king impatiently; "is it an auctioneer's catalogue of goods to be sold that you are hurrying over? Send your companion to me." Another page who stood at the door now entered, and to him the king gave the petition. This second page began by hemming and clearing his throat in such an affected

manner that the king jocosely asked him if he had not slept in the public garden with the gate open the night before.

5. The second page had a good share of self-conceit, however, and so was not greatly disconcerted by the king's jest. He determined that he would avoid the rock on which his companion had been wrecked. So he began reading the petition with great formality and deliberation, emphasizing every word, and prolonging the articulation of every syllable. But his manner was so tedious that the king cried out, "Stop! are you reciting a lesson in the elementary sounds? Out of the room! But no; stay! Send me that little girl who is sitting there by the fountain."

6. The girl thus pointed out by the king was a daughter of one of the laborers employed by the royal gardener, and she had come to help her father weed the flower beds. It chanced that, like many of the poor people of Prussia even in that day, she had received a good education. She was somewhat alarmed when she found herself in the king's presence, but was reassured when the king told her that he only wanted her to read, as his eyes were weak.

7. Now Ernestine (for this was the name of the little girl) was so fond of reading aloud that frequently many of the poor people in the neighborhood would assemble at her father's house to hear her; and those who could not read themselves, would bring to her letters from distant friends or children to decipher. She thus acquired the habit of reading various sorts of handwriting promptly and well.

8. The king gave her the petition, and she rapidly glanced through the opening lines to get some idea of what it was about. As she read, her eyes began to glisten and her breast to heave. "What is the matter?" asked the king; "don't you know how to read?" "O yes, sire," she replied, addressing him with the title usually applied to him, "I will now read it, if you please."

9. The two pages were about to leave the room. "Remain," said the king. The little girl began to read the petition. It was

from a poor widow whose only son had been drafted to serve in the army, although his health was delicate, and his pursuits had been of a character to unfit him for military life. His father had been killed in battle, and the son was ambitious to become a portrait painter.

10. The writer had told her story in a simple, concise manner, which carried to the heart a conviction of its truth; and Ernestine read it with so much feeling, and with an articulation so just, in tones so pure and distinct, that when she had finished, the king, into whose eyes the tears had started, exclaimed, "O! now I understand what it is all about; but I might never have known—certainly, I never should have felt—its meaning, had I trusted to these young gentlemen, whom I now dismiss from my service for one year, recommending them to occupy the time in learning to read."

11. "As for you, my young lady," continued the king, "I know you will ask no better reward for your trouble than to be the instrument in carrying to this poor widow my order for her son's immediate discharge. Let me see if you can write as well as you can read. Take this pen and write as I dictate." He then dictated an order, which Ernestine wrote and he signed. Calling one of his guards, he bade him accompany the girl and see that the order was executed.

12. How much happiness was Ernestine the means of bestowing through her good elocution united to the happy circumstance that brought it to the knowledge of the king! First, there were the poor neighbors to whom she could give instruction and entertainment. Then there was the poor widow who sent the petition, and who not only regained her son, but received through Ernestine an order for him to paint the king's likeness, so that the poor boy rose to great distinction and had more orders than he could attend to. Words could not express his gratitude and that of his mother, to the little girl.

13. And Ernestine had, moreover, the satisfaction of aiding her father to rise in the world, so that he became the king's chief gardener. The king did not forget her, but had her well educated at his own expense. As for the two pages, she was indirectly the means of benefiting them also; for, ashamed of their bad reading, they began studying in earnest, till they overcame the faults that had offended the king. Both finally rose to distinction, one as a lawyer, the other as a statesman; and they owed their advancement in life chiefly to their good elocution.

—*Anonymous.*

Exercise for Conversation and Study

Where is Prussia? Name and locate its capital. What were the bad points in the boys' reading? What were the good points in Ernestine's reading? What did the art of good reading accomplish for Ernestine and others? Did she read according to the Scriptures? Neh. 8:8.

Word Study*

1. Frederick
1. Prussia
1. manuscript
2. corridor
3. articulate
4. jocosely
5. deliberation
6. reassured
7. decipher
8. petition
9. pursuits
10. conviction
11. instrument
12. distinction
13. elocution

*In this and all succeeding "word studies," divide the given list of words into syllables, indicate the diacritical marks, pronounce, define, and learn to spell the words. Define the words according to their meaning in the reading lesson. The numbers refer to the paragraph in which the word occurs.

VOCAL PHYSIOLOGY

I. THE VOCAL ORGANS

> "*And the Lord God . . . breathed into his nostrils the breath of life, and man became a living soul.*"

As we use the vocal organs in reading and speaking, how important it is that we have some knowledge of their structure and function in order that we may better understand how to use and preserve them. This study we term Vocal Physiology. In part, these organs consist of:—

1. The *bellows,* called the *lungs.*
2. The *vibrator,* called the *glottis.*
3. The *reflector,* called the *pharynx.*
4. The *articulators.* the *organs of the mouth,* used in forming words.

The following is a brief description of the organs of voice and the functions of each:—

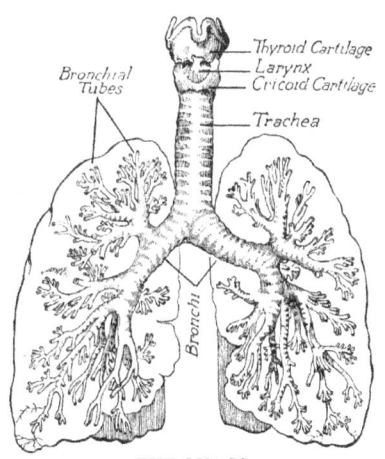

THE LUNGS

1. *The Lungs.* The lungs are at the base of the vocal instrument, and consist of spongy matter wherein the air is stored. The lungs are the bellows, and furnish the air necessary for producing sound waves. They consist of two lobes, one on each side of the chest. As the chest expands, the lungs become inflated with air; as it contracts, a part of the air is expelled.

2. *The Larynx.* This is a cartilaginous box situated above the lungs. It is easily located on the projection called "Adam's apple."

In this box every vocal sound is produced. It is open at both ends, and communicates by its lower opening directly with the lungs through the trachea.

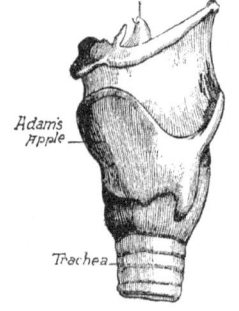

THE LARYNX

3. *The Trachea.* The trachea is a flexible, elastic tube, composed of rings of cartilage, or gristle. These rings are not complete, being open at the back, like a horseshoe, thus allowing the enclosed membrane to sink into a groove, in which the esophagus partly lies. The trachea divides, and forms the bronchial tubes.

4. *The Bronchi.* These are very small tube divisions of the trachea. These tubes divide and subdivide until they end in the minute cells in the lungs. The trachea, bronchial tubes, and lung cells are similar in construction to an inverted tree with its trunk, branches, and leaves.

5. *The Pharynx.* The upper opening of the larynx communicates with the pharynx. In the act of swallowing, this opening between the larynx and pharynx (the glottis) is closed by a leaf-like projection called the epiglottis. The pharynx is a large cavity above the larynx, which forms the back part of the mouth. It is limited in the rear by a muscular wall, in front by the pillars of the fauces. It may be likened to an inverted sack with several openings, or passages. It opens downward into the larynx, forward into the mouth and the two naval cavities, and by the Eustachian tubes into the ear. The pharynx, with the mouth and other cavities of the head, performs the office of a resonator, or tone magnifier, giving greater power and richness to the tones produced in the larynx by the vocal cords.

6. *The Vocal Cords.* These are situated in the larynx. They consist of two ligaments, or bands, of fibrous tissue attached in front to the lower part of the thyroid cartilage, and backward to the two arytenoid cartilages. These ligaments, when inactive, as

in ordinary breathing or whispering, are separated from each other. This opening, or separation, is called the glottis.

7. *The Glottis.* The lips of the glottis, which are separated in ordinary breathing, approach when about to produce a sound, and close the opening with the degree of energy demanded by the character of the sound and the power with which it is to be uttered.

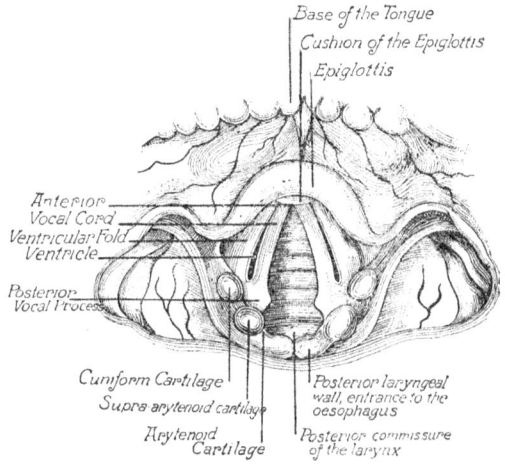

THE VOCAL CORDS

The lips of the glottis being forced upward by the pressure of air from below, give way and allow some of the air to escape, but they immediately return to their original contact and repeat the action. These intermittent emissions or explosions of air, when regular and sufficiently rapid, produce tone. This action is illustrated by the action of the lips of a cornet player.

8. *The Diaphragm.* This is a circular sheet of muscle which forms a partition between the thorax (chest) and the abdomen. In shape it resembles an inverted basin, and yet it is capable of being flattened into the form of an inverted plate. This muscle is at-

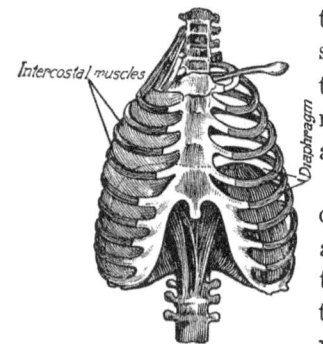

THE CHEST

tached to the spine, the lower part of the sternum, and to the lower ribs. In respiration it works together with the intercostal muscles in compressing the air in the lungs and forcing it through the larynx.

9. *The Intercostal Muscles.* These muscles are short, strap-like muscles connecting all the ribs on both sides of the body. By their contraction the ribs are elevated at their front extremities, each pair being raised a little more than the pair above it.

THE SCRIPTURES AND THE SAVIOUR*

"All Scripture is given by inspiration of God."
"The Father sent the Son to be the Saviour of the world."

1. The majesty of the Scriptures strikes me with astonishment, and the sanctity of the gospel addresses itself to my heart. Look at the volumes of the philosophers, with all their pomp; how contemptible do they appear in comparison with this! Is it possible that a book at once so simple and so sublime can be the work of man?

2. Can He who is the subject of its history be Himself a mere man? Was His the tone of an enthusiast, or of an ambitious sectary? What sweetness! What purity in His manners! What an affecting gracefulness in His instructions! What sublimity in His maxims! What profound wisdom in His discourses! What presence of mind, what sagacity and propriety in His answers! How great the command over His passions! Where is the man,

---

* An extract from the writings of Rousseau, a French author of distinction, but a noted infidel.

where the philosopher, who could so live, suffer, and die, without weakness, and without ostentation?

3. When Plato described his imaginary good man covered with all the disgrace of crime, yet worthy of all the rewards of virtue, he described exactly the character of Jesus Christ. The resemblance was so striking it could not be mistaken, and all the Fathers of the church perceived it. What prepossession, what blindness must it be, to compare the son of Sophronius to the Son of Mary! What an immeasurable distance between them! Socrates, dying without pain, and without ignominy, easily supported his character to the last; and if his death, however easy, had not crowned his life, it might have been doubted whether Socrates with all his wisdom was anything more than a mere sophist.

4. He invented, it is said, the theory of moral science. Others, however, had before him put it in practice, and he had nothing to do but to tell what they had done, and to reduce their examples to precept. Aristides had been just before Socrates defined what justice was. Leonidas had died for his country before Socrates made it a duty to love one's country. Sparta had been temperate before Socrates eulogized sobriety; and before he celebrated the praises of virtue, Greece abounded in virtuous men.

5. But from whom of all His countrymen, could Jesus have derived that sublime and pure morality of which He only has given us both the precepts and example? In the midst of the most licentious fanaticism, the voice of the sublimest wisdom was heard; and the simplicity of the most heroic virtue crowned one of the humblest of all the multitude.

6. The death of Socrates, peacefully philosophizing with his friends, is the most pleasant that could be desired. That of Jesus, expiring in torments, outraged, reviled, and execrated by a whole nation, is the most horrible that could be feared. Socrates, in receiving the cup of poison, blessed the weeping executioner who pre-

sented it; but Jesus, in the midst of excruciating torture, prayed for His merciless tormentors.

7. Yes! if the life and death of Socrates were those of a sage, the life and death of Jesus were those of a God. Shall we say that the evangelical history is a mere fiction? It does not bear the stamp of fiction, but the contrary. The history of Socrates, which nobody doubts, is not as well attested as that of Jesus Christ. Such an assertion in fact only shifts the difficulty, without removing it. It is more inconceivable that a number of persons should have agreed to fabricate this Book, than that one only should have furnished the subject of it.

8. The Jewish authors were incapable of the diction, and strangers to the morality, contained in the gospel, the marks of whose truths are so striking, so perfectly inimitable, that the inventor would be a more astonishing man than the hero.

—*Rousseau.*

Exercise for Conversation and Study

How is it possible for an infidel to approve the writings of the Scriptures? Ps. 76:10. What steps did France take in repudiating the Scriptures and the true God? What is the origin of the Scriptures? 2 Peter 1:19-21; 1 Peter 1:10-12; 2 Tim. 3:16, 17. Where was Jesus born? Was His birthplace foretold? Give reference. How long did the Saviour live among men? What noted historian gives an account of the life and work of Christ? What is the strongest evidence to you of the infallibility and inspiration of the Scriptures?

Word Study

1. Scriptures	4. Sparta	6. executioner
1. sanctity	4. sobriety	6. excruciating
2. enthusiast	5. fanaticism	7. evangelical
2. sagacity	5. licentious	7. inconceivable
3. ignominy	6. execrated	7. Socrates

VOCAL PHYSIOLOGY

II. THE BREATHING PROCESS

"Let everything that hath breath praise the Lord."

The Organs of Respiration. The lungs constitute the breathing apparatus, and contain the air, which is necessary to the production of sound. In order that the air may be admitted into, and expelled from, the lungs, it must traverse the nostrils (or, improperly, the mouth), the pharynx, glottis, and trachea. The admission of the air is called *inspiration,* or *inhalation.* The expulsion is called *expiration,* or *exhalation.*

Inspiration. In the inhaling process, the cavity of the chest is enlarged, thus tending to create a vacuum around the pleura. The resistance being removed, the air rushes through the nostrils, trachea, and bronchial tubes into the lungs cells, thus expanding the lungs, which fill the enlarged cavity containing the lungs. This enlargement is produced by a double action: (1) The depression of the diaphragm by the contraction of its radiating fibers and by an outward movement of the abdomen, enlarges the chest downward. (2) The ribs are moved upward and outward by the contraction of the intercostal and pectoral muscles, and thus the chest is enlarged upward.

Expiration. Expiration, or the exhaling process, is the exact opposite of inspiration. When the various organs have completed the movements of inspiration, they react by their own elastic force. This reaction is aided by other organs, as the intestines, which have been crowded upon, and by the weight of the ribs; thus the air is driven or squeezed out of the lungs.

The Diaphragm in Breathing. The diaphragm is the most important organ used in breathing, and is the one that should be most relied on and cultivated for all vocal purposes, and for improving the health. It is impossible to overestimate the value of the full use of the diaphragm. Women are especially prone, through improper dressing or other bad habits, to err in the use of this powerful organ of voice. Feeble health and feeble voices are but the natural result of disuse or abuse of the organs of voice. In the first attempt to produce a sound, the diaphragm flattens, the stomach slightly protrudes, and the breath is introduced at will through the nose, through the mouth, or through both at once. During this partial inspiration, which is called *abdominal,* the ribs do not move, nor are the lungs filled to their full capacity, to obtain which the diaphragm must and does contract completely. Then, and only then, are the ribs raised, while the stomach is drawn in. This inspiration—in which the lungs have their free action from side to side, from front to back, from top to bottom—is complete and is termed *thoracic-intercostal* respiration. If by compression of any kind the lower ribs are prevented from expanding, the breathing becomes sternal or clavicular.

Breathing Exercises

The following breathing exercises will, if faithfully practiced, greatly increase the power to read, speak, or sing with ease:—

1. Draw the breath slowly through the nostrils, then, through a very minute opening of the lips, exhale freely. Remember that the Lord breathed into man's "nostrils [not his mouth] the breath of life," and this process of inspiration should be faithfully adhered to.

2. Breathe freely through the nostrils, then exhale slowly through the same small opening.

3. Breathe freely and retain the breath during ten seconds or longer.

4. Inhale and exhale freely, gradually increasing in the rate, but stop the exercises as soon as you feel a dizzy sensation.

A good time to take these exercises is just after retiring at night, and before rising in the morning.

THE GREAT EARTHQUAKE

> "*And I beheld when He had opened the sixth seal, and, lo, there was a great earthquake.*"

1. "In no part of the volcanic region of southern Europe has so tremendous an earthquake occurred in modern times as that which began on the first of November, 1755, at Lisbon. A sound of thunder was heard underground, and immediately afterward a violent shock threw down the greater part of that city. In the course of about six minutes, sixty thousand persons perished. The sea first retired, and laid the bar dry; it then rolled in, rising fifty feet above its ordinary level. The mountains of Arrabida, Estrella, Julio, Marvan, and Cintra, being some of the largest in Portugal, were impetuously shaken, as it were from their very foundations; and some of them opened at their summits, which were split and rent in a wonderful manner, huge masses of them being thrown down into the subjacent valleys."* It is also said that flames, supposed to have been electric, appeared to issue from these mountains. Vast columns of smoke also rolled forth, but clouds of dust may have given rise to this appearance.

2. "The terror of the people was beyond description. Nobody wept; it was beyond tears. They ran hither and thither, delirious with horror and astonishment, beating their faces and breasts, crying, 'Misericordia! the *world's at an end!*' Mothers forgot their children, and ran about loaded with crucified images. Unfortunately, many ran to the churches for protection; but in vain was the sacrament exposed; in vain did the poor creatures embrace the altars; images, priests, and people were buried in one common ruin."**

3. "The most extraordinary circumstance which occurred at Lisbon during the catastrophe was the subsidence of the new quay,

---
* From a description given by Sir Charles Lyell.
** From "Wonders of the World" by Sears.

SEQUOIA HIGH SCHOOL, REDWOOD, CAL., AFTER THE GREAT EARTHQUAKE OF APRIL 18, 1906

built entirely of marble, at an immense expense. A great concourse of people had collected there for safety, as a spot where they might be beyond the reach of falling ruins; but suddenly the quay sank down with all the people on it, and not one of the dead bodies ever floated to the surface. A great number of boats and small vessels anchored near it, all full of people, were swallowed up as in a whirlpool. No fragment of these wrecks ever rose again to the surface, and the water in the place where the quay had stood is stated, in many accounts, to be unfathomable; but Whitehurst says he ascertained it to be one hundred fathoms. . . .

4. "The great area over which this Lisbon earthquake extended is very remarkable. The movement was most violent in Spain, Portugal, and the north of Africa; but nearly the whole of Europe, and even the West Indies, felt the shock on the same day. A

seaport called St. Ubes, about twenty miles south of Lisbon, was engulfed. At Algiers and Fez in Africa, the agitation of the earth was equally violent; and at a distance of eight leagues from Morocco, a village the inhabitants of which numbered about eight or ten thousand persons, together with all their cattle, were swallowed up. Soon after, the earth closed again over them.

5. "The shock was felt at sea, on the deck of a ship to the west of Lisbon, and produced very much the same sensation as on dry land. Off St. Lucas, the captain of the ship 'Nancy' felt his vessel so violently shaken that he thought she had struck the ground, but, on heaving the lead, found a great depth of water. Captain Clark, from Denia, in latitude 36 deg. 24 min. N., between nine and ten in the morning, had his ship shaken and strained as if she had struck upon a rock. Another ship, forty leagues west of St. Vincent, experienced so violent a concussion that the men were thrown a foot and a half perpendicularly up from the deck. In Antigua and Barbados, as also in Norway, Sweden, Germany, Holland, Corsica, Switzerland, and Italy, tremors and slight oscillations of the ground were felt.

6. "The agitation of lakes, rivers, and springs in Great Britain was remarkable. At Loch Lomond in Scotland, for example, the water, without the least apparent cause, rose against the banks, and then subsided below its usual level. The greatest perpendicular height of this swell was two feet four inches. It is said that the movement of the earthquake was undulatory, and that it traveled at the rate of twenty miles a minute. A great wave swept over the coast of Spain, and it is said to have been sixty feet high at Cadiz. At Tangier, in Africa, it rose and fell eighteen times on the coast; at Funchal, in Madeira, it rose full fifteen feet perpendicularly above high-water mark, although the tide, which ebbs and flows there seven feet, was then at half ebb. Besides entering the city and committing great havoc, it overflowed other seaports

in the island. At Kinsale, in Ireland, a body of water rushed into the harbor, whirled around several vessels, and poured into the market place."*

7. If the reader will look on his atlas at the countries above mentioned, he will see how large a portion of the earth's surface was agitated by this awful convulsion. Other earthquakes may have been as severe in particular localities, but no other one of which we have any record, combining so great extent with such a degree of severity, has ever been felt on this earth.

—*Uriah Smith.*

Exercise for Conversation and Study

Locate on the map: Portugal, Lisbon, Algiers, Morocco, Cadiz, Tangier, Ireland, West Indies, Norway, and Sweden. Was this earthquake local or general in its extent? What is a league? a fathom? To what measurements are the use of these terms restricted? What is the cause of earthquakes? Are they predicted in prophecy? What prophecy speaks of the earthquake of this lesson? Will there be another great earthquake just before the second coming of Christ? Give Scripture references.

Practice faithfully, night and morning, the four breathing exercises given under "The Breathing Process."

Word Study

1. Lisbon	3. catastrophe	6. Madeira
1. impetuously	4. Portugal	6. havoc
2. delirious	4. leagues	6. Tangier
2. sacrament	5. sensation	7. earthquake
3. extraordinary	5. concussion	7. convulsion

---

* From a description by Sir Charles Lyell.

THE BOBOLINK

*"Praise the Lord from the earth,
ye birds of wing."*

1. The happiest bird of our spring, however, and one that rivals the European lark in my estimation, is the boblincoln, or bobolink, as he is commonly called. He arrives at that choice portion of our year, which, in this latitude, answers to the description of the month of May so often given by the poets. With us it begins about the middle of May, and lasts until nearly the middle of June. Earlier than this, winter is liable to return on its traces, and to blight the opening beauties of the year; and later than this, begin the parching, panting, and dissolving heats of summer. But in this genial interval, Nature is in all her freshness and fragrance; "the rain is over and gone, the flowers appear on the earth, the time of the singing of birds is come, and the voice of the turtledove is heard in our land."

2. The trees are now in their fullest foliage and brightest verdure; the woods are gay with the clustered flowers of the laurel; the air is perfumed with the sweetbrier and the wild rose; the meadows are enameled with clover blossoms; while the young apple, the peach, and the plum begin to swell, and the cherry to glow among the green leaves.

3. This is the chosen season of revelry for the bobolink. He comes amid the pomp and fragrance of the season; his life seems all sensibility and enjoyment, all song and sunshine. He is to be found in the soft bosoms of the freshest and sweetest meadows, and is most in song when the clover is in blossom. He perches on the topmost twig of a tree, or on some long, flaunting weed, and as he rises and sinks with the breeze, pours forth a succession of rich, tinkling notes, crowding one upon another like the outpouring melody of the skylark, and possessing the same rapturous character.

4. Sometimes he pitches from the summit of a tree, begins his song as soon as he gets upon the wing, and flutters tremulously down to the earth, as if overcome with ecstasy at his own music. Sometimes he is in pursuit of his mate, always in full song, as if he would win her by his melody, and always with the same appearance of intoxication and delight. Of all the birds of our groves and meadows, the bobolink was the envy of my boyhood. He crossed my path in the sweetest weather and the sweetest season of the year, when all nature called to the fields, and the rural feeling throbbed in every bosom, but when I, luckless urchin! was doomed to be mewed up, during the livelong day, in a schoolroom.

5. It seemed as if the little varlet mocked at me as he flew by in full song, and sought to taunt me with his happier lot. O, how I envied him! No lessons, no task, no school; nothing but holiday, frolic, green fields, and fine weather. Had I been then more versed in poetry, I might have addressed him in the words of Logan to the cuckoo:—

> "Sweet bird, thy bower is ever green,
> Thy sky is ever clear;
> Thou hast no sorrow in thy song,
> No winter in thy year.
>
> "O, could I fly, I'd fly with thee!
> We'd make, on joyful wing,
> Our annual visit round the globe,
> Companions of the spring."

6. Further observation and experience have given me a different idea of this feathered voluptuary, which I will venture to impart for the benefit of my young readers who may regard him with the same unqualified envy and admiration that I once indulged. I have shown him only as I saw him at first, in what

I may call the poetical part of his career, when he, in a manner, devoted himself to elegant pursuits and enjoyments, and was a bird of music, and song, and taste, and sensibility, and refinement. While this lasted he was sacred from injury; the very schoolboy would not fling a stone at him, and the merest rustic would pause to listen to his strain.

7. But mark the difference. As the year advances, as the clover blossoms disappear, and the spring fades into summer, he gradually gives up his elegant tastes and habits, doffs his poetical suit of black, assumes a russet, dusty garb, and sinks to the gross enjoyment of common, vulgar birds. His notes no longer vibrate on the ear; he is stuffing himself with the seeds of the tall weeds on which he lately swung and chanted so melodiously. He has become a "bon vivant," a "gourmand;" with him now there is nothing like the "joys of the table." In a little while he grows tired of plain, homely fare, and is off on a gastronomic tour in quest of foreign luxuries.

8. We next hear of him, with myriads of his kind, banqueting among the reeds of the Delaware, and grown corpulent with good feeding. He has changed his name in traveling. Boblincoln no more, he is the reedbird now, the much-sought-for tidbit of Pennsylvania epicures, the rival in unlucky fame of the ortolan! Wherever he goes, pop! pop! pop! every rusty firelock in the country is blazing away. He sees his companions falling by thousands around him. Does he take warning and reform? Alas! not he. Again he wings his flight. The rice swamps of the South invite him. Among them he gorges himself almost to bursting; he can scarcely fly for corpulency. He has once more changed his name, and is now the famous ricebird of the Carolinas. Last stage of his career; behold him spitted, with dozens of his corpulent companions, and served up, a vaunted dish, on some Southern table.

9. Such is the story of the bobolink; once spiritual, musical,

admired, the joy of the meadows, and the favorite bird of the spring; finally, a gross little sensualist, who expiates his sensuality in the larder. His story contains a moral, worthy the attention of all little birds and little boys, warning them to keep to those refined and intellectual pursuits which raised him to so high a pitch of popularity during the early part of his career, but to eschew all tendency to that gross and dissipated indulgence which brought this mistaken little bird to an untimely end.

—*Washington Irving.*

Exercise for Conversation and Study

Trace on the map the route of the bobolink in its journeyings. Does it visit your community? If so, when does it come, and when does it depart? How is it enabled to take these long trips without losing its way? What comparison is made in Jer. 8:7? What Bible writer wrote the quotation in the latter part of paragraph 1? Describe the scene pictured in these words.

Continue to practice the breathing exercises mentioned in the previous lesson.

Word Study

1. estimation
1. genial
2. verdure
2. enameled
3. flaunting
3. rapturous
4. intoxication
4. rural
5. varlet
5. cuckoo
6. voluptuary
7. gastronomic
8. corpulent
8. Pennsylvania
9. expiates

JEHOVAH REIGNETH

> *"In its wide range of style and subjects, the Bible has something to interest every mind and to appeal to every heart."*

1. O come, let us sing unto Jehovah;
   Let us make a joyful noise to the Rock of our salvation.
   Let us come before His presence with thanksgiving,
   Let us make a joyful noise unto Him with psalms.

2. For Jehovah is a great God,
   And a great King above all gods.
   In His hand are the deep places of the earth;
   The heights of the mountains are His also.
   The sea is His, and He made it;
   And His hands formed the dry land.

3. O come, let us worship and bow down;
   Let us kneel before Jehovah our Maker;
   For He is our God,
   And we are the people of His pasture, and the sheep of His hand.

4. To-day, O, that ye would hear His voice!
   Harden not your heart as at Meribah,
   As in the day of Massah in the wilderness;
   When your fathers tempted Me,
   Proved Me, and saw My work.

5. Forty years long was I grieved with that generation,
   And said, "It is a people that do err in their heart,
   And they have not known My ways;"
   Wherefore I swear in My wrath,
   That they should not enter into My rest.

—*Psalm 95.*

Exercise for Conversation and Study

Who is the author of this psalm? What evidently were the feelings of the author when he wrote stanza one? What style of expression must be used in order to convey its wonderful thoughts to others? What caused David to break forth with such ecstasy of feeling and expression? Stanza two. What gave him such a vivid sense of God's greatness? Stanza two. Have you been impressed in the same way by beholding the works of God? After the invitation to praise the Lord, what other invitation is given? Why? Stanza three. In view of God's greatness and His loving watch-care over His people, what earnest exhortation follows the invitation to praise and worship? Stanza four. What warning does He give to those who are tempted to be unappreciative? Stanza five. How is David's experience as a shepherd boy among the hills of Judea breathed into this beautiful psalm?

Continue to practice twice a day the four breathing exercises.

Word Study

1. salvation   2. heights   4. Meribah   4. wilderness
1. presence   3. worship   4. tempted   5. generation
1. thanksgiving 3. pasture   5. grieved   5. psalms

VOCAL PHYSIOLOGY

III. VOCALIZATION

"Joy and gladness shall be found therein, thanksgiving, and the voice of melody."

In ordinary respiration the vocal cords lie relaxed and flattened against the walls of the larynx, and only a slight rustling sound, if any, is produced by the friction of the air passing from the lungs.

The process of producing voice is called *vocalization;* and an intelligent understanding of this process depends upon a knowledge of the structure of the voice-box, the larynx. In structure the larynx consists of a framework of cartilages: The *thyroid*, the *cricoid*, the two *arytenoids*, surmounted by two nodules, called the *cartilages of Santorim*, and the *epiglottis*. These cartilages are movable by means of appropriate muscles. The interior of the larynx narrows toward the center to a mere chink, or fissure, called the *glottis*. This opening, which can be seen with the laryngoscope, is bounded by two edges, placed one on the right and the other on the left. These edges constitute the lips of the glottis. Posteriorly they are formed by the internal surface of the arytenoid cartilages, and in front by the vocal cords. The vocal cords are two deep folds of mucous membrane. In each of them, immediately beneath the edge of the fold, lies a band of elastic tissue, known as the inferior thyro-arytenoid ligament, or *true cord;* the outer side of this fold is filled by the internal thyro-arytenoid muscle; at a little distance above these folds are placed two others, called *false cords;* which are separated from the former by two cavities—the *ventricles*. The air in these cavities aids greatly in reinforcing the sounds produced by the vocal cords.

Briefly described, the process of vocalization is as follows: By contraction of proper muscles in the larynx, the two arytenoid cartilages, sitting on the back margin of the cricoid, are moved toward each other, thus bringing the vocal cords near together.

At the same time, the thyroid cartilage is drawn downward and slightly forward, thereby tightening the cords. The outward current of breath, driven against and between the now tense folds of membrane, sets them into a more or less rapid vibration, somewhat similar to that of the reeds in an accordian. This vibration is communicated to the confined column of air, as by the reed of a clarinet; and the air waves thus set in motion are strengthened by the pharynx, and ultimately affect the ear of the hearer. The result of all this is a *vocal tone*, more or less pure, or in other words, *voice*.

The voice instrument is the most powerful of all musical instruments. In it are combined the three principles on which all musical instruments are constructed: the wind, reed, and stringed. For this reason there are such great possibilities in the development of the human voice.

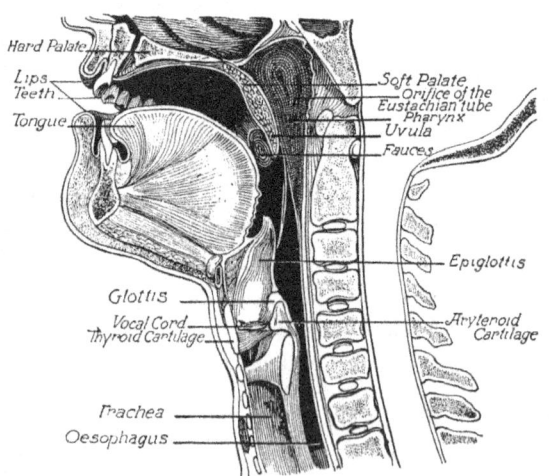

THE VOCAL ORGANS

CHARLES II AND WILLIAM PENN

"There is nothing so kingly as kindness;
And nothing so royal as truth."

King Charles. Well, friend William, I have sold you a noble province in North America; but still, I suppose you have no thoughts of going thither yourself.

Penn. Yes, I have, I assure thee, friend Charles; and I am just come to bid thee farewell.

K. C. What! venture yourself among the savages of North America! Why, man, what security have you that you will not be in the war-kettle in two hours after setting foot on their shores?

P. The best security in the world.

K. C. I doubt that, friend William; I have no idea of any security, against those cannibals, but in a regiment of good soldiers, with their muskets and bayonets. And mind, I tell you beforehand, that, with all my good will for you and your family, to whom I am under obligations, I will not send a single soldier with you.

P. I want none of thy soldiers, Charles; I depend on something better than thy soldiers.

K. C. Ah! what may that be?

P. Why, I depend upon themselves; on the working of their own hearts; on their notions of justice; on their moral sense.

K. C. A fine thing, this same moral sense, no doubt; but I fear you will not find much of it among the Indians of North America.

P. And why not among them, as well as others?

K. C. Because, if they had possessed any, they would not have treated my subjects so barbarously as they have done.

P. That is not proof of the contrary, friend Charles. Thy subjects were the aggressors. When thy subjects first went to North America, they found these poor people the fondest and kindest creatures in the world. Every day they would watch for them to come ashore, and hasten to meet them, and feast them on the best fish, and venison, and corn, which were all they had. In return for this hospitality of the savages, as we call them, thy subjects, termed Christians, seized on their country and rich hunting grounds for farms for themselves. Now, is it to be wondered at that these much injured people should have been driven to desperation by such injustice; and that, burning with revenge, they should have committed some excesses?

K. C. Well, then, I hope you will not complain when they come to treat you in the same manner.

P. I am not afraid of it.

K. C. Ah! how will you avoid it? You mean to get their hunting grounds, too, I suppose?

P. Yes, but not by driving these poor people away from them.

K. C. No, indeed? How then will you get their lands?

P. I mean to buy their lands of them.

K. C. Buy their lands of them? Why, man, you have already bought them of me.

P. Yes, I know I have, and at a dear rate, too; but I did it only to get thy good will, not that I thought thou hadst any right to their lands.

K. C. How, man? no right to their lands?

P. No, friend Charles, no right, no right at all. What right hast thou to their lands?

K. C. Why, the right of discovery, to be sure; the right which the pope and all Christian kings have agreed to give one another.

P. The right of discovery? A strange kind of right, indeed. Now, suppose, friend Charles, that some canoe load of these Indians, crossing the sea, and discovering this island of Great Britain, were to claim it as their own, and set it up for sale over thy head, what wouldest thou think of it?

K. C. Why—why—why—I must confess, I should think it a piece of great impudence in them.

P. Well, then, how canst thou, a Christian, and a Christian prince, too, do that which thou so utterly condemnest in these people, whom thou callest savages? Yes, friend Charles; and suppose, again, that these Indians, on thy refusal to give up thy island of Great Britain, were to make war on thee, and having weapons more destructive than thine, were to destroy many of thy subjects, and drive the rest away—wouldest thou not think it horribly cruel?

K. C. I must say, friend William, that I should; how can I say otherwise?

P. Well, then, how can I, who call myself a Christian, do what I should abhor even in the heathen? No; I will not do it. But I will buy the right of the proper owners, even of the Indians themselves. By doing this I shall imitate God Himself, in His justice and mercy, and thereby insure His blessing on my colony, if I should ever live to plant one in North America.

—*Anonymous.*

Exercise for Conversation and Study

Who was Charles II? Who was William Penn? What part of the United States was purchased and settled by him? From whom did he purchase his lands? What state is named in his honor? What city? Write a brief account of the experiences of William Penn in his dealings with the Indians, and the results that followed.

It is important that the breathing exercises be faithfully continued.

Word Study

savages	aggressors	utterly
cannibals	Christians	justice
security	revenge	abhor
bayonets	complain	colony
province	desperation	imitate

WILLIAM PENN'S TREATY WITH THE AMERICAN INDIANS

> *"If it be possible, as much as lieth in you, live peaceably with all men."*

1. The country assigned to him by the royal charter was yet full of its original inhabitants; and the principles of William Penn did not allow him to look upon that gift as a warrant to dispossess the first proprietors of the land. He had accordingly appointed his commissioners, the preceding year, to treat with them for the fair purchase of a part of their lands, and for their joint possession of the remainder; and the terms of the settlement being now nearly agreed upon, he proceeded, very soon after his arrival, to conclude the settlement and solemnly to pledge his faith and to ratify and confirm the treaty in sight both of the Indians and planters.

2. For this purpose a grand convocation of the tribes had been appointed near the spot where Philadelphia now stands, and it was agreed that he and the presiding sachems should meet and exchange faith under the spreading branches of a prodigious elm tree that grew on the bank of the river. On the day appointed, accordingly, an innumerable multitude of Indians assembled in that neighborhood, and were seen, with their dark visages and brandished arms, moving in vast swarms in the depth of the woods which then overshaded the whole of that now cultivated region.

3. On the other hand, William Penn with a moderate attendance of friends advanced to meet them. He came, of course, unarmed, in his usual plain dress, without banners, or mace, or guard, or carriages; and only distinguished from his companions by wearing a blue sash of silk network (which, it seems, is still preserved by Mr. Kett of Seething Hall, near Norwich), and by having in his hand a roll of parchment on which was engrossed the confirmation of the treaty of purchase and amity. As soon as he drew near the spot where the sachems were assembled, the whole multitude of Indians threw down their weapons, and seated

themselves on the ground in groups, each under his own chieftain; and the presiding chief intimated to William Penn that the nations were ready to hear him.

4. Having been thus called upon, he began. The Great Spirit, he said, who made them and him, who rules the heaven and the earth, and who knows the innermost thoughts of man, knew that he and his friends had a hearty desire to live in peace and friendship with them, and to serve them to the utmost of their power. It was not their custom to use hostile weapons against their fellow creatures, for which reason they had come unarmed. Their object was not to do injury, and thus provoke the Great Spirit, but to do good. They were then met on the broad pathway of good faith and good will, so that no advantage was to be taken on either side, but all was to be openness, brotherhood, and love.

5. After these and other words, he unrolled the parchment, and, by means of the same interpreter, conveyed to them, article by article, the conditions of the purchase, and the words of the compact then made for their eternal union. Among other things, they were not to be molested in their lawful pursuits even in the territory they had alienated, for it was to be common to them and the English. They were to have the same liberty to do all things therein relating to the improvement of their grounds, and the providing of sustenance for their families, which the English had. If any disputes should arise between the two, they should be settled by twelve persons, half of whom should be English, and half Indians.

6. He paid them for the land, and made them many presents besides from the merchandise which had been spread before them. Having done this, he laid the roll of parchment on the ground, observing again that the ground should be common to both people. He then added that he would not do as the Marylanders did; that is, call them children or brothers only, for often parents were liable

to whip their children too severely, and brothers sometimes would differ; neither would he compare the friendship between them to a chain, for the rain might sometimes rust it, or a tree might fall and break it; but he would consider them as the same flesh and blood with the Christians, and the same as if one man's body were to be divided into two parts. He then took up the parchment and presented it to the sachem who bore the horn in the chaplet, and desired him and the other sachems to preserve it carefully for three generations, that their children might know what had passed between them, just as if he himself had remained with them to repeat it.

7. The Indians in return made long and stately harangues, of which, however, no more seems to have been remembered than that "they pledged themselves to live in love with William Penn and his children as long as the sun and moon should endure." And thus ended this famous treaty of which Voltaire has remarked, with so much truth and severity, "that it was the only one ever concluded between savages and Christians that was not ratified by an oath—and the only one that never was broken!"

8. Such, indeed, was the spirit in which the negotiation was entered into, and the corresponding settlement conducted, that, for the space of more than seventy years, and so long indeed as the Quakers retained the chief power in the government, the peace and amity which had been thus solemnly promised and concluded were never violated; and a large and most striking, though solitary example afforded of the facility with which they who are really sincere and friendly in their own views may live in harmony with those who are supposed to be peculiarly fierce and faithless.

9. We can not bring ourselves to wish that there were no one but Quakers in the world, because we fear that it would be insupportably dull; but when we consider what tremendous evils daily arise from the petulance and profligacy, the ambition and

irritability, of sovereigns and ministers, we can not help thinking it would be the most efficacious of all reforms to choose all those ruling personages out of that plain, pacific, and sober-minded sect.
—*Edinburgh Review.*

Exercise for Conversation and Study

To what religious sect did William Penn belong? Describe some of the peculiarities of this sect as regards their language, dress, and manner of conducting religious meetings. What is their attitude toward war? Is the sect strong in numbers, and where do the Quakers live at the present time?

"Breathe deep and forge ahead." Your success in reading depends upon it. Make drawings of the larynx, showing its construction.

Word Study

1. assigned	3. amity	6. merchandise
1. proprietors	3. sachems	7. ratified
1. Indians	4. hostile	7. harangues
2. prodigious	5. interpreter	8. Quakers
2. brandished	5. alienated	9. irritability

THE WINGED WORSHIPERS

[Two swallows that flew into a church during service suggested the poem that follows.]

> Yea, the sparrow hath found an house,
> And the swallow a nest for herself,
> Where she may lay her young, even Thine altars,
> O Lord of hosts, my King, and my God.
> —Psalm 84:3.

1. Gay, guiltless pair,
   What seek ye from the fields of heaven?
   Ye have no need of prayer,
   Ye have no sins to be forgiven.

2. Why perch ye here,
   Where mortals to their Maker bend?
   Can your pure spirits fear
   The God ye never could offend?

3. Ye never knew
   The crimes for which we come to weep;
   Penance is not for you,
   Blessed wand'rers of the upper deep.

4. To you 'tis given
   To wake sweet nature's untaught lays;
   Beneath the arch of heaven
   To chirp away a life of praise.

5. Then spread each wing,
   Far, far above, o'er lakes and lands,
   And join the choirs that sing
   In yon blue dome not reared with hands.

6. Or, if ye stay
   To note the consecrated hour,
   Teach me the airy way,
   And let me try your envied power.

7. Above the crowd,
   On upward wings, could I but fly,
   I'd bathe in yon bright cloud,
   And seek the stars that gem the sky.

8. 'Twere heaven indeed,
   Through fields of trackless light to soar,
   On nature's charms to feed,
   And nature's own great God adore.
   —*Charles Sprague.*

Exercise for Conversation and Study

Commit to memory the verse of the psalm at the beginning of the lesson. Give an oral description of the scene pictured in this verse. What suggested to the poet the thoughts of this poem? Explain the beautiful expressions: "fields of heaven;" "blessed wanderers;" "upper deep;" "airy way;" "fields of trackless light."

If you have been faithful in practicing the breathing exercises, keep right on; for you will need all the breathing power that you can command before finishing the lessons in this book.

Word Study

1. prayer	4. beneath	7. upward
1. guiltless	5. choirs	7. crowd
2. mortals	6. consecrated	8. soar
3. penance	6. envied	8. adore

VOCAL PHYSIOLOGY

IV. THE ORGANS OF SPEECH AND HEARING

"I will be with thy mouth, and teach thee what thou shalt say."

The organs of speech are those organs which are employed in modifying the breath, vocalized or unvocalized, for the purpose of expressing thought. They are the tongue, lips, palate, teeth, and nasal passages. By various combinations with one another, they obstruct the outward movement of the breath from the pharynx, and so give rise to a great variety of modifications of the natural, or fundamental, tone of the voice. In whispering, unvocalized breath is modified or affected by these organs to suit the purposes of speech.

The Tongue. This is not the simple, paddle-shaped organ which it is commonly supposed to be from observation of its upper surface, but rather a thick, cushion-shaped mass of fibers in apparently complete confusion, but really so disposed as to be capable of producing motion in any and every direction or several directions.

The Palate. This is the roof of the mouth. The fixed front portion is called the *hard palate.* Continuous with it is a yielding muscular and membranous awning, separating the mouth from the nasal passages and the upper part of the pharynx. This is the *soft palate.* Dependent from this is a conical appendage called the *uvula.* The soft palate is capable of depression and other movements.

The Nasal Passages. These admit of closure at their inner extremities by the action of the soft palate. The presence or absence of this closure is very essential to the production of certain sounds.

The Lips and Teeth. These need no description. The former are of great importance in articulation; the latter of but little. The distinctive and crowning process of speech is that of articulation, a process as complex and intricate as it is essential. The tongue, by its power of manifold motion, moves forward and backward, narrows and widens, arches and flattens in its several parts; the lips open and contract; the palate rises and lowers; the nasal passages are closed and unclosed; the teeth approach and separate,—all these movements take place in ever-varying combination, shaping the column of vibrating breath; and from each separate combination results a sound of distinct and recognizable quality, capable of appropriation as a thought-symbol.

The Ear. This is not an organ for the production of the voice, but is its receiving instrument. Sound waves in the air, or other mediums, are focused by the external ear upon the tympanum, a cavity covered by a thin membrane similar in its arrangement and function to the head of a drum. A number of small bones in contact with the inner side of this membrane transmit the vibrations to the internal ear, where the auditory nerves communicate with the brain.

In summing up we find that the diaphragm and other muscles, by their alternate movements, operate the lungs. The breath, forced from the lungs, passes through the bronchi and trachea into the larynx. The vocal cords, when tensely drawn across the cavity of the larynx, set the column of breath into vibration. This vibration, increased by the resonating action of the pharynx and other cavities, is communicated to the external air, and at length falls as a tone upon the listening ear.

THE STEAMBOAT TRIAL

> *"The way of a ship in the midst of the sea."*

1. The Bible everywhere conveys the idea that this life is but a time of probation, of trial and discipline, which is intended to prepare us for the life to come. In order that all, even the youngest of my readers, may understand what is meant by this, I shall illustrate it by some familiar examples, drawn from the actual business of life.

2. When a large steamboat is built, with the intention of having her employed upon the waters of a large river, she must be proved before put to service. Before trial, it is somewhat doubtful whether she will succeed. In the first place, it is not absolutely certain whether her machinery will work at all. There may be some flaw in the iron, or an imperfection in some part of the workmanship which will prevent the motion of her wheels. Or, if this is not the case, the power of the machinery may not be sufficient to propel her through the water with such force as to overcome the current; or when brought to encounter the rapids at some narrow passage in the stream, she may not be able to force her way against their resistance.

3. The engineer, therefore, resolves to try her in all these respects, that her security and her power may be properly proved, before she is intrusted with her valuable cargo of human lives. He cautiously builds a fire under her boiler; he watches with eager interest the rising of the steam gauge, and scrutinizes every part of the machinery as it gradually comes under the control of the tremendous power which he is apprehensively applying.

4. With what interest does he observe the first stroke of the ponderous piston! And when, at length, the fastenings of the boat are let go, and the motion is communicated to the wheels, and the mighty mass slowly moves away from the wharf, how

deep and eager an interest does he feel in all her movements and every indication he can discover of her future success!

5. The engine, however, works imperfectly, as every one must on its first trial; and the object in this experiment is not to gratify idle curiosity, by seeing that she will move, but to discover and remedy every little imperfection, and to remove every obstacle that prevents more entire success. For this purpose you will see our engineer examining most minutely and most attentively every part of her complicated machinery. The crowd on the wharf may be simply gazing on her majestic progress as she moves off from the shore, but the engineer is within, looking with faithful examination into all the minutiæ of the motion.

6. He scrutinizes the action of every lever and the friction of every joint; here, he oils a bearing; there, he tightens a nut; one part of the machinery has too much play, and he confines it; another, too much friction, and he loosens it; now, he stops the engine; now, reverses her motion; and again, sends the boat forward in her course. He discovers, perhaps, some great improvement of which she is susceptible, and when he returns to the wharf and has extinguished her fire, he orders from the machine shop the necessary alteration.

7. The next day he puts his boat to trial again, and she glides over the water more smoothly and swiftly than before. The jar that he had noticed is gone, and the friction reduced; the beams play more smoothly, and the alteration which he had made produces a more equable motion in the shaft, or gives greater effect to the stroke of the paddles upon the water.

8. When at length her motion upon the smooth surface of the river is such as to satisfy him, he turns her course, we will imagine, toward the rapids, to see how she will sustain a greater trial. As he increases her steam to give her power to overcome the new force with which she has to contend, he watches with eager interest her boiler, inspects the gauge and safety valve, and, from

her movements under the increased pressure of her steam, he receives suggestions for further improvements or for precautions that will insure greater safety.

9. These he executes, and thus he may go on for many days, or even weeks, trying and examining for the purpose of improvement every working of that mighty power to which he knows hundreds of lives are soon to be intrusted. This now is probation; trial for the sake of improvement. And what are its results? Why, after this course has been thoroughly and faithfully pursued, this floating palace receives upon her broad deck, and in her carpeted and curtained cabin, her four or five hundred passengers, who pour along in one long procession of happy groups, over the bridge of planks; father and son, mother and children, young husband and wife, all with implicit confidence trusting themselves and their dearest interest to her power.

10. See her sail away! How beautiful and yet how powerful are all her motions! That beam glides up and down gently and smoothly in its grooves, and yet, gentle as it seems, hundreds of horses could not hold it still; there is no apparent violence, but every movement is with irresistible power. How graceful is her form, and yet how mighty is the momentum with which she presses on her way!

11. Loaded with life, and herself the very symbol of life and power, she seems something ethereal, unreal, which, ere we look again, will have vanished away. And though she has within her bosom a furnace glowing with furious fires, and a reservoir of death, the elements of most dreadful ruin and conflagration, of destruction most complete and agony the most unutterable, and though her strength is equal to the united energy of two thousand men, she restrains it all.

12. She was constructed by genius, and has been tried and improved by fidelity and skill; and one man governs and controls her, stops her and sets her in motion, turns her this way and that,

as easily and certainly as the child guides the gentle lamb. She walks over the one hundred and sixty miles of her route without rest and without fatigue; and the passengers, who have slept in safety in her berths with destruction by water without and by fire within, defended only by the plank from the one and by a sheet of copper from the other, land at the appointed time in safety.

13. My reader, you have within you susceptibilities and powers of which you have little present conception; energies which are hereafter to operate in producing fullness of enjoyment or horrors of suffering, of which you can now form scarcely a conjecture. You are now on trial. God wishes you to prepare yourself for safe and happy action. He wishes you to look within, to examine the complicated movements of your heart, to detect what is wrong, to modify what needs change, and to rectify every irregular motion.

14. You go out to try your moral powers upon the stream of active life, and then return to retirement to improve what is right and remedy what is wrong. Renewed opportunities of moral practice are given you that you may go from strength to strength, until every part of that complicated moral machinery, of which the human heart consists, will work as it ought to work, and is prepared to accomplish the mighty purposes for which your powers are designed. You are on trial, on probation, now. You will enter upon active service in another world.

—*Abbott.*

Exercise for Conversation and Study

What part of the steamboat has guiding power? What organ of the human body has great controlling power? James 3:5. What is the moral lesson in this scripture? Who invented the first steamboat? On what body of water was the first trip made? Was the science of navigation well understood in the days of Solomon? Prov. 30:18, 19. Were ships used at that time for commercial purposes? 1 Kings 9:26-28; 22:48; 2 Chron. 9:21. How were they propelled? To what extent are ships used at the present time for carrying on commerce? Name the important shipbuilding cities of the world. Explain the following texts of scripture: Gen. 49:13; Judges 5:17; Rev. 18:17-19.

With the aid of a mirror, locate as many as possible of the organs of speech, and make a diagrammatic drawing showing the position of each. Be conscientious in continuing the breathing exercises.

Word Study

1. probation
2. propel
2. machinery
3. engineer
3. gauge
3. apprehensively

3. scrutinizes
4. ponderous
5. experiment
5. minutiæ
6. susceptible
6. alteration

8. precaution
11. conflagration
12. genius
13. conjecture
14. complicated
14. remedy

THE BIBLE AS AN EDUCATOR

"The knowledge of the Holy is understanding."

1. For the mind and the soul, as well as for the body, it is God's law that strength is acquired by effort. It is exercise that develops. In harmony with this law, God has provided in His Word the means for mental and spiritual development.

2. The Bible contains all the principles that men need to understand in order to be fitted either for this life or for the life to come. And these principles may be understood by all. No one with a spirit to appreciate its teachings can read a single passage from the Bible without gaining from it some helpful thought. But the most valuable teaching of the Bible is not to be gained by occasional or disconnected study. Its great system of truth is not so presented as to be discerned by the hasty or careless reader. Many of its treasures lie far beneath the surface, and can be obtained only by diligent research and continuous effort. The truths that go to make up the great whole must be searched out and gathered up, "here a little, and there a little."

3. When thus searched out and brought together, they will be found to be perfectly fitted to one another. Each gospel is a supplement to the others, every prophecy an explanation of another, every truth a development of some other truth. The types of the Jewish economy are made plain by the gospel. Every principle in the Word of God has its place, every fact its bearing. And the complete structure, in design and execution, bears testimony to its Author. Such a structure no mind but that of the Infinite could conceive or fashion.

4. In searching out the various parts and studying their relationship, the highest faculties of the human mind are called into intense activity. No one can engage in such study without developing mental power.

5. And not alone in searching out truth and bringing it together does the mental value of Bible study consist. It consists also in the effort required to grasp the themes presented. The mind occupied with commonplace matters only, becomes dwarfed and enfeebled. If never tasked to comprehend grand and far-reaching truths, it after a time loses the power of growth. As a safeguard against this degeneracy, and a stimulus to development, nothing else can equal the study of God's Word. As a means of intellectual training, the Bible is more effective than any other book, or all other books combined. The greatness of its themes, the dignified simplicity of its utterances, the beauty of its imagery, quicken and uplift the thoughts as nothing else can. No other study can impart such mental power as does the effort to grasp the stupendous truths of revelation. The mind thus brought in contact with the thoughts of the Infinite can not but expand and strengthen.

6. And even greater is the power of the Bible in the development of the spiritual nature. Man, created for fellowship with God, can only in such fellowship find his real life and development. Created to find in God his highest joy, he can find in nothing else

that which can quiet the cravings of the heart, can satisfy the hunger and thirst of the soul. He who with sincere and teachable spirit studies God's Word, seeking to comprehend its truths, will be brought into touch with its Author; and, except by his own choice, there is no limit to the possibilities of his development.

7. In its wide range of style and subjects, the Bible has something to interest every mind and appeal to every heart. In its pages are found history the most ancient, biography the truest to life, principles of government for the control of the state, for the regulation of the household,—principles that human wisdom has never equaled. It contains philosophy the most profound, poetry the sweetest and the most sublime, the most impassioned and the most pathetic. Immeasurably superior in value to the productions of any human author are the Bible writings, even when thus considered; but of infinitely wider scope, of infinitely greater value, are they when viewed in relation to the grand central thought. Viewed in the light of this thought, every topic has a new significance. In the most simply-stated truths are involved principles that are as high as heaven and that compass eternity.

—*Mrs. E. G. White.*

Exercise for Conversation and Study

In what ways is a knowledge of the Scriptures profitable? 2 Tim. 3: 16, 17. Commit this scripture to memory. When should one begin to gain a knowledge of the Bible? Verse 15. What are the two main divisions of the Bible? Name the books of the Old and New Testaments, and give the number of chapters in each book. Select portions of the Bible that treat on the following subjects mentioned in paragraph seven: history, biography, government, philosophy, and poetry. Select passages that express joy, sorrow, indignation, hope, despair, courage. Select scriptures that possess beautiful imagery. See "Poetry and Song" in *Education.*

Word Study
1. acquired
1. spiritual
2. principles
2. occasional
3. supplement
3. prophecy
4. faculties
5. stupendous
5. truths
5. degeneracy
5. Infinite
6. development
7. style
7. pathetic
7. biography

SOUND

I. KINDS OF SOUNDS

"Blessed is the people that know the joyful sound."

In previous lessons we have learned something of the structure and operation of the vocal organs, and the next thing in order is the character and value of the sounds produced. As an introduction, definitions are given of sound, tone, and noise.

Sound is the effect produced upon the auditory nerve by vibrations of the air or other conducting media.

Water and solid substances, as wood or metal, are good conductors, or media, of sound waves; but usually, if not always, a greater or less portion of air enters into the chain of communication. Sounds are classified as tones and noises.

A *tone* is a sound produced by regular, or periodical, vibrations of the sounding body. It admits of uniform continuation, and is usually agreeable to the ear.

A *noise* is a sound produced by irregular, or nonperiodical, vibrations—the motions of the sounding body changing irregularly. A combination of coincident or discordant tones, as when the keys of a piano are all struck at once, is also a noise.

A waterfall, for instance, or a machine in motion, has its uniform tone or keynote, usually, however, rendered almost unnoticeable by the multitude of discordant noises—splashings, thumpings, etc.—which accompany and overpower it.

Voice is tone produced by the mutual action of the larynx and the breath from the lungs.

It is perhaps possible, though exceedingly uncommon and unnatural, to produce voice with the in-going breath. The pure, unmixed, unobstructed product of the larynx is the sound heard in the English word *ah* when clearly uttered. It is the same in all persons without distinction of age, sex, or race. It is capable, however, of extensive variation in pitch, this being the sole modification of voice which the unaided larynx can affect.

The volume, or quantity, of voice depends upon the amount and the rate of expulsion of the out-going breath. It is controlled chiefly by the diaphragm and the abdominal muscles.

Speech is either voice or breath modified by articulation for the purpose of expressing thought.

Singing without words, the wailing of an infant, etc., are examples of voice without speech. Ordinary whispering is speech without voice. Common speech employs a mixture of vocalized and unvocalized breath duly articulated, a combination of tones and noises.

An oral element, or elementary sound, is, strictly speaking, a sound of human speech which can not be analyzed, or separated into parts. It is produced with a single and fixed position of the organs of speech.

In common speech, however, the term has been loosely applied, also to certain couplets or combinations of sound, as the diphthongs. This leads to the expression "compound element," a contradiction of terms, but too firmly established by usage, perhaps, to be abolished.

The number of oral elements, including compounds according to the popular usage above mentioned, is about forty-five.

The number of possible speech sounds is almost infinite. Alexander Ellis, the great English phonologist, has invented a notation for about four hundred of them.

61

COURAGE TO DO RIGHT

"Have courage, my boy, to say No!"

1. I was sitting by a window in the second story of one of the large boarding houses at Saratoga Springs, thinking of absent friends, when I heard shouts of children from the piazza beneath me.

"O, yes; that's capital! so we will! Come on, now! There's William Hale! Come on, William, we are going to have a ride on the Circular Railway. Come with us."

"Yes, if my mother is willing. I will run and ask her," replied William.

2. "O! O! so you must run and ask your ma! Great baby, run along to your ma! Aren't you ashamed? I didn't ask my mother."

"Nor I," "Nor I," added half a dozen voices.

"Be a man, William," cried the first voice; "come along with us, if you do not want to be called a coward as long as you live; don't you see we are all waiting?"

3. I leaned forward to catch a view of the children, and saw William standing with one foot advanced, and his hand firmly clinched, in the midst of the group. He was a fine subject for a painter at that moment. His flushed brow, flashing eye, compressed lip, and changing cheek, all told how the word coward was rankling in his breast. "Will he indeed prove himself one by yielding to them?" thought I. It was with breathless interest I listened for his answer; for I feared that the evil principle in his heart would be stronger than the good. But no.

4. "I will not go without asking my mother," said the noble boy, his voice trembling with emotion; "and I am no coward, either. I promised her I would not leave the house without permission, and I should be a base coward if I were to tell her a wicked lie."

5. I saw him in the evening in the crowded parlor. He was walking by his mother's side, a stately matron, clad in widow's

mourning. Her gentle and polished manners, the rich, full tones of her sweet voice, showed her to be a lady of refinement and culture. It was with evident pride that she looked on her graceful boy, whose face was one of the finest I ever saw, fairly radiant with animation and intelligence.

6. Well might she be proud of such a son, one who could dare to do right when all were tempting to do wrong. I shall probably never see the brave boy again; but my heart breathed a prayer that that spirit, now so strong in its integrity, might never be sullied by worldliness and sin; never, in coming years, be overcome when tempted to do evil.

7. Then, indeed, will he be a joy to the widow's heart, a pride and ornament to his native land. Our country needs such stout, brave hearts, that can stand fast when the whirlwind of temptation gathers thick and strong around them; she needs men who from infancy upward have scorned to be false and recreant to duty.

8. Would you, young friend, be a brave man and a blessing to your country?—Be truthful, never tell a lie, or deceive in any manner; and then, if God spares your life, you will be a stouthearted man, a strong and fearless champion of the truth.

—*Anonymous.*

Exercise for Conversation and Study

Which one of the Ten Commandments did William keep when he refused to follow the advice of his companions? Commit it to memory. What will be the result of keeping this commandment? Eph. 6:2, 3. Paragraph one contains several capital letters; give the reason for the use of each.

With the organ, piano, or some other musical instrument, produce a tone; a noise. Produce the same with the vocal instrument.

Word Study

1. piazza	3. clinched	5. evident	7. temptation
1. Saratoga	3. compressed	5. animation	7. recreant
2. ashamed	3. rankling	6. sullied	8. champion
2. coward	4. permission	6. probably	8. deceive

ODE TO A WATERFOWL

> *"Yea, the stork in the heaven knoweth her appointed times;*
> *And the turtle, and the crane, and the swallow observe the time of their coming;*
> *But My people know not the judgment of the Lord."*

1. Whither, midst falling dew,
    While glow the heavens with the last steps of day,
    Far, through their rosy depths, dost thou pursue
        Thy solitary way?

2. Vainly the fowler's eye
    Might mark thy distant flight to do thee wrong,
    As, darkly painted on the crimson sky,
        Thy figure floats along.

3. Seek'st thou the plashy brink
    Of weedy lake, or marge of river wide,
    Or where the rocking billows rise and sink
        On the chafed ocean side?

4. There is a Power whose care
    Teaches thy way along that pathless coast,
    The desert and illimitable air—
        Lone wandering, but not lost.

5. All day thy wings have fanned,
    At that far height, the cold, thin atmosphere,
    Yet stoop not, weary, to the welcome land,
        Though the dark night is near.

6. And soon that toil shall end;
    Soon shalt thou find a summer home, and rest,

And scream among thy fellows; reeds shall bend,
Soon, o'er thy sheltered nest.

7. Thou'rt gone, the abyss of heaven
Hath swallowed up thy form; yet on my heart
Deeply hath sunk the lesson thou hast given,
And shall not soon depart.

8. He who, from zone to zone,
Guides through the boundless sky thy certain flight,
In the long way that I must tread alone,
Will lead my steps aright.
—*William Cullen Bryant.*

Exercise for Conversation and Study

What is the name of the waterfowl that is the subject of this beautiful poem? What expressions in the poem helped you to suggest its name? Explain the following rhetorical expressions: "steps of day," "rosy depths," "solitary way," "crimson sky," "plashy brink," "chafed ocean side," "cold, thin atmosphere," "welcome land," "abyss of heaven." Why is "Power" capitalized in the fourth stanza? What lesson does the waterfowl teach? Commit to memory Jer. 8:7. Read and give the thoughts contained in Job 39:26, 27.

Pronounce the word *ah* at different pitches, and with varied degrees of force. Remember that the diaphragm is to be used *chiefly* in producing tone.

Word Study

1. pursue	3. marge	6. scream
1. solitary	4. illimitable	6. sheltered
2. distant	5. atmosphere	7. abyss
2. crimson	5. fanned	8. zone

SOUND

II. CLASSIFICATION OF ORAL ELEMENTS

The oral elements admit of classification in several different ways, or modes, varying according to the basis of classification employed. The most familiar classification is that into vocals, subvocals, and aspirates.

A *vocal*, or vowel sound, is a tone of the voice but little or not at all modified, or interrupted, by the organs of speech.

A *subvocal* is a tone of the voice greatly modified, or interrupted, by the organs of speech.

An *aspirate* is a mere breathing, more or less modified by the organs of speech.

Vocals, subvocals, and aspirates, are also called, with great propriety, tonics, subtonics, and atonics.

Vocals, or tonics, are vocal tones nearly pure; *i. e.*, but little mixed with mere noise.

Subvocals, or subtonics, are impure tones, or tones so greatly mixed with noise, the rustling of breath against the organs, etc., that the noise predominates more or less over the tone. The tone is covered by the noise and becomes undertone.

Aspirates, or atonics, contain no vocal tone, being produced with the vocal cords in a state of inaction.

It will thus be seen that this classification is based upon the amount of vocal tone—much, little, or none—which the sound contains.

A *vowel* is a letter used ordinarily to represent a vocal, or tonic, sound.

A *consonant* is a letter used ordinarily to represent a subvocal or an aspirate sound.

The English vowels are *a, e, i, o, u,* and sometimes *w* and *y*. A more scientific statement would add to *y*, also *l, n,* and *r*.

Cognates are those pairs of consonant sounds, one subvocal and one aspirate, which are produced with the organs of speech in the same or very nearly the same position for both; as b and p, v and f.

A *diphthong* (*di*, double; *pthongos*, voice) is a combination of two vocals, or vowel sounds, in one utterance, or syllable. When both vowels are sounded, as *ou* in out and *oi* in oil, it is called a *proper diphthong;* when only one is sounded, it is called a *vowel digraph*, or *improper diphthong;* as *ai* in rain, *eo* in people.

A *triphthong* is a combination of three vowel sounds in a single syllable; as, *eye*, *eiu* in adieu, *eau* in beau. Some scholars do not recognize the term triphthong, classing all triphthongs as trigraphs.

A *digraph* is a combination of two letters to represent one sound. These letters may be vowels or consonants; hence we may have vowel digraphs (which are sometimes called "improper diphthongs"), as *ai* in said, or consonant digraphs, as *ph* in phiz.

A *trigraph* is a combination of three letters to represent one sound; as *sch* in schist, *eau* in beau.

Another classification of the oral elements is that based upon the kind of modification which the sounds receive; that is, upon the special organs of speech used in forming them. The several classes take their names from the organ most prominently in use.

A *labial* is a speech-sound modified chiefly by the lips; as the sounds of o, b, and p.

A *palatal* is a sound modified chiefly by the palate; as the sounds of e, g, and k.

A *lingual* is a sound modified chiefly by the tongue; as the sounds of l, d, and t.

The lips, being two and external, are more independent than other organs in their action. The tongue and palate assist each other, the sound being named, or classed, according to the greater prominence of either organ in the work of modification.

The teeth also assist in the formation of certain sounds, which may therefore be called *labio-dentals*, *linguo-dentals*, etc.

Sounds which owe their peculiar quality in part to an openness of the nasal passages, are called *nasals;* as the sounds of *m* and *n.*

THE SHIELD OF OMNIPOTENCE

*"God is our refuge and strength,
A very present help in trouble."*

1. He that dwelleth in the secret place of the Most High
   Shall abide under the shadow of the Almighty.
   I will say of Jehovah, He is my refuge and my fortress;
   My God, in whom I trust.

2. For He will deliver thee from the snare of the fowler,
   And from the deadly pestilence.
   He will cover thee with His pinions,
   And under His wings shalt thou take refuge;
   His truth is a shield and a buckler.

3. Thou snalt not be afraid for the terror by night,
   Nor for the arrow that flieth by day;
   For the pestilence that walketh in darkness,
   Nor for the destruction that wasteth at noonday.

4. A thousand shall fall at thy side,
   And ten thousand at thy right hand;
   But it shall not come nigh thee.
   Only with thine eyes shalt thou behold,
   And see the reward of the wicked.

5. For Thou, O Jehovah, art my refuge!
   Thou hast made the Most High thy habitation:
   There shall no evil befall thee;
   Neither shall any plague come nigh thy tent.

6. For He will give His angels charge over thee,
To keep thee in all thy ways.
They shall bear thee up in their hands,
Lest thou dash thy foot against a stone.

7. Thou shalt tread upon the lion and adder;
The young lion and the serpent shalt thou trample under foot.
Because he hath set his love upon Me, therefore will I deliver him;
I will set him on high, because he hath known My name.

8. He shall call upon Me, and I will answer him,
I will be with him in trouble;
I will deliver him, and honor him.
With long life will I satisfy him,
And show him My salvation.

—*Psalm 91.*

Exercise for Conversation and Study

Who wrote this prophetic psalm? To what time does it apply? Read Revelation, chapters 15 and 16. Name the ten plagues that were visited on Egypt. Name the seven last plagues. When will they be visited upon the earth? How great will be their destruction? The people of God will appreciate the promises of this psalm in the time of the plagues. Would it not be well to memorize it?

Make out a list of the digraphs and trigraphs you can find in this and previous lessons.

Word Study

1. Almighty	3. destruction	6. against
1. fortress	4. thousand	7. serpent
2. pestilence	4. reward	7. trample
2. pinions	5. refuge	8. satisfy
3. arrow	5. plague	8. salvation

SOUND

III. QUALITY OF ORAL SOUNDS

Long and *short* are terms which apply only to vocals. Vowel sounds differ from subvocals in that they are less interrupted by the organs of speech. They differ from each other in quantity, or duration, and in quality. With reference to quality they are classified as long and short.

Long vowel sounds are those which may be, and usually are, prolonged in their utterance; as *a* in *pay*, and *oo* in *woo*.

Short vowel sounds are those which, in ordinary speech, do not admit of prolongation, as *i* in *fit*, *o* in *not*. In the English language they are peculiarly abrupt, or "explosive," in their utterance. The prolonging of a short sound results in "drawling."

Each vowel has a "regular" long and short sound, which in most cases it represents, and one or more "occasional," or irregular sounds. The regular long and short sounds of a given vowel in English are not necessarily, nor even usually, the natural correlatives of each other.

LONG SOUNDS			SHORT SOUNDS		
ā,	as in	fāme	ă,	as in	făt
ä,	" "	fäther	ȧ,	" "	ȧsk
a̤,	" "	fa̤ll	ĕ,	" "	mĕt
â,	" "	fâre	ĭ,	" "	pĭt
ē,	" "	mēte	ŏ,	" "	cŏffee
ẽ,	" "	vẽrse	o͝o,	" "	fo͝ot
ī,	" "	mīne	ŭ,	" "	ŭp
ō,	" "	tōne			
o͞o,	" "	bo͞ot			
ū,	" "	tūne			
û,	" "	ûrge			
ou,	" "	sour			
oi,	" "	oil			

Correlative Long and Short Sounds

LONG			SHORT		
â,	as in	câre	ĕ,	as in	mĕt
ä,	" "	fäther	ȧ,	" "	ȧsk
a̤,	" "	fa̤ll	ŏ,	" "	ŏn
ē,	" "	mēte	ĭ,	" "	mĭt
o͞o,	" "	bo͞ot	o̵o̵,	" "	fo̵o̵t
û,	" "	ûrge	ŭ,	" "	ŭp

Quality. Vowel sounds differ in quality according to the different positions of the organs during their utterance, every new adjustment of the organs producing a distinct effect upon the ear.

The various terms, as flat, grave, broad, obtuse, etc., which have been used to indicate quality of sounds, are rather misleading than useful.

The study and discrimination of the nicer and more difficult shades of sound, and of the configurations by which they are produced, is a matter of much importance to scientific students of language.

Semivowels are those sounds which, in their degree of modification, stand on the border line between vocals and subvocals, and are thus capable of use in either class. They are the sounds of *w, y, l, n,* and *r,* and perhaps even that of *m.* The term semivocal is not extremely accurate; but for the want of a better is used here, and is likely to continue in use, with a more scientific application than formerly.

CHARACTER OF THE PURITAN FATHERS

"Give me liberty or give me death!"

1. One of the most prominent features which distinguished our forefathers, was their determined resistance to oppression. They seemed born and brought up for the high and special purpose of showing to the world that the civil and religious rights of man, the rights of self-government, of conscience and independent thought, are not merely things to be talked of and woven into theories; but to be adopted with the whole strength and ardor of the mind, felt in the profoundest recesses of the heart, carried into the general life, and made the foundation of practical usefulness, visible beauty, and true nobility.

2. Liberty, with them, was an object of too serious desire and stern resolve to be personified, allegorized, and enshrined. They made no goddess of it, as the ancients did; they had no time nor inclination for such trifling; they felt that liberty was the simple birthright of every human creature; they called it so; they claimed it as such; they reverenced and held it fast as the unalienable gift of the Creator, which was not to be surrendered to power, nor sold for wages.

3. It was theirs, as men; without it they did not esteem themselves men; more than any other privilege or possession, it was essential to their happiness, for it was essential to their original nature; and therefore they preferred it above wealth, and ease, and country; and that they might enjoy and exercise it fully, they forsook houses, and lands, and kindred, their homes, their native soil, and their fathers' graves.

4. They left all these; they left England, which, whatever it might have been called, was not to them a land of freedom; they launched forth on the pathless ocean,—the wide, fathomless ocean, soiled not by the earth beneath, and bounded all round and above only by heaven. It seemed to them like that better and sublimer

PILGRIMS GOING TO CHURCH
BOUGHTON 1834—

freedom, which their country knew not, but of which they had the conception and image in their hearts; and after a toilsome and painful voyage, they came to a hard and wintry coast, unfruitful and desolate, but unguarded and boundless. Its calm silence interrupted not the ascent of their prayers; it had no eyes to watch, no ears to hearken, no tongue to report of them. Here, again, there was an answer to their souls' desire, and they were satisfied and gave thanks; they saw that they were free, and the desert smiled.

5. I am telling an old tale; but it is one that must be told when we speak of those men. It is to be added that they transmitted their principles to their children, and that, peopled by such a race, our country was always free. So long as its inhabitants were unmolested by the mother country in the exercise of their important rights, they submitted to the form of English government; but when those rights were invaded, they spurned away even the form.

6. This act was the Revolution, which came naturally and spontaneously, and had nothing in it of the wonderful or unforeseen. The wonder would have been if it had not occurred. It was indeed a happy and glorious event, but by no means unnatural; and I intend no slight to the revered actors of the Revolution, when I assert that their fathers before them were as free as they—every whit as free.

7. The principles of the Revolution were not the suddenly acquired property of a few bosoms; they were abroad in the land ages before; they had always been taught, like the truths of the Bible. They had descended from father to son, down from those primitive days when the pilgrim, established in his simple dwelling, and seated at his blazing fire, piled high from the forest which shaded his door, repeated to his listening children the story of his wrongs and his resistance, and bade them rejoice, though the wild winds and the wild beasts were howling without, for they had nothing to fear from great men's oppression.

8. Here are the beginnings of the Revolution. Every settler's hearth was a school of independence; the scholars were apt, and the lessons sunk deeply; and thus it came that our country was always free. It could not be other than free.

9. As deeply seated as was the principle of liberty and resistance to arbitrary power in the breasts of the Puritans, it was not more so than their piety and sense of religious obligation. They were emphatically a people whose God was the Lord. Their form of government was as strictly theocratical, if direct communication be excepted, as was that of the Jews; insomuch that it would be difficult to say where there was any civil authority among them entirely distinct from ecclesiastical jurisdiction.

10. Whenever a few of them settled a town, they immediately gathered themselves into a church; their elders were magistrates, and their code of laws was the Pentateuch. These were forms, it is true, but forms which faithfully indicated principles and feelings; for no people could have adopted such forms who were not thoroughly imbued with the spirit, and bent on the practice, of religion.

11. God was their king; and they regarded Him as truly and literally so as if He had dwelt in a visible palace in the midst of their state. They were His devoted, resolute, humble subjects; they undertook nothing which they did not beg of Him to prosper; they accomplished nothing without rendering to Him the praise; they suffered nothing without carrying their sorrows to His throne; they ate nothing which they did not implore Him to bless.

12. Their piety was not merely external; it was sincere; it had the proof of a good tree in bearing good fruit; it produced and sustained a strict morality. Their tenacious purity of manners and speech obtained for them in the mother country their name of Puritans, which, though given in derision, was as honorable an appellation as was ever bestowed by man on man.

13. That there were hypocrites among them, is not to be doubted; but they were rare. The men who voluntarily exiled themselves to an unknown coast, and endured there every toil and hardship for conscience' sake, that they might serve God in their own manner, were not likely to set conscience at defiance, and make the service of God a mockery. They were not likely to be, neither were they, hypocrites. I do not know that it would be arrogating too much for them, to say that on the extended surface of the globe there was not a single community of men to be compared with them in the respects of deep religious impressions and an exact performance of moral duty.

—*Greenwood.*

Exercise for Conversation and Study

Why were the early settlers of New England called Puritans? What caused them to leave their native land? When did they reach America, and where did they land? What holiday had its origin with the Puritan Fathers, and what were the conditions connected with its first observance? What prophecy in the Scriptures foretells the rise and development of a nation in new territory, having for its basic principles civil and religious liberty? Rev. 13:12. What document was prepared that emphasized these principles, and who were some of the leading men that figured prominently in laying the foundation stones of this new government and nation—the United States? Memorize the passage in the Declaration of Independence that declares the equality of all mankind. What scriptures echo the same truth?

Study carefully the long vowel sounds, and make a list of the words in the lesson that contain these sounds.

Word Study

1. prominent
1. oppression
2. liberty
2. unalienable
3. original
4. launched
4. ascent
5. government
6. Revolution
6. spontaneously
7. pilgrim
8. independence
9. Puritans
12. tenacious
13. hypocrite

THE GOODLY LAND

"Behold, I make all things new."

1. The wilderness and the dry land shall be glad;
   And the desert shall rejoice, and blossom as the rose.
   It shall blossom abundantly, and rejoice even with joy and singing;
   The glory of Lebanon shall be given unto it,
   The excellency of Carmel and Sharon;
   They shall see the glory of Jehovah,
   The excellency of our God.

2. Strengthen ye the weak hands,
   And confirm the feeble knees.
   Say to them that are of a fearful heart, "Be strong, fear not;
   Behold your God will come with vengeance,
   With the recompense of God;
   He will come and save you."

3. Then the eyes of the blind shall be opened,
   And the ears of the deaf shall be unstopped.
   Then shall the lame man leap as a hart,
   And the tongue of the dumb shall sing:
   For in the wilderness shall waters break out,
   And streams in the desert.

4. And the glowing sand shall become a pool,
   And the thirsty ground springs of water:
   In the habitation of jackals, where they lay,
   Shall be grass with reeds and rushes.

5. And a highway shall be there, and a way,
   And it shall be called The Way of Holiness;

The unclean shall not pass over it; but it shall be for the redeemed:
The wayfaring men, yea, fools, shall not err therein.

6. No lion shall be there,
Nor shall any ravenous beast go up thereon;
They shall not be found there:
But the redeemed shall walk there;
And the ransomed of Jehovah shall return,
And come with singing unto Zion;
And everlasting joy shall be upon their heads;
They shall obtain gladness and joy,
And sorrow and sighing shall flee away.

—*Isaiah 35.*

Exercise for Conversation and Study

When will this prophecy have its fulfillment? What animals are mentioned in the prophecy? Describe the habits and disposition of each. What truth is emphasized by the reference made to these creatures? What other animals are spoken of elsewhere, by the same prophet? Isa. 11:6-9; 65:25. What changes will take place in the surface of the earth? What is a desert? Locate on the map the Sahara, and the Great American Deserts. What is Lebanon? Carmel? Sharon? Locate each.

Study carefully the short vowel sounds and make a list of the words in the lesson that contain these sounds.

Word Study

1. Lebanon	3. wilderness	6. ravenous
1. Carmel	4. habitation	6. redeemed
1. excellency	4. jackals	6. ransomed
2. vengeance	5. wayfaring	6. Zion
2. recompense	5. Holiness	6. Jehovah

SOUND

IV. DESCRIPTION OF ENGLISH SOUNDS

A brief description of each of the sounds recognized by the English dictionaries is here given as possibly the most practical and serviceable part of these studies. It is thought best to take them up in the order in which they naturally occur in the several series as exhibited in the accompanying diagram.

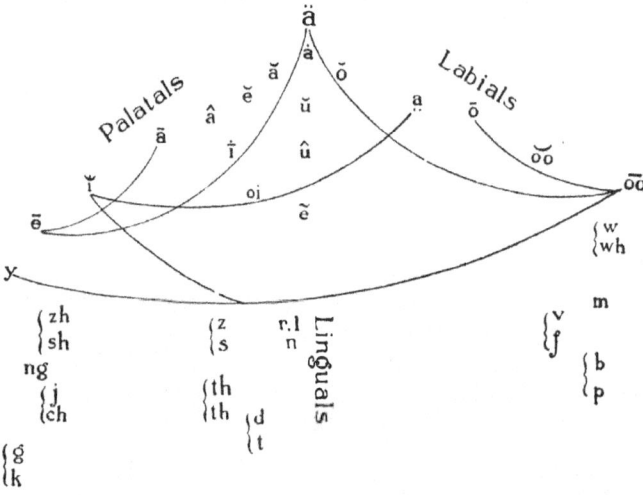

This diagram is, in the main, self-explanatory to one acquainted with Webster's notation.

Starting with the pure, open tone *ah*, the sounds in each series are arranged in the order of openness, downward direction indicating increase of closure.

Consonant sounds are placed beside that to which they are the most closely related.

If the student will produce, successively, all the sounds of each series in the downward order, he can not fail to observe the gradual and uninterrupted closure of the organs concerned.

The Vowel Sounds. A, as in *ah, far* (ä). Italian *a*. This is the fundamental tone of the human voice, the pure product of the vocal organs. Its proper production requires an extreme openness of the organs of speech, allowing the column of fully vocalized breath to pass without obstruction at any point. All other vocals and the subvocals may be considered as simply modifications of this tone.

A, as in *ask* (ȧ). Short Italian *a*. This sound differs from the preceding one in quantity, being short, or explosive. When perfectly produced, it requires the same extreme openness of the organs as the full Italian *a;* but it is liable, even in the hands of good speakers, to a slight modification by closure. In instruction, however, the full openness should be insisted upon.

Uneducated [or careless] speakers often use, in place of this elegant sound, in words like dance, grass, etc., a corruption or drawling of the short *a*, a coarse and most disagreeable error.

Labials. O, as in *on, coffee* (ŏ) ; *a*, as in *what* (ạ). Short *o;* (short, broad *a*). This sound so closely resembles the short Italian *a*, as to be very often confounded with it. Its proper utterance requires that the column of vocalized breath should be slightly obstructed by contraction of the lips, drawing the corners of the mouth slightly toward each other. The sound closely resembles that of *a* in *fall*, but is short, or explosive, admitting of no prolongation.

Much care should be taken with this sound; for, while it is one of the finest in the language, it is probably the most abused— the pronunciation of such words as *not, what, fog, watch*, etc., with the sound of Italian *a* more or less shortened, being the invariable custom of the majority of people in some localities, especially in the northwestern states.

A as in *awe* (a̦) ; *o* as in *or* (ô). Broad *a*. Broad *a* resembles Italian *a* in quantity, being long; but it is modified by a contraction and consequent projection of the lips, which lengthens the cavity of resonance.

The position of the lips is a trifle closer than that for short *o*, from which sound this differs but slightly, except in duration.

O, as in *ho* (ō). Long *o*. This sound is a labial. It begins with a position of the lips somewhat closer than that for broad *a*, which position is still further closed during the continuance of the tone, which vanishes in the sound of *oo*, as in *coo*.

OO, as in *foot* (o̤o) ; *o*, as in *wolf* (o̦) ; *u*, as in *put* (u̦). Short *oo* (*u* medial). A still closer lip position than the one for beginning long *o*, with an explosive emission of voice, gives the short vocal known as short *oo*, heard in *foot*, *push*.

OO, as in *boot* (ōō) ; *o*, as in *do* (o̦) ; *u* as in *rude* (u̦). Long *oo* (slender *o*). A prolongation of the vocal tone with a slightly closer position than for the preceding sound (short *oo*), yields the sound heard in *coo, do*. It is the closest of the labial vocals, the next stage of lip closure resulting in the sound of *w*.

This sound is often indolently contracted into the short *oo* in such words as *broom, room, soon,* and even *food*. To pronounce these with the sound of *oo* in *foot* is grossly negligent, though only too common.

Ou, as in *sound; ow,* as in *cow*. If the lips change from extreme openness, as in *ah,* to the extreme closeness of *oo* while the vocal tone continues, the result will be the labial diphthong *ou*, which, therefore, may be considered as the sum of the whole series just discussed. Its analysis is **ou**=ä+**ōō**.

A caution is here necessary. Many speakers begin this diphthong with the sound of short *a*, as *caou* for *cow*.

THE SEA AND ITS USES

> "*All the rivers run into the sea;*
> *Yet the sea is not full;*
> *Unto the place from whence the*
> *rivers come,*
> *Thither they return again.*"

1. The sea is the world's fountain of life and health and beauty, and if it were taken away, the grass would perish from the mountains, the forests would crumble on the hills. Water is as indispensable to all life, vegetable or animal, as the air itself. This element of water is supplied entirely by the sea. The sea is the great, inexhaustible fountain which is continually pouring up into the sky precisely as many streams, and as large, as all the rivers of the world are pouring into the sea.

2. The sea is the real birthplace of the clouds and the rivers, and out of it come all the rains and dews of heaven. Instead of being a waste and an incumbrance, therefore, it is a vast fountain of fruitfulness, and the nurse and mother of all the living. Out of its mighty breast come the resources that feed and support the population of the world. We are surrounded by the presence and bounty of the sea.

3. It looks upon us from every violet in our garden bed; from every spire of grass that drops upon our passing feet the beaded dew of the morning; from the bending grain that fills the arm of the reaper; from bursting presses, and from barns filled with plenty; from the broad foreheads of our cattle and the rosy faces of our children.

4. It is the sea that feeds us. It is the sea that clothes us. It cools us with the summer cloud, and warms us with the blazing fires of winter. We make wealth for ourselves and for our children out of its rolling waters, though we may live a thousand leagues away from its shore, and never have looked upon its crested beauty or listened to its eternal anthem.

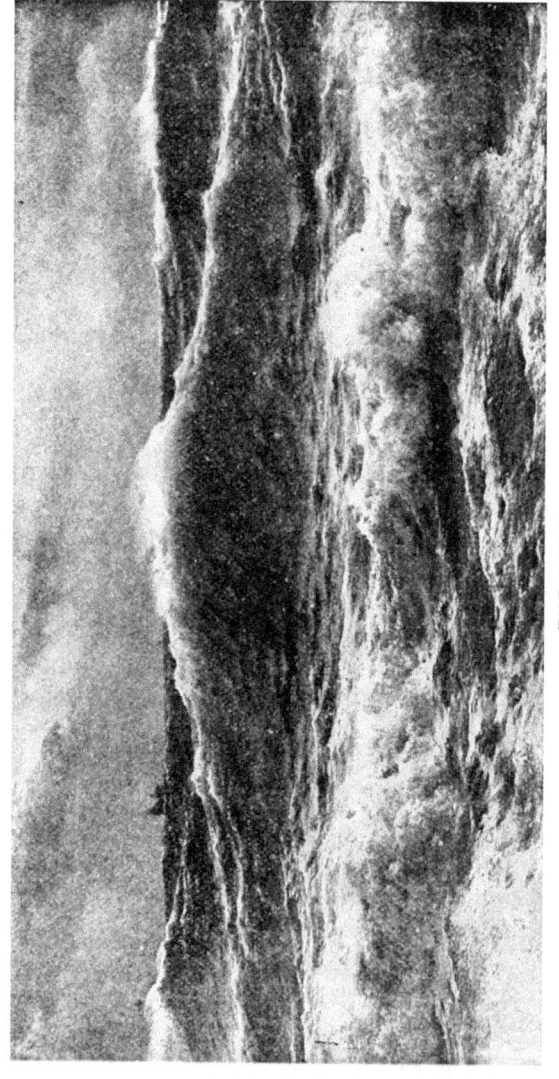

THE OCEAN

5. Thus the sea, though it bears no harvest on its bosom, yet sustains all the harvests of the world. It, like a desert itself, makes all the other wildernesses of the earth to bud and blossom as the rose. Though its own waters are as salt and wormwood, it makes the clouds of heaven to drop with sweetness, opens springs in the valleys and rivers among the hills.

6. The sea is a perpetual source of health to the world. Without it there could be no drainage for the lands. It is the scavenger of the world. The sea is also set to purify the atmosphere. The winds, whose wings are heavy and whose breath is sick with the malaria of the lands over which they have blown, are sent out to range over these mighty pastures of the deep, to plunge and play with the rolling billows and dip their pinions over and over in its healing waters.

7. There they rest when they are weary; there they rouse themselves when they are refreshed. Thus their whole sustenance is drenched, and bathed, and washed, and winnowed, and sifted through and through by this glorious baptism. Thus they fill their mighty lungs once more with the sweet breath of the ocean, and, striking their wings for the shore, they go breathing health and vigor.

8. The ocean is not the idle creature that it seems, with its vast and lazy length stretched between continents, with its huge bulk sleeping along the shore, or tumbling in aimless fury from pole to pole. It is a mighty giant, who, leaving his cozy bed, comes up upon the land to spend his strength in the service of man. Thus the sea keeps all our mills and factories in motion. Thus the sea spins our thread and weaves our cloth.

9. It is the sea that cuts our iron bars like wax, rolls them out into proper thinness, or piles them up in the solid shaft, strong enough to be the pivot of a revolving planet. It is the sea that tunnels the mountain, and bores the mine, and lifts the coal from

its sunless depth, and the ore from its rocky bed. It is the sea that lays the iron track, that builds the iron horse, that fills his nostrils with fiery breath, and sends his tireless hoofs thundering across the longitudes. It is the power of the sea that is doing for man all these mightiest works that would else be impossible.

10. "There is a pleasure in the pathless woods,
    There is a rapture on the lonely shore,
    There is a society where none intrudes
      By the deep sea, and music in its roar.
    I love not man the less, but Nature more,
    From these our interviews, in which I steal
      From all I may be, or have been before,
    To mingle with the universe, and feel
    What I can ne'er express, yet can not all conceal.

11. "Roll on, thou deep and dark blue ocean—roll;
    Ten thousand fleets sweep over thee in vain;
    Man marks the earth with ruin—his control
      Stops with the shore;—upon the watery plain
      The wrecks are all thy deed, nor doth remain
    A shadow of man's ravage, save his own;
      When, for a moment, like a drop of rain,
    He sinks into the depths with bubbling groan,
    Without a grave, unknelled, uncoffined, and unknown."
    —*Selected.*

Exercise for Conversation and Study

When were the seas created? Gen. 1:9, 10. What Bible writer speaks of the circulation of the waters in the sea? Eccl. 1:7. What keeps the sea from overflowing the land? Job 38:8, 10. What name is applied to the large bodies of water separating the continents? Name and locate the five oceans. Why is the water in the ocean salt? Enumerate the blessings bestowed by the sea. Who made it? Ps. 95:3-5. Who then is really the Author of all its blessings? James 1:17.

From this and previous lessons, select ten words for each of the following sounds:—

ä, long Italian; ŏ, short o; ȧ, short Italian; ạ, broad a.

Word Study

1. indispensable
1. inexhaustible
2. resources
2. population
2. incumbrance
4. leagues
4. anthem
5. valleys
6. perpetual
6. scavenger
7. drenched
7. baptism
8. continents
9. nostrils
9. longitudes

THE TALENT OF SPEECH

"A word fitly spoken is like apples of gold in baskets of silver."

1. The power of speech is a talent that should be diligently cultivated. Of all the gifts we have received from God, none is capable of being a greater blessing than this. With the voice we convince and persuade; with it we offer prayer and praise to God, and with it we tell others of the Redeemer's love. How important, then, that it be so trained as to be most effective for good.

2. The culture and right use of the voice are greatly neglected, even by persons of intelligence and Christian activity. There are many who read or speak in so low or so rapid a manner that they can not be readily understood. Some have a thick, indistinct utterance; others speak in a high key, in sharp, shrill tones, that are painful to the hearers. Texts, hymns, and the reports and other papers presented before public assemblies are sometimes read in such a way that they are not understood, and often so that their force and impressiveness are destroyed.

3. This is an evil that can and should be corrected. On this point the Bible gives instruction. Of the Levites who read the

Scriptures to the people in the days of Ezra, it is said, "They read in the Book in the law of God distinctly, and gave the sense, and caused them to understand the reading."

4. By diligent effort all may acquire the power to read intelligibly, and to speak in a full, clear, round tone, in a distinct and impressive manner. By doing this we may greatly increase our efficiency as workers for Christ.

5. Every Christian is called to make known to others the unsearchable riches of Christ; therefore he should seek for perfection in speech. He should present the Word of God in a way that will commend it to the hearers. God does not design that His human channels shall be uncouth. It is not His will that man shall belittle or degrade the heavenly current that flows through Him to the world.

6. We should look to Jesus, the perfect pattern; we should pray for the aid of the Holy Spirit, and in His strength, we should seek to train every organ for perfect work.

7. Especially is this true of those who are called to public service. Every minister and every teacher should bear in mind that he is giving to the people a message that involves eternal interests. The truth spoken will judge them in the great day of final reckoning. And with some souls the manner of the one delivering the message will determine its reception or rejection. Then let the word be so spoken that it will appeal to the understanding and impress the heart. Slowly, distinctly, and solemnly should it be spoken, yet with all the earnestness which its importance demands.

8. The right culture and use of the power of speech has to do with every line of Christian work; it enters into the home life, and into all our intercourse with one another. We should accustom ourselves to speak in pleasant tones, to use pure and correct language, and words that are kind and courteous. Sweet, kind words are as dew and gentle showers to the soul. The Scripture says of Christ that grace was poured into His lips, that He might "know

how to speak a word in season to him that is weary." And the Lord bids us, "Let your speech be alway with grace," "that it may minister grace unto the hearers."

9. In seeking to correct or reform others, we should be careful of our words. They will be a savor of life unto life or of death unto death. In giving reproof or counsel, many indulge in sharp, severe speech, words not adapted to heal the wounded soul. By these ill-advised expressions the spirit is chafed, and often the erring ones are stirred to rebellion. All who would advocate the principles of truth need to receive the heavenly oil of love. Under all circumstances reproof should be spoken in love. Then our words will reform, but not exasperate. Christ by His Holy Spirit will supply the force and the power. This is His work.

10. Not one word is to be spoken unadvisedly. No evil speaking, no frivolous talk, no fretful repining, no impure suggestion, will escape the lips of him who is following Christ. The apostle Paul, writing by the Holy Spirit, says, "Let no corrupt communication proceed out of your mouth." A corrupt communication does not mean only words that are vile. It means any expression contrary to holy principles and pure and undefiled religion. It includes impure hints and covert insinuations of evil. Unless instantly resisted, these lead to great sin.

11. Upon every family, upon every individual Christian, is laid the duty of barring the way against corrupt speech. When in the company of those who indulge in foolish talk, it is our duty to change the subject of conversation if possible. By the help of the grace of God we should quietly drop words or introduce a subject that will turn the conversation into a profitable channel.

12. It is the work of parents to train their children to proper habits of speech. The very best school for this culture is the home life. From the earliest years the children should be taught to speak respectfully and lovingly to their parents and to one another.

They should be taught that only words of gentleness, truth, and purity must pass their lips. Let the parents themselves be daily learners in the school of Christ. Then by precept and example they can teach their children the use of "sound speech, that can not be condemned." This is one of the greatest and most responsible of their duties.

13. As followers of Christ we should make our words such as to be a help and an encouragement to one another in the Christian life. Far more than we do, we need to speak of the precious chapters in our experience. We should speak of the mercy and loving-kindness of God, of the matchless depths of the Saviour's love. Our words should be words of praise and thanksgiving. If the mind and heart are full of the love of God, this will be revealed in the conversation. It will not be a difficult matter to impart that which enters into our spiritual life. Great thoughts, noble aspirations, clear perceptions of truth, unselfish purposes, yearnings for piety and holiness, will bear fruit in words that reveal the character of the heart-treasure. When Christ is thus revealed in our speech, it will have power in winning souls to Him.

14. We should speak of Christ to those who know Him not. We should do as Christ did. Wherever He was, in the synagogue, by the wayside, in the boat thrust out a little from the land, at the Pharisee's feast, or the table of the publican, He spoke to men of the things pertaining to the higher life. The things of nature, the events of daily life, were bound up by Him with the words of truth. The hearts of His hearers were drawn to Him; for He had healed their sick, had comforted their sorrowing ones, and had taken their children in His arms and blessed them. When He opened His lips to speak, their attention was riveted upon Him, and every word was to some soul a savor of life unto life.

15. So it should be with us. Wherever we are, we should watch for opportunities of speaking to others of the Saviour. If we follow Christ's example in doing good, hearts will open to us as they

did to Him. Not abruptly, but with tact born of divine love, we can tell them of Him who is the "Chiefest among ten thousand," and the One "altogether lovely." This is the very highest work in which we can employ the talent of speech. It was given to us that we might present Christ as the sin-pardoning Saviour.
—*Mrs. E. G. White.*

Exercise for Conversation and Study

Name and locate the organs of speech. In your own language describe the action of these organs in producing speech. For what purpose has God given the talent of speech? Mention some of the ways that this talent is misused. What are the characteristics of a well-trained voice? Can all improve their voices by diligent, painstaking effort? What is the purpose of your reading class? Mention some of the most common mistakes made in reading.

Make out lists of words containing the following vowel sounds: ŏ, o͝o, o͞o, and ou. Drill carefully on the production of the vowel sounds studied.

Word Study

1. diligent	4. efficiency	10. insinuations
1. persuade	5. degrade	12. condemned
2. culture	7. especially	13. yearnings
2. indistinct	8. accustom	14. synagogue
3. instruction	9. exasperate	14. Pharisees
4. impressive	9. advocate	15. Saviour

SOUND

V. DESCRIPTION OF ENGLISH SOUNDS (CONTINUED)

Palatals. This series of sounds might with greater accuracy be termed *linguo-palatals*, since the part played by the tongue is so great; but the simpler term has the sanction of high authority, at least.

A, as in *at* (ă). Short *a*. This simple and familiar sound differs but little in position from the short Italian *a*, though quite distinct to the ear. A slightly different adjustment of the soft palate from that for *ah*, and a slight lifting of the blade of the tongue, constitute its peculiarity. Like other short sounds it should receive a neat and elegant utterance, any prolongation of it destroying its true character.

E, as in *met* (ĕ). Short *e*. A still closer approach of tongue and palate than that required for short *a*, is necessary for the production of short *e*, the tongue being thrust well forward, and its middle portion considerably arched. The only caution needful is that against prolongation in speaking. It may be prolonged in singing, however.

A, as in *care* (â); *e*, as in *there* (ê). Circumflex *a*. This sound has been thought by some to be identical with the preceding one, short *e*. It differs from it, when correctly uttered, in being somewhat closer and in admitting of moderate prolongation. It occurs in accented syllables only before the sound of *r*. It is a simple element, and constitutes the radical, or initial, part of long *a*, heard in *pay*.

A, as in *pay* (ā); *e*, as in *prey* (ē). Long *a*. Long *a* is a linguopalatal. It begins with the preceding sound in the series, *a*, as in *care*, and closes with the sound of *e*, in *me*. This involves a considerable closure of the palate and tongue during the utterance of the sound. In the utterance of *a*, in *care*, the tongue is immediately drawn back and narrowed to form the palatal *r;* but in forming long *a* the tongue is pressed still farther forward, and is crowded against the upper teeth to form the vanishing element. In unaccented syllables the vanish is sometimes omitted.

I, as in *it* (ĭ) ; *y,* as in *abyss* (y̆). Short *i*. This sound most resembles that of *e,* in *me*. It is slightly more open in its formation, being in closeness midway between the radical and the vanishing parts of long *a*. It is a true abrupt, or short sound; and even when prolonged, it is still distinct from long *e*.

E, as in *me* (ē) ; *i,* as in *pique* (ī). Long *e*. This is the closest of the palatal vocals, the next stage of palatal closure yielding the semi-vowel *y,* as in *yet*. For the formation of long *e,* the edges of the tongue are pressed against the teeth, while its middle portion is almost in contact with the palate throughout its whole length, thus leaving a very thin passage for the breath.

I, as in *ice* (ī) ; *y,* as in *my* (ȳ). Long *i*. This is a palatal. For its production, the tongue and palate are placed in the extreme open position of Italian *a* and closed, during vocalization, to the extreme close position of long *e*. Thus, like *ou,* it is the sum of a series of sounds. Its analysis is usually given as: ī=ä+ē, which is practically correct. A common fault in its utterance consists in not beginning with a sufficiently open position of the mouth.

U, as in *use, tune* (ū) ; *ew,* as in *new* (ew̄). Long *u*. Long *u* presents two distinct phases to the ear, as heard in the words *use* and *tune.* If the palate and tongue be placed in the close and tense position required for the sound of *y* in *yet,* and then open while the lips close to the position of *oo* in *woo,* the resulting voice-sound will be that of long *u* at the beginning of a syllable, as in *union, use,* etc. In any other place than the beginning of a syllable, however, it is almost impossible to form the *y* sound perfectly; hence, a more open position is substituted, that of short *i,* as in *it;* and the *u* becomes a combination of the short *i,* and the long *oo,* the *i* accented, but very quickly uttered. But for this change from *y* to short *i,* the words *tune* and *duke* would become, in most mouths, *choon* and *jook*. Long *u* is one of the most difficult and trying sounds of our language. Its analysis may be represented thus: $\bar{u} = \bar{e} + \overline{oo}$.

Oi, as in *oil;* *oy*, as in *boy*. Its position is that for broad *a*, as in *awe*, changing to that of the close palatal, short *i;* $\mathbf{oi} = \hat{o} + \breve{i}$.

MAN THE LIFEBOAT

"And so it came to pass that they escaped all safe to land."

1. Man the lifeboat! Man the lifeboat!
   Hearts of oak, your succor lend!
   See the shattered vessel stagger;
   Quick, O quick, assistance send!

2. See, they launch the gallant lifeboat!
   See, they ply the lusty oar!
   Round them rage the foamy breakers,
   Cheers attend them from the shore.

3. Now the fragile bark is hanging
   On the billow's giddy height;
   Now to fearful depths descending,
   While we sicken at the sight.

4. Courage! courage!—she's in safety;
   For again her buoyant form
   Mounts and mocks the dashing surges,
   Like the petrel in the storm.

5. With her precious cargo freighted,
   Now the lifeboat nears the shore;

Parents, brethren, friends, embracing
Those they thought to see no more.

6. Blessings on the dauntless spirits,
Dangers thus who nobly brave;
Ready life and limb to venture,
So they may a brother save!

—*Selected.*

Exercise for Conversation and Study

What is the scene here described by the poet? Learn what you can of the construction of a lifeboat. What are lifeboat stations? Where and how are they operated? Read the lesson as nearly as possible, with the same feeling and emotion, as if you were an eyewitness of this scene. Why is the exclamation point used in the first and second stanzas and not in the third and fifth? Read the second and third stanzas together. Should both be read with the same expression? Why? What shipwreck is referred to by the line at the head of the lesson, and where is the incident recorded? Relate it in your own words.

Write out lists of words containing the following vowel sounds: ă, ĕ, â. Be very careful to acquire the habit of correctly pronouncing all these vowel sounds.

Word Study

1. succor	3. fragile	5. freighted
1. assistance	3. giddy	5. embracing
2. launch	4. petrel	6. dauntless
2. gallant	4. buoyant	6. spirits
2. breakers	5. precious	6. venture

DANIEL IN A HEATHEN SCHOOL

"Dare to be a Daniel,
Dare to stand alone;
Dare to have a purpose firm,
Dare to make it known."

1. In the third year of the reign of Jehoiakim king of Judah came Nebuchadnezzar king of Babylon unto Jerusalem, and besieged it. And the Lord gave Jehoiakim king of Judah into his hand, with part of the vessels of the house of God: which he carried into the land of Shinar to the house of his god; and he brought the vessels into the treasure-house of his god.

2. And the king spake unto Ashpenaz the master of his eunuchs, that he should bring certain of the children of Israel, and of the king's seed, and of the princes; children in whom was no blemish, but well favored, and skillful in all wisdom, and cunning in knowledge, and understanding science, and such as had ability in them to stand in the king's palace, and whom they might teach the learning and tongue of the Chaldeans.

3. And the king appointed them a daily provision of the king's meat, and of the wine which he drank: so nourishing them three years, that at the end thereof they might stand before the king. Now among these were of the children of Judah, Daniel, Hananiah, Mishael, and Azariah: unto whom the prince of the eunuchs gave names: for he gave unto Daniel the name of Belteshazzar; and to Hananiah, of Shadrach; and to Mishael, of Meshach; and to Azariah, of Abed-nego.

4. But Daniel purposed in his heart that he would not defile himself with the portion of the king's meat, nor with the wine which he drank: therefore he requested of the prince of the eunuchs that he might not defile himself. Now God had brought Daniel into favor and tender love with the prince of the eunuchs.

5. And the prince of the eunuchs said unto Daniel, "I fear my lord the king, who hath appointed your meat and your drink:

for why should he see your faces worse liking than the children which are of your sort? then shall ye make me endanger my head to the king."

6. Then said Daniel to Melzar, whom the prince of the eunuchs had set over Daniel, Hananiah, Mishael, and Azariah, "Prove thy servants, I beseech thee, ten days; and let them give us pulse to eat, and water to drink. Then let our countenances be looked upon before thee, and the countenance of the children that eat of the portion of the king's meat; and as thou seest, deal with thy servants." So he consented to them in this matter, and proved them ten days.

7. And at the end of ten days their countenances appeared fairer and fatter in flesh than all the children which did eat the portion of the king's meat. Thus Melzar took away the portion of their meat, and the wine that they should drink; and gave them pulse. As for these four children, God gave them knowledge and skill in all learning and wisdom, and Daniel had understanding in all visions and dreams.

8. Now at the end of the days that the king had said he should bring them in, then the prince of the eunuchs brought them in before Nebuchadnezzar. And the king communed with them; and among them all was found none like Daniel, Hananiah, Mishael, and Azariah: therefore stood they before the king. And in all matters of wisdom and understanding, that the king enquired of them, he found them ten times better than all the magicians and astrologers that were in all his realm. And Daniel continued even unto the first year of King Cyrus.

—*Daniel 1.*

Exercise for Conversation and Study

Locate Babylon on the map. Relate briefly how Daniel and his companions came to be in Babylon. What were the entrance requirements of the royal school of Babylon? (Read paragraph two.) How would you stand such a test? Where had they received an education to enable them to meet these entrance requirements? How did they pass their final examinations at the end of the three years' course? How did their knowledge compare with that of other students in the same school? (Read paragraph eight.) What was the secret of the success of those four Hebrew youth in their efforts to gain an education in a heathen school? (Read paragraph seven.) What incident in this lesson shows that Daniel and his companions believed in the harmonious development of the physical, mental, and moral powers in the gaining of an education? Does a Christian education fit one for the proper discharge of the duties of this life, as well as for the life to come? Prove your answer by referring to later experiences in the life of Daniel. Read with proper expression the stanza at the head of this lesson.

Make list of words containing the following vowel sounds: $\bar{a}$, $\breve{i}$, $\bar{e}$.

Word Study

1. Nebuchadnezzar
1. Jehoiakim
1. Judah
2. Ashpenaz
2. Israel
2. Chaldeans
3. Daniel
3. Hananiah
3. Mishael
3. Azariah
3. Belteshazzar
3. Shadrach
3. Abed-nego
4. eunuchs
6. Melzar
8. astrologers
8. magicians
8. Cyrus

SOUND

VI. DESCRIPTION OF ENGLISH SOUNDS (CONTINUED)

Linguals

The linguals differ from the palatals in the relative prominence of the tongue as a modifying instrument. This is more plainly seen in the consonant than in the vowel sounds of the series.

U, as in *up* ($\breve{u}$); O, as in *son* ($\dot{o}$). Short *u*. This is an open sound, being, like short *a* and short *o*, but one remove from Italian *a*, though in a different direction. The slight closure necessary to transform short Italian *a* into short *u*, is effected by a slight elevation of the base of the tongue. The sound is one of easy utterance, requiring little muscular effort, and therefore liable to intrude itself into many places where it does not belong, to the exclusion of more elegant sounds, especially in unaccented syllables. The excessive use of it is a mark of laziness and barbarous negligence in speech.

U, as in urge (û) ; o, as in *word* (ŏ). Circumflex *u*. A slightly greater elevation of the back part of the tongue toward the soft palate than that for short *u*, with prolongation of the tone, gives the sound of *u* heard before *r* final, or *r* followed by another consonant. It is a comparatively open sound, and easy of utterance, differing from short *u* to the ear, chiefly in its greater duration.

E, as in *verse* (ẽ) ; *i*, as in *girl* (ĩ). Tilde *e*. This is a close lingual sound, the tongue being well raised in all its forward part, while the teeth are brought nearer together than for the preceding sound (*u* in *urge*). It has been described as an intermediate between short *e*, as in *merry*, and the *u* in *urge;* though it is commonly confused by great numbers of people with the latter sound. The distinction between the two is insisted upon by such authorities as Webster and Smart.

The direction to be given to students is: Keep a close position of all the organs, and form the sound well forward in the mouth. The *u* sound can be made with an open mouth; this can not.

Semivowels

As the difference between vocals and subvocals is only a difference in degree of modification or obstruction by the organs of speech, it is natural that there should be a stage of uncertainty, a sort of borderland between them. Hence some writers, with much reason, recognize these sounds which lie along this borderline as a separate class, under the name of semivowels.

W. The labial semivowel is represented in English by the letter *w*. It is formed by a lip-closure so extreme as to lessen the purity of the tone considerably below that of long *oo*, though not so far as to prevent prolongation of the sound.

Y. The palatal semivowel is the sound of *y* in *yet*, which bears the same close relation to long *e* that *w* does to long *oo*. The position of the organs is similar to that for long *e*, but one degree closer, reducing the tone to a mere buzz or hum. The tongue is slightly drawn back from the *e* position, and the pressure against the teeth is increased.

R. Closely related to the sound of *e* in *her* (tilde *e*), are the two sounds of *r*. The lingual *r*, heard at the beginning or anywhere before the vowel sound of a syllable, is formed by placing the tongue well forward and turned upward so that the breath is passed over its extreme tip, producing a very slight trill, or vibration. The position differs from that of tilde *e* in the turning up of the tip of the tongue. The palatal, or uvular *r*, heard at the end of a syllable, or whenever not immediately followed by a vowel, as in *far*, *farm*, can be produced without the aid of the tip of the tongue, being formed farther back in the mouth.

This is clearly a different sound from the lingual *r*, but the two are not discriminated by some ears. The common and disagreeable error of failing to sound the palatal *r*, giving *fahmah* for *farmer*, etc., is usually taken as an evidence of affectation. It is often, however, a matter of innocent, ignorant habit rather than affectation.

L. The sound of *l* is of about the same closeness as the lingual *r*, the tip of the tongue, however, being placed against the upper teeth or the roof of the mouth, and the breath allowed to escape over the edges of the tongue. It is the semivowel character of *l* which allows it to become the vocal basis of a syllable, as in *able*, *shovel*, etc., in which the *e* is entirely mute, and yet the words are dissyllables.

N. The nasal sound of *n* in *nail*, has the same peculiarity as the foregoing, often constituting a syllable of itself, as in *heaven*, *cotton*, where the preceding vowel is silent.

In the production of this sound, the tongue is placed against the hard palate in such a way as wholly to obstruct the oral passages, the breath escaping through the nasal passages instead.

Semivowels { Labial, w.
Palatal, y.
Lingual, r, l, n.

THE STARS

"They that be wise shall shine as the brightness of the firmament; And they that turn many to righteousness as the stars forever and ever."

1. It is the Christian's privilege to revel in the consolations of this marvelous promise. A conception of its magnitude can be gathered only from the stellar worlds themselves. What are these stars, in the likeness of which the teachers of righteousness are to shine forever and ever? How much of brightness, and majesty, and length of days is involved in this comparison!

2. The sun of our own solar system is one of these stars. If we compare it with this globe upon which we live (our handiest standard of measurement), we find it an orb of no small magnitude and magnificence. Our earth is eight thousand miles in diameter; but the sun's diameter is eight hundred eighty-five thousand six hundred eighty miles. In size it is one and one-half million times larger than our globe; and in the matter of its substance it would balance three hundred fifty-two thousand worlds like ours. What immensity is this!

3. Yet this is far from being the largest or the brightest of the orbs which drive their shining chariots in myriads through the heavens. His proximity (he being only some ninety-five million miles from us) gives him with us a controlling presence and in-

fluence. But far away in the depths of space, so far that they appear like mere points of light, blaze other orbs of vaster size and greater glory. The nearest fixed star, Alpha Centauri, in the southern hemisphere, is found, by the accuracy and efficiency of modern instruments, to be nineteen thousand million miles away; but the polestar system is fifteen times as remote, or two hundred eighty-five thousand million miles; and it shines with a luster equal to that of eighty-six of our suns. Others are still larger, as, for instance, Vega, which emits the light of three hundred forty-four of our suns; Capella, four hundred thirty; Arcturus, five hundred sixteen; and so on, till at last we reach the great star Alcyone, in the constellation of the Pleiades, which floods the celestial spaces with a brilliancy twelve thousand times that of the ponderous orb which lights and controls our solar system! Why, then, does it not appear more luminous to us?—Ah! its distance is twenty-five million diameters of the earth's orbit; and the latter is one hundred ninety million miles! Figures are weak to express such distances. It will be sufficient to say that its glowing light must traverse space as light only travels,—one hundred ninety-two thousand miles a second,—for a period of more than seven hundred years, before it reaches this distant world of ours!

4. Some of these monarchs of the sky rule singly, like our own sun. Some are double; that is, what appears to us like one star is found to consist of two stars—two suns with their retinue of planets, revolving around each other; others are triple; some are quadruple; and one, at least, is sextuple.

5. Besides this, they show all the colors of the rainbow. Some systems are white, some blue, some red, some yellow, some green; and this means differently colored days for the planets of those systems. Castor gives his planets green days. The double polestar gives his yellow. In some, the different suns belonging to the same system are variously colored. Says Dr. Burr, "And, as if to make that Southern Cross the fairest object in all the heavens, we find

in it a group of more than a hundred variously colored red, green, blue, and bluish-green suns, so closely thronged together as to appear in a powerful telescope like a superb bouquet or piece of fancy jewelry."*

6. And what of the age of these glorious bodies? A few years pass away, and all things earthly gather the mold of age, and the odor of decay. How much in this world has perished entirely! But the stars shine on as fresh as in the beginning. Centuries and cycles have gone by, kingdoms have arisen and slowly passed away; we go back beyond the dim and shadowy horizon of history, go back even to the earliest moment introduced by revelation, when order was evoked from chaos, and "the morning stars sang together, and all the sons of God shouted for joy"—even then the stars were on their stately marches, and how long before this we know not; for astronomers tell us of nebulæ lying on the farthest outposts of telescopic vision, whose light in its never-ceasing flight would consume five million years in reaching this planet. So ancient are these stellar orbs! Yet their brightness is not dimmed, nor their force abated. The dew of youth still seems fresh upon them. No broken outline shows the foothold of decay; no faltering motion reveals the decrepitude of age. Of all things visible, these stand next to the Ancient of Days; and their undiminished glory is a prophecy of eternity.

7. And thus shall they who turn many to righteousness shine in a glory that shall bring joy even to the heart of the Redeemer; and thus shall their years roll on forever and ever.

—*Uriah Smith.*

Exercise for Conversation and Study

Commit to memory the lines at the head of this lesson. Where in the Bible may they be found? Are we invited to study the stars? Isa. 40:26. How were they created? Ps. 33:6, 9. Are there many of them? How are they upheld? Heb. 1:1-3; Col. 1:16, 17. What is

---
* In "Ecce Coelum," p. 136.

said of God's knowledge of the starry hosts? Ps. 147:4, 5; Isa. 40:26. How much knowledge have you of the starry heavens? With the aid of the teacher locate the following constellations: Big Dipper, Little Dipper, Cassiopeia, Lyra, Orion, and Pleiades; and the bright stars Vega, Arcturus, Polaris, Capella, Sirius, Castor, and Pollux. Which of these constellations and stars are spoken of in the Bible? Who is called the Bright and Morning Star? What thought do you get from reading Job 38:4-7? What are the morning stars mentioned in this scripture?

Select lists of words containing the vowel sounds û, ŭ, ē. Pronounce the words carefully and note which of the organs of speech are used most in producing the sounds.

Word Study

1. conception
1. magnitude
1. stellar
1. comparison
2. magnificence
2. diameter
2. immensity
3. orbs
3. myriads
3. proximity
3. Vega
3. Capella
3. Arcturus
3. Pleiades
4. retinue
5. Castor
6. astronomers
6. horizon
6. nebulæ
6. Ancient
7. righteousness

DECISIVE INTEGRITY

"The just man walketh in his integrity;
His children are blessed after him."

1. The man who is so conscious of the rectitude of his intentions as to be willing to open his bosom to the inspection of the world, is in possession of the strongest pillars of a decided character. The course of such a man will be firm and steady, because he has nothing to fear from the world, and is sure of the approbation and support of heaven; while he who is conscious of secret and dark designs, which, if known, would blast him, is perpetually shrinking and dodging from public observation, and is afraid of all around, and much more of all above him.

2. Such a man may, indeed, pursue his iniquitous plans steadily; he may waste himself to a skeleton in the guilty pursuit; but it is impossible that he can pursue them with the same health-inspiring confidence and exulting alacrity with him who feels, at every step, that he is in the pursuit of honest ends, by honest means. The clear, unclouded brow, the open countenance, the brilliant eye that can look an honest man steadfastly yet courteously in the face, the healthfully beating heart, and the firm, elastic step, belong to him whose bosom is free from guile, and who knows that all his purposes are pure and right.

3. Why should such a man falter in his course? He may be slandered; he may be deserted by the world; but he has that within him that will keep him erect, and enable him to move onward in his course with his eyes fixed on heaven, which he knows will not desert him.

4. Let your first step, then, in that discipline which is to give you decision of character, be the heroic determination to be honest men, and to preserve this character through every vicissitude of fortune, and in every relation that connects you with society. I do not use this phrase, "honest men," in the narrow sense merely of meeting your pecuniary engagements, and paying your debts; for this the common pride of gentlemen will constrain you to do.

5. I use it in the larger sense of discharging all your duties, both public and private, both open and secret, with the most scrupulous, heaven-attesting integrity; in that sense, further, which drives from the bosom all little, dark, crooked, sordid, debasing considerations of self, and substitutes in their place a bolder, loftier, and nobler spirit; one that will dispose you to consider yourselves as born, not so much for yourselves, as for your country and your fellow creatures, and which will lead you to act on every occasion, sincerely, justly, generously, magnanimously.

6. There is a morality on a larger scale, perfectly consistent with a just attention to your own affairs, which it would be the height of folly to neglect: a generous expansion, a proud elevation,

and a conscious greatness of character, which is the best preparation for a decided course in every institution into which you can be thrown; and it is to this high and noble tone of character that I would have you aspire.

7. I would not have you resemble those weak and meager streamlets which lose their direction at every impediment that presents itself, and stop, and turn back, and creep around, and search out every little channel through which they may wind their feeble and sickly course. Nor yet would I have you resemble the headlong torrent that carries havoc in its mad career.

8. But I would have you be like the ocean, that noblest emblem of majestic decision, which in the calmest hour, still heaves its resistless might of waters to the shore, filling the heavens, day and night, with the echoes of its sublime declaration of independence, and tossing and sporting on its bed with an imperial consciousness of strength that laughs at opposition. It is this depth, and weight, and power, and purity of character, that I would have you resemble; and I would have you, like the waters of the ocean, to become purer by your own action.
—*Wirt.*

Exercise for Conversation and Study

What promise does the Lord make to the just man? Prov. 20:7. What Bible character held fast his integrity under great afflictions? Give a brief account of Job's trials and affliction. How was his steadfast integrity rewarded? Job 42:12-17.

Select words containing the semi-vowels w, y, l, r, n, and note the position of the organs of speech in producing the sounds.

Word Study

1. conscious	3. erect	6. morality
1. rectitude	4. decision	6. elevation
1. inspection	4. discipline	7. impediment
2. iniquitous	4. pecuniary	7. torrent
2. alacrity	5. scrupulously	8. emblem
2. courteously	5. magnanimously	8. imperial

SOUND

VII. DESCRIPTION OF ENGLISH SOUNDS (CONTINUED)

Other Subvocals

As already defined, subvocals are tones produced in the larynx, but greatly modified in the mouth. They are thus impure tones, or, as the name implies, *undertones*.

Vocals are also subject to obstruction, as we have seen, but not to the same degree. The obstruction of the breath gives rise to friction and a mingling of mere noise with the tone. When this admixture of noise reaches such a degree as to predominate over, and partially obscure, the tone, the sound is called subvocal.

Labials

V. If the edges of the upper teeth be placed upon the lower lip, and the vocalized breath forced between the teeth, the sound of the letter *v* will be produced. This sound would be more correctly named *labio-dental*.

M. Let the lips be closed entirely and the vocalized breath be allowed to pass only through the nose. The resulting sound is that of *m*. It differs from that of *n* only in its initial quality and not in its continuation. This sound is sometimes ranked among the semivowels, since it is possible for it to serve as the vowel element of a syllable, as in the common contraction *yes'm* and the ejaculation *m'h'm*. These are hardly legitimate words, however.

B. If, now, the nasal passages be covered with the soft palate, while the action of the larynx continues, we have the sound of the letter *b*, a sound requiring complete contraction of the organs and so not capable of prolongation. The common error in its separate production consists in allowing the lips to part, thus not producing the sound of *b* alone, but in connection with a neutral vowel—a combination best represented by the syllable *buh*.

Palatals

Zh. The sound usually represented by z before long u, as in *azure*, or by z or s before i, as in *osier*, is produced with the blade of the tongue in close proximity to the hard palate and the teeth shut or nearly so. It is a simple element, produced without change of position, though tongue, teeth, and palate conjoin in its formation. It is thus not a pure but mixed palatal.

This sound has been treated as a compound of z and y, but the fact seems to be that the utterance of z and y in succession is impossible without a hiatus, and this element, somewhat similar to them both, is substituted for them. Though known as the sound of zh, it is never represented by that combination of letters, which, indeed, does not occur in the English language. The sound might with more propriety be called the second sound of z.

J. The sound of j is also a mixed palatal. It has generally been considered a compound of the sound of d and the one just discussed, zh. It is undoubtedly a compound, a subvocal diphthong, so to speak; but the analysis mentioned, $d+zh$, is of doubtful accuracy. $D+y$ would seem to be nearer the truth; but the second element is, in all probability, a sound that does not occur separately in our language. The sound of j differs from that of zh in the still greater elevation of the tongue, forming a temporary contact with the hard palate, which is then suddenly broken, the closed teeth parting at the same instant and allowing the breath to escape forcibly. When j is uttered without a vowel immediately ensuing, it is inevitably followed, or closed, by the sound of its aspirate cognate, ch.

Ng, N. The second, or palate, sound of n, usually called ng, is produced by bringing the soft palate and the back part of the tongue into complete contact, compelling the breath to escape through the nose, as in m and n.

From being produced so far back, it is often called a guttural, or throat sound. It is very often displayed by the first, or common, sound of *n* in the mouths of negligent and indolent speakers. Though often represented by the digraph *ng*, it is frequently represented by *n* alone, as in *fin-ger, lin-ger*, etc., in which words the *g* has its own sound and forms no part of the representation of this sound.

G. With the base of the tongue and the soft palate in perfect contact, close also the nasal passages. The attempt to vocalize will result in the sound of *g* as in *gate*, which occupies the same place in the palatal series as *b* in the labial—the last, or closest, subvocal. The letter *g* is unfortunately often used to represent the more open sound of *j*.

THE TOWN PUMP

"If any man thirst, let him come unto Me, and drink."

1. Noon, by the north clock! Noon, by the east! High noon, too, by those hot sunbeams that fall scarcely aslope upon my head, and almost make the water bubble and smoke in the trough under my nose. Truly, we public characters have a tough time of it! And among all the town officers chosen at the yearly meeting, where is he that sustains for a single year the burden of such manifold duties as are imposed in perpetuity upon the Town Pump?

2. The title of town treasurer is rightfully mine, as guardian of the best treasure the town has. The overseers of the poor ought to make me their chairman, since I provide bountifully for the pauper without expense to him that pays taxes. I am at the head of the fire department, and one of the physicians of the board of health. As a keeper of the peace, all water drinkers confess me equal to the constable. I perform some of the duties of the town clerk, by promulgating public notices when they are pasted on my front.

3. To speak within bounds, I am chief person of the munici-

pality, and exhibit, moreover, an admirable pattern to my brother officers by the cool, steady, upright, downright, and impartial discharge of my business, and the constancy with which I stand to my post. Summer or winter, nobody seeks me in vain; for all day long I am seen at the busiest corner, just above the market, stretching out my arms to rich and poor alike; and at night I hold a lantern over my head to show where I am, and to keep people out of the gutters.

4. At this sultry noontide, I am cupbearer to the parched populace, for whose benefit an iron goblet is chained to my waist. Like a dramseller on the public square on muster day, I cry aloud to all and sundry, in my plainest accents and at the very tiptop of my voice: "Here it is, gentlemen! Here is the good liquor! Walk up, walk up, gentlemen, walk up, walk up! Here is the superior stuff! Here is the unadulterated ale of father Adam! Better than Cognac, Hollands, Jamaica, strong beer, or wine of any price; here it is, by the hogshead or the single glass and not a cent to pay. Walk up, gentlemen, walk up, and help yourselves!"

5. It were a pity if all this outcry drew no customers. Here they come. A hot day, gentlemen. Quaff, and away again, so as to keep yourselves in a nice, cool sweat. You, my friend, will need another cupful to wash the dust down your throat, if it be as thick there as it is on your cowhide shoes. I see that you have trudged half a score of miles to-day, and, like a wise man, have passed by the taverns, and stopped at the running brooks and well curbs. Otherwise, betwixt heat without and fire within, you would have been burnt to cinder, or melted down to nothing at all—in the fashion of a jellyfish.

6. Drink, and make room for the other fellow who seeks my aid to quench the fiery fever of last night's potations, which he drained from no cup of mine. Welcome, most rubicund sir! You and I have been strangers hitherto; nor, to confess the truth, will my nose be anxious for a closer intimacy till the fumes of your breath be a little less potent.

7. Mercy on you, man! The water absolutely hisses down your red-hot gullet, and is converted quite into steam in the miniature Tophet which you mistake for a stomach. Fill again, and tell me on the word of an honest toper, did you ever, in cellar, tavern, or any other kind of dramshop, spend the price of your children's food for swig half so delicious? Now for the first time these ten years you know the flavor of cold water. Good-by; and whenever you are thirsty, recollect that I keep a constant supply at the old stand.

8. Who next? O, my little friend, you are just let loose from school, and come here to scrub your blooming face, and drown the memory of certain taps of the ferrule, and other schoolboy troubles in a draught from the Town Pump. Take it, pure as the current of your young life; take it, and may your heart and tongue never be scorched with a fiercer thirst than now.

9. There, my dear child, put down the cup and yield your place to this elderly gentleman, who treads so tenderly over the paving stones that I suspect he is afraid of breaking them. What! he limps by without so much as thanking me, as if my hospitable offers were meant only for people who have no wine cellars.

10. Well, well, sir, no harm done, I hope! Go, draw the cork, tip the decanter; but when your great toe shall set you a-roaring, it will be no affair of mine. If gentlemen love the pleasant titillations of the gout, it is all one to the Town Pump. This thirsty dog, with his red tongue lolling out, does not scorn my hospitality, but stands on his hind legs and laps eagerly out of the trough. See how lightly he capers away again! Jowler, did your worship ever have the gout?

11. Your pardon, good people! I must interrupt my stream of eloquence, and spout forth a stream of water to replenish the trough for this teamster and his two yoke of oxen, who have come all the way from Staunton, or somewhere along that way. No part of my business gives me more pleasure than the watering of

cattle. Look! how rapidly they lower the watermark on the sides of the trough, till their capacious stomachs are moistened with a gallon or two apiece, and they can afford time to breathe with sighs of calm enjoyment! Now they roll their quiet eyes around the brim of their monstrous drinking vessel. An ox is your true toper.

12. I hold myself the grand reformer of the age. From my spout, and such spouts as mine, must flow the stream that shall cleanse our earth of a vast portion of its crime and anguish, which have gushed from the fiery fountains of the still. In this mighty enterprise, the cow shall be my great confederate. Milk and water!

13. Ahem! Dry work this speechifying, especially to all unpracticed orators. I never conceived till now what toil the temperance lecturers undergo for my sake. Do, some Christian, pump a stroke or two, just to wet my whistle. Thank you, sir. But to proceed.

14. The Town Pump and the Cow! Such is the glorious partnership that shall finally monopolize the whole business of quenching thirst. Blessed consummation! Then Poverty shall pass away from the land, finding no hovel so wretched where her squalid form may shelter itself. Then Disease, for lack of other victims, shall gnaw his own heart and die. Then Sin, if she do not die, shall lose half her strength.

15. Then there shall be no war of households. The husband and the wife, drinking deep of peaceful joy, a calm bliss of temperate affections, shall pass hand in hand through life, and lie down, not reluctantly, at its protracted close. To them the past will be no turmoil of mad dreams, nor the future an eternity of such moments as follow the delirium of a drunkard. Their dead faces shall express what their spirits were, and are to be, by a lingering smile of memory and hope. —*Nathaniel Hawthorne.*

Exercise for Conversation and Study

Note the vigorous style of expression in this speech of the Town

Pump. Read it with life and animation. Carefully examine a pump, noting its parts. Describe the pumping operation and explain the principles underlying it. What is the composition of water? What are its properties which make it the best of all beverages? Of what is water a symbol? Rev. 22:17; John 4:5-12; 7:37.

Pronounce carefully the linguals *th, z, d,* and the aspirates *f (ph), p, h, sh, ch, k, th, s, t.* Pronounce words in which they are used.

Word Study

1. manifold	6. potations	11. capacious
1. perpetuity	6. rubicund	11. monstrous
2. treasurer	7. miniature	12. confederate
2. promulgating	8. ferrule	14. monopolize
3. municipality	9. hospitable	14. consummation
4. unadulterated	10. titillations	15. turmoil
5. taverns	11. eloquence	15. delirium

"THE LIVING WATER"

"Ho! every one that thirsteth, come ye to the waters."

Jesus answered and said unto her, "If thou knewest the gift of God and who it is that saith unto thee, 'Give Me to drink;' thou wouldest have asked of Him, and He would have given thee living water."

The woman saith unto Him, "Sir, Thou hast nothing to draw with, and the well is deep: from whence then hast Thou that living water?" . . .

Jesus answered and said unto her, "Whosoever drinketh of this water shall thirst again: but whosoever drinketh of the water that I shall give him, shall never thirst; but the water that I shall give him shall be in him a well of water springing up into everlasting life."

And the Spirit and the Bride say, "Come!" And let him that heareth, say, "Come!" And let him that is athirst, come. And whosoever will, let him take of the water of life freely.

—*Bible.*

SOUND

VIII. DESCRIPTION OF ENGLISH SOUNDS (CONCLUDED)

Linguals

Th. The subvocal *th*, as in *this* (**th**), is a linguo-dental. Although the occasion of so much trouble to foreigners learning our language, it is of the easiest production. Place the tip of the tongue under and against the edges of the upper teeth, and expel the vocalized breath between the teeth. The above simple direction, aided by reasonable attention and perseverance, will enable any person, whose mouth has not become actually ossified, to acquire this sound perfectly.

Z. To produce the sound of *z*, as in *buzz*, the tongue takes the same general position as for the trilled *r;* but the tip is a little less elevated, and is brought very near to the teeth, which are nearly or quite closed. The close resemblance of this position to that for *th*, accounts for the Frenchman's treatment of that sound, *th*, in speaking English.

D. Place the tip of the tongue against the hard palate, so as completely to obstruct the oral passage, the position for *n;* close the nasal passages also, permitting no breath to escape. The attempt to vocalize will then result in the sound of the letter *d*, the last subvocal in the lingual series. Like *b* and *g*, it is non-continuant.

In attempting to produce this sound separately, the same error is made that was mentioned in connection with *b*. The organs are allowed to part, permitting the breath to escape and form the syllable *duh*. Let no breath escape until the tone has ceased.

Aspirates

Wh. If unvocalized breath be expelled with the lips closely contracted, as for the semivowel *w*, the sound produced is that represented by *wh*, as in *what*, a labial aspirate.

It has been a disputed point whether this sound is simply a whispered w or a compound, $h+w$, the w of the compound being the full subvocal. The editors of Webster have seemed to waver on this point, but such phonologists as Ellis and Bell pronounce it to be a distinct and simple aspirate. A failure to discriminate between this sound and its cognate w, constitutes one of the peculiarities of the English Cockney dialect, in which *when, what, which,* become *wen, wat, wich.*

F (Ph). The labio-dental aspirate f, is the cognate of v. The lower lip is placed against the upper teeth, and unvocalized breath expelled.

P. If the unvocalized breath be accumulated behind the closed lips and they be suddenly parted, the puff of escaping air yields the sound of the letter p, a labial aspirate.

H. The forcible aspiration known as the sound of h, is usually classified as a palatal. It is, however, somewhat anomalous in character, being capable of production in any of the vowel positions indifferently, as can be seen by uttering the words *aha, aho,* and similar combinations, in which the whole is produced without change of position. It is simply a sudden expulsion of the breath with any open position of the organs, and the Greeks were consistent in rejecting it as an independent sound, and denying it a letter for its representation.

Sh. The mixed palatal *sh*, the cognate of *zh*, is clearly a single element. The blade of the tongue is well arched toward the hard palate, the teeth are nearly or quite closed, and the breath is thus expelled with much friction, giving a highly aspirated sound. This sound is represented in English orthography by a great number of symbols, mostly digraphs, as, *sh, ci, ti, ch,* etc.

Ch. The sound of *ch*, heard in *child, chin,* is the cognate of j, and, like it, a compound difficult of analysis. The analysis, $ch+t+y$, is probably nearer the truth than the more common one, $ch=t+sh$; but its relation to either one of these combinations is, doubtless, that of similarity rather than identity. In its formation the tip of the tongue is placed against the hard palate, and the teeth shut. The closed organs are then suddenly parted, and the escaping breath yields the sound of *ch*.

K. The sound of *k*, often represented by other letters, as *c*, *ch*, *gh*, is the only purely palatal aspirate in our language, though several are found in other languages, as the German.

For its production the soft palate is made to meet the base of the tongue, the nasal passages being also closed—the same position as that for its cognate *g*. When this complete closure is suddenly broken by the unvocalized breath, the sound of *k* results.

Th (aspirate). This sound differs from the subvocal *th* only in the lack of vocality. The tip of the tongue is placed under the edges of the upper teeth, and the breath is blown out between the teeth. It is a linguo-dental. The substitution of this sound for that of *s* constitutes the fault known as lisping. The simple direction for its cure is: Keep the tongue within the teeth while sounding *s*.

S. If the tip of the tongue be turned slightly upward near the upper teeth, as for *z*, and unvocalized breath be passed over it, the sound of *s* will be the result. It is a fine, sharp whistle. The common mouth, however, too often renders it as a coarse hiss.

T. The letter *t* represents the sound of the puff of breath set free by the sudden parting of the middle closure of the mouth, that formed by the close contact of the tip of the tongue with the hard palate. If the sound of *d* be produced, and the breath be then blown out, it yields this sound, the pure lingual aspirate.

THE BELLS

> "And even things without life giving sound, whether pipe or harp, except they give a distinction in the sounds, how shall it be known what is piped or harped?"

(An excellent poem for exercise in expression.)

1. Hear the sledges with the bells—
    Silver bells—
What a world of merriment their melody foretells!
    How they tinkle, tinkle, tinkle,
        In the icy air of night!
    While the stars that oversprinkle
    All the heavens, seem to twinkle
        With a crystalline delight;
    Keeping time, time, time,
    In a sort of Runic rhyme,
To the tintinnabulation that so musically wells
    From the bells, bells, bells, bells,
        Bells, bells, bells—
From the jingling and the tinkling of the bells.

2. Hear the mellow wedding bells,
        Golden bells!
What a world of happiness their harmony foretells!
    Through the balmy air of night
    How they ring out their delight!
        From the molten-golden notes,
            And all in tune,
        What a liquid ditty floats
    To the turtledove that listens, while she gloats
            On the moon!

3.   O, from out the sounding cells,
What a gush of euphony voluminously wells!
         How it swells!
         How it dwells
      On the Future! how it tells
      Of the rapture that impels
    To the swinging and the ringing
       Of the bells, bells, bells—
    Of the bells, bells, bells, bells,
         Bells, bells, bells—
To the rhyming and the chiming of the bells.

4.   Hear the loud alarum bells—
         Brazen bells!
What a tale of terror, now, their turbulency tells!
       In the startled ear of night
    How they scream out their affright!
       Too much horrified to speak,
       They can only shriek, shriek, shriek,
         Out of tune,
In a clamorous appealing to the mercy of the fire,
In a mad expostulation with the deaf and frantic fire,
       Leaping higher, higher, higher,
         With a desperate desire,
         And a resolute endeavor
         Now—now to sit or never,
By the side of the pale-faced moon.

5.   O, the bells, bells, bells!
      What a tale their terror tells
         Of despair!
      How they clang, and clash, and roar!
      What a horror they outpour

On the bosom of the palpitating air!
  Yet the ear, it fully knows,
    By the twanging
    And the clanging,
  How the danger ebbs and flows;
  Yet the ear distinctly tells
    In the jangling
    And the wrangling,
  How the danger sinks and swells,
By the sinking or the swelling in the anger of the bells—
    Of the bells—
    Of the bells, bells, bells, bells,
      Bells, bells, bells—
  In the clamor and the clangor of the bells!

—*E. A. Poe.*

Exercise for Conversation and Study

In this poem, the author was trying to reproduce in verse the music made by various kinds of bells. The meaning of his verses is thus of much less importance than the sound. Do you think the poet has been successful with the sleigh bells and the fire bells? Which is the more effective?

The poet's success in producing the sound of the bells was due in part to his skill in the use of appropriate figurative language, in part to the movement of the verse, and very largely to his choice of words. Which words seem to you to give the sound they describe?

Study the "Chart of Vocals and Vowel Substitutes" with a view of committing it to memory.

Word Study

1. sledges	2. liquid	4. shriek
1. crystalline	3. euphony	4. expostulation
1. Runic	3. voluminously	5. palpitating
1. tintinnabulation	3. rhyming	5. distinctly
2. balmy	4. alarum	5. clangor

SOUND

IX. TABLE OF ENGLISH SOUNDS

Tables of English sounds, as presented by Webster's Dictionary, are here given for convenience of reference. Each sound should be studied carefully with respect to its physical character, as given under "Description of English Sounds" in preceding lessons.

CHART OF VOCALS AND VOWEL SUBSTITUTES

Symbol	Name	Key-word	Substitute Symbol	Key-word
ā	Long	māte	e̱	pre̱y
ă	Short	măt		
â	Circumflex	câre	ê	whêre
ä	Italian	fär		
ȧ	Short Italian	ȧsk		
a̤	Broad	a̤we	ô	nôr
ē	Long	mē	ï	marïne
ĕ	Short	mĕt		
ẽ	Tilde	vẽrse	{ ĩ ã ỹ	{ bĩrd scholãr mỹrrh
ī	Long	thīne	ȳ	mȳ
ĭ	Short	tĭn	y̌	aby̌ss
ō	Long	bōne		
ŏ	Short	cŏffee	a̤	wha̤t
o͞o	Long	bo͞ot	{ o̤ ṳ	{ do̤ rṳde
o͝o	Short	fo͝ot	{ o̤ ṳ	{ wo̤lf pṳsh
ū	Long	tūne		
ŭ	Short	ŭp	ȯ	dȯne
û	Circumflex	ûrge	õ	wõrd
ou		sound	ow	cow
oi		oil	oy	boy

CHART OF CONSONANT SOUNDS

Symbol	Key-word	Substitute	Symbol	Key-word	Substitute
b	bet		p	pet	
d	dot		t	tin	ed, th
ḡ	ḡet		k	kit	c, ch, gh, q
			h	hat	
j	jet	ġ	ch	chin	
l	lid				
m	mit				
n	not				
ṉ	fiṉger	**ng**			
r	rat, tar				
th	**th**at		th	thin	
v	vat		f	fat	ph, gh
w	woe		wh	when	
y	yet				
z	buzz	ṣ	s	sin	ç
z(zh)	azure	si, zi	sh	shot	ci, c, ce, ch, si, ti, sch

THE FUTURE INHERITANCE

> *"Eye hath not seen, nor ear heard, neither have entered into the heart of man, the things which God hath prepared for them that love Him."*

1. A fear of making the future inheritance seem too material has led many to spiritualize away the very truths which lead us to look upon it as our home. Christ assured His disciples that He went to prepare mansions for them in the Father's house. Those who accept the teachings of God's Word will not be wholly ignorant concerning the heavenly abode. And yet, "eye hath not seen, nor ear heard, neither have entered into the heart of man, the things which God hath prepared for them that love Him." Human language is inadequate to describe the reward of the righteous. It will be known only to those who behold it. No finite mind can comprehend the glory of the Paradise of God.

2. In the Bible the inheritance of the saved is called a country. There the heavenly Shepherd leads His flocks to fountains of living waters. The tree of life yields its fruit every month, and the leaves of the tree are for the service of the nations. There are ever-flowing streams, clear as crystal, and beside them waving trees cast their shadows upon the paths prepared for the ransomed of the Lord. There the widespreading plains swell into hills of beauty, and the mountains of God rear their lofty summits. On those peaceful plains, beside those living streams, God's people, so long pilgrims and wanderers, shall find a home.

3. "My people shall dwell in a peaceable habitation, and in sure dwellings, and in quiet resting-places." "Violence shall no more be heard in thy land, wasting nor destruction within thy borders; but thou shalt call thy walls Salvation, and thy gates Praise." "They shall build houses, and inhabit them; and they shall plant vineyards, and eat the fruit of them. They shall not build, and another inhabit; they shall not plant, and another eat: . . . Mine elect shall long enjoy the work of their hands."

4. There, "the wilderness and the solitary place shall be glad for them; and the desert shall rejoice, and blossom as the rose." "Instead of the thorn shall come up the fir tree, and instead of the brier shall come up the myrtle tree." "The wolf also shall dwell with the lamb, and the leopard shall lie down with the kid; . . . and a little child shall lead them." "They shall not hurt nor destroy in all My holy mountain," saith the Lord.

5. Pain can not exist in the atmosphere of heaven. There will be no more tears; no funeral trains, no badges of mourning. "There shall be no more death, neither sorrow, nor crying, . . . for the former things are passed away." "The inhabitant shall not say, 'I am sick;' the people that dwell therein shall be forgiven their iniquity."

6. There is the New Jerusalem, the metropolis of the glorified new earth, "a crown of glory in the hand of the Lord, and a royal diadem in the hand of thy God." "Her light was like unto a stone most precious, even like a jasper stone, clear as crystal." "The nations of them which are saved shall walk in the light of it; and the kings of the earth do bring their glory and honor into it." Saith the Lord, "I will rejoice in Jerusalem, and joy in My people." "The tabernacle of God is with men, and He shall dwell with them, and they shall be His people, and God Himself shall be with them, and be their God."

7. In the city of God "there shall be no night." None will need or desire repose. There will be no weariness in doing the will of God and offering praise to His name. We shall ever feel the freshness of the morning, and shall ever be far from its close. "And they need no candle, neither light of the sun; for the Lord God giveth them light." The light of the sun will be superseded by a radiance which is not painfully dazzling, yet which immeasurably surpasses the brightness of our noontide. The glory of God and the Lamb floods the holy city with unfading light. The redeemed walk in the sunless glory of perpetual day.

8. "I saw no temple therein; for the Lord God Almighty and the Lamb are the temple of it." The people of God are privileged to hold open communion with the Father and the Son. Now we "see through a glass, darkly." We behold the image of God reflected, as in a mirror, in the works of nature and in His dealings with men; but then we shall see Him face to face, without a dimming veil between. We shall stand in His presence, and behold the glory of His countenance

9. There the redeemed shall "know, even as also they are known." The loves and sympathies which God Himself has planted in the soul, shall there find truest and sweetest exercise. The pure communion with holy beings, the harmonious social life with the blessed angels and with the faithful ones of all ages, who have washed their robes and made them white in the blood of the Lamb, the sacred ties that bind together "the whole family in heaven and earth,"—these help to constitute the happiness of the redeemed.

10. There, immortal minds will contemplate with never-failing delight the wonders of creative power, the mysteries of redeeming love. There is no cruel, deceiving foe to tempt to forgetfulness of God. Every faculty will be developed, every capacity increased. The acquirement of knowledge will not weary the mind or exhaust the energies. There the grandest enterprises may be carried forward, the loftiest aspirations reached, the highest ambitions realized; and still there will arise new heights to surmount, new wonders to admire, new truths to comprehend, fresh objects to call forth the powers of mind and soul and body.

11. All the treasures of the universe will be open to the study of God's redeemed. Unfettered by mortality, they wing their tireless flight to worlds afar,—worlds that thrilled with sorrow at the spectacle of human woe, and rang with songs of gladness at the tidings of a ransomed soul. With unutterable delight the children of earth enter into the joy and wisdom of unfallen beings. They share the treasures of knowledge and understanding gained through

ages upon ages in contemplation of God's handiwork. With undimmed vision they gaze upon the glory of creation,—suns and stars and systems, all in their appointed order circling the throne of Deity. Upon all things, from the least to the greatest, the Creator's name is written, and in all are the riches of His power displayed.

12. And the years of eternity, as they roll, will bring richer and still more glorious revelations of God and of Christ. As knowledge is progressive, so will love, reverence, and happiness increase. The more men learn of God, the greater will be their admiration of His character. As Jesus opens before them the riches of redemption, and the amazing achievements in the great controversy with Satan, the hearts of the ransomed thrill with more fervent devotion, and with more rapturous joy they sweep the harps of gold; and ten thousand times ten thousand and thousands of thousands of voices unite to swell the mighty chorus of praise.

13. "And every creature which is in heaven, and on the earth, and under the earth, and such as are in the sea, and all that are in them, heard I saying, 'Blessing, and honor, and glory, and power, be unto Him that sitteth upon the throne, and unto the Lamb forever and ever.'"

14. The great controversy is ended. Sin and sinners are no more. The entire universe is clean. One pulse of harmony and gladness beats through the vast creation. From Him who created all, flow life and light and gladness, throughout the realms of illimitable space. From the minutest atom to the greatest world, all things, animate and inanimate, in their unshadowed beauty and perfect joy, declare that God is love.

— *Mrs. E. G. White.*

Exercise for Conversation and Study

Where in the Old Testament do we find the promise of a new earth? Where in the New Testament? Will the new earth be as real as the one on which we live? How will it compare with our earth in respect to things which it contains? What will be the condition of the animal kingdom? The plant kingdom? Of man? How will the redeemed occupy their time? Isa. 65:21-24. How will the new earth be brought into existence? 2 Peter 3:10-14. Make a list of the most beautiful rhetorical expressions contained in this lesson.

Study the "Chart of Vowel Sounds" with a view of committing it to memory.

Word Study

1. inadequate
1. ignorant
2. Shepherd
3. peaceable
4. leopard
6. metropolis
6. tabernacle
7. radiance
7. immeasurably
8. communion
9. sympathies
10. exhaust
11. universe
11. unutterable
12. achievements

VOCAL SYMBOLS

The art of representing speech-sounds to the eye by distinct and appropriate symbols, is called phonotypy.

This term, originally given to a particular system of speech-symbols, may now be appropriately applied to the whole art of phonetic representation.

The ancient Phœnicians are credited with making the first analysis of the sounds of speech, and with the adoption of a phonetic system of characters for the representation of the several sounds. This was an inconceivably great step in linguistic science, but one which has not been repeated. The present English alphabetic notation of sounds, or orthography, is no advance from the Phœnician system, but the reverse. It is, indeed, so imperfectly phonetic and so utterly unscientific as scarcely to deserve mention under this head—except for some consideration of its defects.

THE DEFECTS OF OUR ENGLISH ALPHABET

1. For the representation of, say forty-five sounds, it furnishes

but twenty-six characters; and of these, three, *c*, *q*, and *x*, are worthless, having no sounds of their own. Consequently one letter, as *a*, must represent several sounds.

2. Our letters are unsteady in their powers, now representing one sound and now another, and often no sound at all. This is a source of great confusion.

3. Our orthography is inconsistent. Similar sounds find no similarity in their symbols, as *v* and *f*, for example. Single letters represent compound sounds, as long *i*, long *u*, and *j;* while digraphs represent single sounds as *th*, *ph*, etc.

4. The letters do not represent the same sounds as in other languages. Thus our long *e* is represented in other languages by *i;* our *oo* sounds, uniformly by *u;* our long *a*, by *e*, and all in a far more symmetrical and consistent manner than in English.

Diacritical Marks. The inadequacy of the English alphabet is such that for the most ordinary purposes it has been found necessary to employ an auxiliary system of diacritical marks—guideboards on the heads of our bewildered letters—a needful makeshift to overcome the incapacity of our orthography for exact representation.

Webster's Dictionary employs the following marks:—

1. Vowel marks
   The macron: ā, ē, ī, ō, ū, ȳ
   The breve: ă, ĕ, ĭ, ŏ, ŭ, y̆
   The circumflex accent: â, ê, ô, û
   The tilde, or wave: ẽ, ĩ, ỹ
   One dot (above or below): ȧ, ȯ, ạ, ọ, ụ
   Two dots (above or below): ä, ï, o̤, ṳ
   Bar below: e̱

2. Consonant Marks
   The bar: ḡ   One dot: ġ
   The dotted bar: s̤, x̤   Bar below: ṉ
   The cedilla: ç, çh   Bar through: **th, c ch**

Most of these marks, and some others, are used in Worcester's Dictionary and in the Gazetteer and Biographical Dictionary of Dr. Thomas, but not always with the same signification.

Significance of the Diacritical Marks. The macron and breve, having been used from time immemorial to indicate the quantity of syllables, are very naturally employed in all dictionaries to indicate the regular long and short sounds of the vowels.

The circumflex accent, long used to indicate "common" quantity, is employed by Webster to denote certain sounds of *a, e, o,* and *u,* before *r*—all long sounds. By Worcester the same mark is used to mark the broad sound of *a* and several substitute sounds, as *i* with the sound of long *e*, etc.

Two dots above the vowel are used by Webster to mark the Italian *a* only; by Worcester, for the same sound and also for the "short and obtuse" sounds of all other vowels followed by a single *r* in accented syllables.

One dot beneath a vowel is used by Worcester uniformly to indicate the obscure sounds of vowels in unaccented syllables, for which Webster, in general, employs no notation, depending upon the application of rules.

The dotted bar, used by Worcester to mark certain vowel sounds, is placed by Webster under *s* and *x* to indicate their use as subvocals (for *z* and *gz*).

For the signification of other marks, as the tilde or wave, the cedilla, etc., the dictionaries named may be consulted.

THE HEAVENLY COUNTRY

> "But now they desire a better country; that is, an heavenly; wherefore God is not ashamed to be called their God; for He hath prepared for them a city."

1. Lonely and weary, by sorrow oppressed,
   Onward we hasten with longings for rest,
   Bidding adieu to the world with its pride,
   Longing to stand by Immanuel's side.
   Though we are pilgrims, before us now rise
   Visions of glory rejoicing our eyes.
   Bright are the crowns that we hope soon to wear,
   Blessed the rest; O, we long to be there!

2. There is the city in splendor sublime;
   O, how its turrets and battlements shine!
   Pearls are its portals, surpassingly bright,
   Jasper its walls, and the Lamb is its light.
   Pathways of gold that blest city adorn,
   Glittering with glory far brighter than morn;
   Angels stand beck'ning us onward to share
   Glory unfading; we long to be there!

3. Rivers are gliding 'mid unfading trees,
   Songs of the ransomed are borne on the breeze;
   Glory-lit mountains resplendent are seen,
   Valleys and hills clad in Eden-like green;
   There shall the glory of God ever be,
   Filling the earth as the waves fill the sea;
   There shall the ransomed, immortal and fair
   Evermore dwell; O, we long to be there!

   —*Anonymous.*

Exercise for Conversation and Study

Study the "Chart of Consonant Sounds" with a view to committing it to memory.

INFLUENCE

> "For none of us liveth to himself,
> and no man dieth to himself."

1. The life of Christ was an ever-widening, shoreless influence, an influence that bound Him to God and to the whole human family. Through Christ, God has invested man with an influence that makes it impossible for him to live to himself. Individually we are connected with our fellow men, a part of God's great whole, and we stand under mutual obligations. No man can be independent of his fellow men; for the well-being of each affects others. It is God's purpose that each shall feel himself necessary to others' welfare, and seek to promote their happiness.

2. Every soul is surrounded by an atmosphere of its own,—an atmosphere, it may be, charged with the life-giving power of faith, courage, and hope, and sweet with the fragrance of love. Or it may be heavy and chill with the gloom of discontent and selfishness, or poisonous with the deadly taint of cherished sin. By the atmosphere surrounding us, every person with whom we come in contact is consciously or unconsciously affected.

3. This is a responsibility from which we can not free ourselves. Our words, our acts, our dress, our deportment, even the expression of the countenance, has an influence. Upon the impression thus made there hang results for good or evil which no man can measure. Every impulse thus imparted is seed sown which will produce its harvest. It is a link in the long chain of human events, extending we know not whither. If by our example we aid others in the development of good principles, we give them power to do good. In their turn they exert the same influence upon others, and they upon still others. Thus by our unconscious influence thousands may be blessed.

4. Throw a pebble into the lake, and a wave is formed, and another and another; and as they increase, the circle widens, until

it reaches the very shore. So with our influence. Beyond our knowledge or control, it tells upon others in blessing or in cursing.

5. Character is power. The silent witness of a true, unselfish, godly life carries an almost irresistible influence. By revealing in our own life the character of Christ, we co-operate with Him in the work of saving souls. It is only by revealing in our life His character that we can co-operate with Him. And the wider the sphere of our influence, the more good we may do. When those who profess to serve God follow Christ's example, practicing the principles of the law in their daily life; when every act bears witness that they love God supremely and their neighbor as themselves, then will the church have power to move the world.

6. But never should it be forgotten that influence is no less a power for evil. To lose one's own soul is a terrible thing; but to cause the loss of other souls is still more terrible. That our influence should be a savor of death unto death is a fearful thought; yet this is possible. Many who profess to gather with Christ are scattering from Him. This is why the church is so weak. Many indulge freely in criticism and accusing. By giving expression to suspicion, jealousy, and discontent, they yield themselves as instruments to Satan. Before they realize what they are doing, the adversary has through them accomplished his purpose. The impression of evil has been made, the shadow has been cast, the arrows of Satan have found their mark. Distrust, unbelief, and downright infidelity have fastened upon those who otherwise might have accepted Christ. Meanwhile the workers for Satan look complacently upon those whom they have driven to skepticism, and who are now hardened against reproof and entreaty. They flatter themselves that in comparison with these souls they are virtuous and righteous. They do not realize that these sad wrecks of character are the work of their own unbridled tongues and rebellious hearts. It is through their influence that these tempted ones have fallen.

7. So frivolity, selfish indulgence, and careless indifference on the part of professed Christians, are turning away many souls from

the path of life. Many there are who will fear to meet at the bar of God the results of their influence.

8. It is only through the grace of God that we can make a right use of this endowment. There is nothing in us of ourselves by which we can influence others for good. If we realize our helplessness and our need of divine power, we shall not trust to ourselves. We know not what results a day, an hour, or a moment may determine, and never should we begin the day without committing our ways to our heavenly Father. His angels are appointed to watch over us, and if we put ourselves under their guardianship, then in every time of danger they will be at our right hand. When unconsciously we are in danger of exerting a wrong influence, the angels will be by our side, prompting us to a better course, choosing our words for us, and influencing our actions. Thus our influence may be a silent, unconscious, but mighty power in drawing others to Christ and the heavenly world.

—Mrs. E. G. White.

Exercise for Conversation and Study

Is it possible for one to live or die without influencing those about him? Rom. 14: 7, 8. What Bible character tried to excuse himself from having any responsibility with reference to his brother? Did the Lord excuse him? In what ways are we our "brother's keeper"? Mention ways of exerting an influence for good, for evil. Give Bible examples of men who exerted a good influence over others; an evil influence. (Read Eze. 3: 15-21.)

In the list of words under "Word Study," mark the vowels and classify the consonants according to classification previously given; as, labials, linguals, aspirates, etc.

Word Study

1. influence
1. mutual
2. atmosphere
2. consciously
2. poisonous
3. responsibility
3. exert
4. circle
5. character
5. sphere
6. criticism
6. infidelity
6. complacently
7. frivolity
8. determine
8. guardianship

THE BRIGHT SIDE

"Every cloud has a silver lining."

1. There is many a rest in the road of life
    If we only would stop to take it,
   And many a tone from the better land,
    If the querulous heart would wake it.
   To the sunny soul that is full of hope,
    And whose beautiful trust ne'er faileth,
   The grass is green and the flowers are bright,
    Though the wintry storm prevaileth.

2. Better to hope, though the clouds hang low,
    And to keep the eyes still lifted,
   For the sweet blue sky will still peep through
    When the ominous clouds are rifted.
   There was never a night without a day,
    Or an evening without a morning;
   And the darkest hour, as the proverb goes,
    Is the hour before the dawning.

3. There is many a gem in the path of life,
    Which we pass in our idle pleasure,
   That is richer far than the jeweled crown,
    Or the miser's hoarded treasure:
   It may be the love of a little child,
    Or a mother's prayer to heaven;
   Or only a beggar's grateful thanks
    For a cup of water given.

4. Better to weave in the web of life
    A bright and golden filling,
   And to do God's will with a ready heart,
    And hands that are swift and willing,

Than to snap the delicate, slender threads
Of our curious lives asunder,
And then blame Heaven for the tangled ends,
And sit and grieve and wonder.

—*Selected.*

VOCAL ARTICULATION

> "*So they read in the Book in the law of God distinctly.*"

Articulation is that action of the tongue and other organs of speech by which each oral element receives its peculiar and proper character.

As the action of the organs is slight for vowel and great for consonant sounds, the chief labor of articulation is found in connection with the latter, some writers even limiting the term articulation to the execution of consonant sounds.

The word is derived from *articulus,* a little joint, and thus literally signifies the jointing of speech. The fitness of this term arises from the natural law of alternation in speech, the continual alternation of open and close sounds.

Good articulation demands, in reading or speaking,—

1. The utterance of all and only the required sounds.
2. The proper separation of the various sounds.
3. The exact and proper utterance of each sound.

The corresponding errors in articulation are: **(1)** Omission, (2) Blending, (3) Substitution.

Carefully drill on the following lists of words, avoiding the errors of articulation pointed out:—

First, from the omission of one or more elements in a word; as,—

an'	for	an*d*	sto'm	for	sto*r*m
frien's	"	frien*ds*	wa'm	"	wa*r*m
blin'ness	"	blin*d*ness	bois t'rous	"	bois t*er* ous

fac's	for	fac*t*s	chick'n	for	chick *e*n
sof'ly	"	sof*tl*y	his t'ry	"	his t*o*ry
fiel's	"	fiel*d*s	nov'l	"	nov *e*l
wil's	"	wil*d*s	trav'l	"	trav *e*l

Secondly, from uttering one or more elements that should not be sounded; as,—

ev *e*n	for	ev'n	rav *e*l	for	rav'l
heav *e*n	"	heav'n	sev *e*n	"	sev'n
tak *e*n	"	tak'n	sof *te*n	"	sof'n
sick *e*n	"	sick'n	of *te*n	"	of'n
driv *el*	"	driv'l	shov *e*l	"	shov'l
grov *e*l	"	grov'l	shriv *e*l	"	shriv'l

Thirdly, from substituting one element for another; as,—

s*e*t	for	s*i*t	bun net	for	bon net
s*e*nce	"	s*i*nce	chil dr*u*n	"	chil dr*e*n
sh*e*t	"	sh*u*t	sul ler	"	*ce*l lar
for g*i*t	"	for g*e*t	mel l*e*r	"	mel l*ow*
*s*rill	"	*sh*rill	pil l*e*r	"	pil l*ow*
*w*irl	"	*wh*irl	mo m*u*nt	"	mo m*e*nt
a g*a*n or ag*a*ne	"	a gain (a g*e*n)	harm l*i*ss	"	harm l*e*ss
h*e*rth	"	hearth (harth)	kind n*i*ss	"	kind n*e*ss
tr*o*f fy	"	tro phy	*w*is per	"	*wh*is per
p*a* rent	"	par ent	sing i*n*	"	sing i*ng*

SOME COMMON ERRORS IN ARTICULATION

Analyze each of the following errors, and determine in what the error consists:—

algebray	for	algebra	bile	for	boil
Ameriky	"	America	bimeby	"	by and by
attackted	"	attacked	ketch	"	catch

childern	for	children	lickrish	for	licorice
drownded	"	drowned	mushmelon	"	muskmelon
equil	"	equal	miskeeter	"	mosquito
ellum	"	elm	mountanious	"	mountainous
forrud	"	forward	nekked	"	naked
figger	"	figure	awnjiz	"	oranges
Febuary	"	February	pleg	"	plague
f'rever'n'ever	"	forever and ever	pillar	"	pillow
git	"	get	perty	"	pretty
holler	"	halloo	pudd'n'	"	pudding
hundered	"	hundred	wich	"	which
I'd 'no	"	I don't know	yep	"	yes

The conditions of good articulation, and so of good pronunciation are,—
 1. Flexibility and vigor of the organs of speech.
 2. An exact knowledge of the peculiar character of each sound in the English language.
 3. A knowledge of the principles, or rules, according to which these sounds are combined.
 4. Careful attention to the daily practical use of this knowledge, converting knowledge into skill.

Flexibility of the organs may be attained by suitable drill exercises; such as the utterance in rapid succession of the sounds of *ah, ee, oo, it, ip, ik, had$\bar{e}$, had$\bar{\imath}$, had$\bar{o}$,* with vigorous and exaggerated facial action.

TEACHING IN PARABLES—PART I

*"I will open My mouth in parables;
I will utter things which have been
kept secret from the foundation of
the world."*

1. In Christ's parable-teaching the same principle is seen as in His own mission to the world. That we might become acquainted with His divine character and life, Christ took our nature, and dwelt among us. Divinity was revealed in humanity; the invisible glory in the visible human form. Men could learn of the unknown through the known; heavenly things were revealed through the earthly; God was made manifest in the likeness of men. So it was in Christ's teaching; the unknown was illustrated by the known; divine truths by earthly things with which the people were most familiar.

2. The Scripture says, "All these things spake Jesus unto the multitude in parables; . . . that it might be fulfilled which was spoken by the prophet, saying, 'I will open My mouth in parables; I will utter things which have been kept secret from the foundation of the world.'" Natural things were the medium for the spiritual; the things of nature and the life-experience of His hearers were connected with the truths of the written Word. Leading thus from the natural to the spiritual kingdom, Christ's parables are links in the chain of truth that unites man with God, and earth with heaven.

3. In His teaching from nature, Christ was speaking of the things which His own hands had made, and which had qualities and powers that He Himself had imparted. In their original perfection, all created things were an expression of the thought of God. To Adam and Eve in their Eden home, nature was full of the knowledge of God, teeming with divine instruction. Wisdom spoke to the eye, and was received into the heart; for they communed with God in His created works. As soon as the holy

pair transgressed the law of the Most High, the brightness from the face of God departed from the face of nature. The earth is now marred and defiled by sin. Yet even in its blighted state, much that is beautiful remains. God's object lessons are not obliterated; rightly understood, nature speaks of her Creator.

4. In the days of Christ these lessons had been lost sight of. Men had well-nigh ceased to discern God in His works. The sinfulness of humanity had cast a pall over the fair face of creation; and instead of manifesting God, His works became a barrier that concealed Him. Men "worshiped and served the creature more than the Creator." Thus the heathen "became vain in their imaginations, and their foolish heart was darkened." So in Israel, man's teaching had been put in the place of God's. Not only the things of nature, but the sacrificial service and the Scriptures themselves,—all given to reveal God,—were so perverted that they became the means of concealing Him.

5. Christ sought to remove that which obscured the truth. The veil that sin has cast over the face of nature, He came to draw aside, bringing to view the spiritual glory that all things were created to reflect. His words placed the teachings of nature as well as of the Bible in a new aspect, and made them a new revelation.

6. Jesus plucked the beautiful lily, and placed it in the hands of children and youth; and as they looked into His own youthful face, fresh with the sunlight of His Father's countenance, He gave the lesson, "Consider the lilies of the field, how they grow [in the simplicity of natural beauty]; they toil not, neither do they spin: and yet I say unto you, that even Solomon in all his glory was not arrayed like one of these." Then followed the sweet assurance and the important lesson, "Wherefore, if God so clothe the grass of the field, which to-day is, and to-morrow is cast into the oven, shall He not much more clothe you, O ye of little faith?"

7. In the sermon on the mount these words were spoken to

others besides children and youth. They were spoken to the multitude, among whom were men and women full of worries and perplexities, and sore with disappointment and sorrow. Jesus continued: "Therefore take no thought, saying, 'What shall we eat?' or, 'What shall we drink?' or, 'Wherewithal shall we be clothed?' (for after these things do the Gentiles seek): for your heavenly Father knoweth that ye have need of all these things." Then spreading out His hands to the surrounding multitude, He said, "But seek ye first the kingdom of God, and His righteousness; and all these things shall be added unto you."

8. Thus Christ interpreted the message which He Himself had given to the lilies and the grass of the field. He desires us to read it in every lily and every spire of grass. His words are full of assurance, and tend to confirm trust in God.

9. So wide was Christ's view of truth, so extended His teaching, that every phase of nature was employed in illustrating truth. The scenes upon which the eye daily rests were all connected with some spiritual truth, so that nature is clothed with the parables of the Master.

10. In the earlier part of His ministry, Christ had spoken to the people in words so plain that all His hearers might have grasped truths which would make them wise unto salvation. But in many hearts the truth had taken no root, and it had been quickly caught away. "Therefore speak I to them in parables," He said; "because they seeing see not; and hearing they hear not, neither do they understand. . . . For this people's heart is waxed gross, and their ears are dull of hearing, and their eyes they have closed."

11. Jesus desired to awaken inquiry. He sought to arouse the careless, and impress truth upon the heart. Parable-teaching was popular, and commanded the respect and attention, not only of the Jews, but of the people of other nations. No more effective method of instruction could He have employed. If His hearers had desired a knowledge of divine things, they might have understood His words; for He was always willing to explain them to the honest inquirer.

12. Again, Christ had truths to present which the people were unprepared to accept, or even to understand. For this reason also He taught them in parables. By connecting His teaching with the scenes of life, experience, or nature, He secured their attention and impressed their hearts. Afterward, as they looked upon the objects that illustrated His lessons, they recalled the words of the divine Teacher. To minds that were open to the Holy Spirit, the significance of the Saviour's teaching unfolded more and more. Mysteries grew clear, and that which had been hard to grasp became evident. —*Mrs. E. G. White.*

Exercise for Conversation and Study

What is a parable? What method of teaching did Christ employ largely when instructing the people? Matt. 13: 24, 35. Was His method of teaching foretold in the Scriptures? Where and by whom? Was Jesus recognized as a great Teacher? Give scriptural proof. What are the advantages of the parable-method of teaching over other methods? Make a list of the parables of Christ. Should the parable-method be used to-day in making plain the principles of the kingdom of heaven? What form of expression did Jesus use in teaching from nature? From the Bible?

Articulation Drill

Articulate the letter *d* in moun*d*, houn*d*, kin*d*, fin*d*, wil*d*, chil*d*, an*d*, han*d*, ban*d*, le*d*, fe*d*, win*d*, soun*d*, sinne*d*. Repeat: A kind hand led the little band through a desert land of wind and sand.

Word Study

1. invisible	4. humanity	8. lilies
1. illustrated	4. sacrificial	9. view
2. parables	5. obscured	10. ministry
2. spiritual	6. beautiful	11. inquiry
2. natural	6. arrayed	11. method
3. qualities	7. multitude	12. objects
3. obliterated	7. perplexities	12. significance

TEACHING IN PARABLES—PART II

"The kingdom of heaven is like."

1. Jesus sought an avenue to every heart. By using a variety of illustrations, He not only presented truth in its different phases, but appealed to the different hearers. Their interest was aroused by figures drawn from the surroundings of their daily life. None who listened to the Saviour could feel that they were neglected or forgotten. The humblest, the most sinful, heard in His teaching a voice that spoke to them in sympathy and tenderness.

2. And He had another reason for teaching in parables. Among the multitudes that gathered about Him, there were priests and rabbis, scribes and elders, Herodians and rulers, world-loving, bigoted, ambitious men, who desired above all things to find some accusation against Him. Their spies followed His steps day after day, to catch from His lips something that would cause His condemnation, and forever silence the One who seemed to draw the world after Him. The Saviour understood the character of these men, and He presented truth in such a way that they could find nothing by which to bring His case before the Sanhedrin. In parables He rebuked the hypocrisy and wicked works of those who occupied high positions, and in figurative language clothed truth of so cutting a character that had it been spoken in direct denunciation, they would not have listened to His words, and would speedily have put an end to His ministry. But while He evaded the spies, He made truth so clear that error was manifested, and the honest in heart were profited by His lessons. Divine wisdom, infinite grace, were made plain by the things of God's creation. Through nature and the experiences of life, men were taught of God. "The invisible things of Him since the creation of the world," were "perceived through the things that are made, even His everlasting power and divinity."

3. In the Saviour's parable-teaching is an indication of what

constitutes the true "higher education." Christ might have opened to men the deepest truths of science. He might have unlocked mysteries which have required many centuries of toil and study to penetrate. He might have made suggestions in scientific lines that would have afforded food for thought and stimulus for invention to the close of time. But He did not do this. He said nothing to gratify curiosity, or to satisfy man's ambition by opening doors to worldly greatness. In all His teaching, Christ brought the mind of man in contact with the Infinite Mind. He did not direct the people to study men's theories about God, His Word, or His works. He taught them to behold Him as manifested in His works, in His Word, and by His providences.

4. Christ did not deal in abstract theories, but in that which is essential to the development of character, that which will enlarge man's capacity for knowing God, and increase his efficiency to do good. He spoke to men of those truths that relate to the conduct of life, and that take hold upon eternity.

5. It was Christ who directed the education of Israel. Concerning the commandments and ordinances of the Lord, He said, "Thou shalt teach them diligently unto thy children, and shalt talk of them when thou sittest in thine house, and when thou walkest by the way, and when thou liest down, and when thou risest up. And thou shalt bind them for a sign upon thine hand, and they shall be as frontlets between thine eyes. And thou shalt write them upon the posts of thy house, and on thy gates." In His own teaching, Jesus showed how this command is to be fulfilled,—how the laws and principles of God's kingdom can be so presented as to reveal their beauty and preciousness. When the Lord was training Israel to be the special representatives of Himself, He gave them homes among the hills and valleys. In their home life and their religious service they were brought in constant contact with nature and with the Word of God. So Christ taught His disciples by the lake, on the mountain side, in the fields and groves, where they

could look upon the things of nature by which He illustrated His teachings. And as they learned of Christ, they put their knowledge to use by co-operating with Him in His work.

6. So through the creation we are to become acquainted with the Creator. The book of nature is a great lesson-book, which in connection with the Scriptures we are to use in teaching others of His character, and guiding lost sheep back to the fold of God. As the works of God are studied, the Holy Spirit flashes conviction into the mind. It is not the conviction that logical reasoning produces; but unless the mind has become too dark to know God, the eye too dim to see Him, the ear too dull to hear His voice, a deeper meaning is grasped, and the sublime, spiritual truths of the written word are impressed on the heart.

7. In these lessons direct from nature, there is a simplicity and purity that makes them of the highest value. All need the teaching to be derived from this source. In itself the beauty of nature leads the soul away from sin and worldly attractions, and toward purity, peace, and God. Too often the minds of students are occupied with men's theories and speculations, falsely called science and philosophy. They need to be brought into close contact with nature. Let them learn that creation and Christianity have one God. Let them be taught to see the harmony of the natural with the spiritual. Let everything which their eyes see or their hands handle be made a lesson in character-building. Thus the mental powers will be strengthened, the character developed, the whole life ennobled.

8. Christ's purpose in parable-teaching was in direct line with the purpose of the Sabbath. God gave to men the memorial of His creative power that they might discern Him in the works of His hand. The Sabbath bids us behold in His created works the glory of the Creator. And it was because He desired us to do this that Jesus bound up His precious lessons with the beauty of natural things. On the holy rest-day, above all other days, we should study

the messages that God has written for us in nature. We should study the Saviour's parables where He spoke them, in the fields and groves, under the open sky, among the grass and flowers. As we come close to the heart of nature, Christ makes His presence real to us, and speaks to our hearts of His peace and love.

9. And Christ has linked His teaching, not only with the day of rest, but with the week of toil. He has wisdom for him who drives the plow and sows the seed. In the plowing and sowing, the tilling and reaping, He teaches us to see an illustration of His work of grace in the heart. So in every line of useful labor and every association of life, He desires us to find a lesson of divine truth. Then our daily toil will no longer absorb our attention and lead us to forget God; it will continually remind us of our Creator and Redeemer. The thought of God will run like a thread of gold through all our homely cares and occupations. For us the glory of His face will again rest upon the face of nature. We shall ever be learning new lessons of heavenly truth, and growing into the image of His purity. Thus shall we "be taught of the Lord;" and in the lot wherein we are called, we shall "abide with God."

—*Mrs. E. G. White.*

Exercise for Conversation and Study

Why did Christ speak to the people in parables? From what sources were the parables drawn? Did Christ have a thorough knowledge of nature and the sciences? How and when did He obtain this knowledge? In what respects did He teach natural science differently from what it is taught to-day? What is the relation of parable-teaching to the Sabbath? What relation does it sustain to the six days of toil? What spiritual lessons are taught by these parables: The Sower, The Leaven, The Wheat and Tares? Make a list of the objects in nature that are used in the Bible as symbols of Christ; of the Christian; of the wicked.

Articulation

Articulate the letter *t* in los*t*, cos*t*, mos*t*, toas*t*, burs*t*, wors*t*, dus*t*, jus*t*, boastes*t*, greates*t*, loudes*t*. Articulate distinctly the *t*'s and *d*'s in the stanza,—

"The heights by great men reached and kept,
Were not attained by sudden flight;
But they while their companions slept
Were toiling upward in the night."

Word Study

1. variety	2. denunciation	6. logical
1. figures	3. science	7. simplicity
1. humblest	3. constitutes	7. contact
2. hypocrisy	4. theories	7. Christianity
2. Herodians	5. ordinances	8. memorial
2. Sanhedrin	5. reveal	8. creative

VOCAL PRONUNCIATION

I. SYLLABICATION

A syllable is a vowel sound which alone, or in combination with one or more consonant sounds, forms a word or a separable part of a word. The letter *l* is to be considered a vowel in the termination *ble* and sometimes in final *el*, the *e* being strictly silent. The letters *n* and *r* also sometimes perform the vowel office, as in *euchre, haven,* etc. The longest syllable in the English language is the word *strength*.

Syllabication is the separating of a word into parts according to the number of its distinct vowel sounds.

Syllabication is the first step toward determining the pronunciation of an unfamiliar word. The difficulty of the process is much increased, in our langauge, by the frequency of silent letters and other irregularities.

The syllabication of words in spelling is of no value to the spelling itself, but it is of great importance. especially to children, as an aid to pronunciation.

Two general principles enter into syllabication,—the phonetic, or division with respect to smoothness and ease of utterance; and the etymological, or separation with respect to the derivation of the word. Unfortunately for us, no specific rules of much practical value can be given, so many exceptions arise from the conflict of the two principles, named from other causes.

Silent letters, or those which are not direct representatives of sounds, constitute one of the chief hindrances to pronunciation. Many of these are as useless as they are annoying, while others perform somewhat the same office as diacritical marks, governing and indicating the sounds of other letters. Thus:—

1. Silent *e* final usually indicates the long sound of the preceding vowel, as in *mete, fane.*

2. The doubling of a consonant usually indicates the short sound of the preceding vowel, as in *fallow, merry.*

3. The silent *u* after *g* indicates the hard sound of that letter, as in *guide, rogue.*

In vowel digraphs, the silent letters serve to indicate the sound of the other, or active vowels; though the great lack of consistency and uniformity in the influence which they exercise, renders them less useful to the learner.

Silent *e* occurs much more frequently than any other silent letter, and exercises a correspondingly great influence upon our orthoepy and orthography. The following rules will be found of practical value:—

Rule 1. *E* final is always silent except in monosyllables containing no other vowel, as *be, we,* and in classical or foreign words, as *Calliope, blasé,* etc.

Rule 2. *E* is usually silent in the termination *ed.*

Exceptions. (1) When preceded by *d* or *t,* the *e* is sounded from physiological necessity, as in *bounded, acted.*

(2) When *ed* is followed by *ly* or *ness*, the *e* has its regular short sound, as in *assuredly, blessedness*.

(3) A number of adjectives, mostly participial, have the short sound of *e*, as in *aged, beloved, blessed, crooked, cursed, dogged, hooked, learned, winged*. As verbs or participles, however, they invariably drop the sound of the *e*.

Rule 3. E is usually silent in the termination *en*, as in *heaven*, which should be pronounced as nearly as possible in one syllable. There are a few exceptional words, like *chicken, kitchen, hyphen;* and the *e* is sounded when preceded by *l, m, n,* or *r*, as in *woolen, siren,* etc.

Rule 4. E, though usually sounded in the termination *el*, is silent in a few words, as *chattel, easel, hazel, ravel, shovel, weasel,* etc.

GOD'S FIRST TEMPLES

*"O Lord, how manifold are Thy works!
in wisdom hast Thou made them all:
the earth is full of Thy riches."*

1. The groves were God's first temples. Ere man learned
To hew the shaft and lay the architrave,
And spread the roof above them,—ere he framed
The lofty vault, to gather and roll back
The sound of anthems,—in the darkling wood,
Amidst the cool and silence, he knelt down
And offered to the Mightiest solemn thanks
And supplication. For his simple heart
Might not resist the sacred influences,
Which from the stilly twilight of the place,
And from the gray old trunks, that, high in heaven,
Mingled their mossy boughs, and from the sound
Of the invisible breath that swayed at once

THE GROVES

RAYSDAEL 1625-1682

All their green tops, stole over him, and bowed
His spirit with the thought of boundless Power
And inaccessible Majesty. Ah! why
Should we, in the world's riper years, neglect
God's ancient sanctuaries, and adore
Only among the crowd, and under roofs
That our frail hands have raised? Let me, at least,
Here, in the shadow of this aged wood,
Offer one hymn; thrice happy, if it find
Acceptance in His ear.

2.   Father, Thy hand
Hath reared these venerable columns: Thou
Didst weave this verdant roof. Thou didst look down
Upon the naked earth, and, forthwith, rose
All these fair ranks of trees. They, in Thy sun
Budded, and shook their green leaves in Thy breeze,
And shot toward heaven. The century-living crow,
Whose birth was in their tops, grew old and died
Among their branches; till, at last, they stood,
As now they stand, massy, and tall, and dark,
Fit shrine for humble worshiper to hold
Communion with his Maker.

3.   These dim vaults,
These winding aisles, of human pomp or pride
Report not. No fantastic carvings show
The boast of our vain race to change the form
Of Thy fair works. . . .

4. Here is continual worship; nature, here,
In the tranquillity that Thou dost love,
Enjoys Thy presence. Noiselessly, around,

From perch to perch, the solitary bird
Passes; and yon clear spring, that, midst its herbs,
Wells softly forth, and wandering steeps the roots
Of half the mighty forest, tells no tale
Of all the good it does.

5.   Thou hast not left
Thyself without a witness, in these shades,
Of Thy perfections. Grandeur, strength, and grace,
Are here to speak of Thee. This mighty oak—
By whose immovable stem I stand, and seem
Almost annihilated—not a prince,
In all that proud old world beyond the deep,
E'er wore his crown as loftily as he
Wears the green coronal of leaves, with which
Thy hand has graced him. Nestled at his root
Is beauty, such as blooms not in the glare
Of the broad sun. That delicate forest flower,
With scented breath, and looks so like a smile,
Seems, as it issues from the shapeless mold,
An emanation of the indwelling Life,
A visible token of the upholding Love
That are the soul of this wide universe.

6. My heart is awed within me, when I think
Of the great miracle that still goes on,
In silence round me—the perpetual work
Of Thy creation, finished, yet renewed
Forever. Written on Thy works, I read
The lesson of Thy own eternity.
Lo! all grow old and die: but see, again,
How on the faltering footsteps of decay,
Youth presses—ever gay and beautiful youth—
In all its beautiful forms. These lofty trees

Wave not less proudly that their ancestors
Molder beneath them. . . .

7. There have been holy men, who hid themselves
Deep in the woody wilderness, and gave
Their lives to thought and prayer, till they outlived
The generation born with them, nor seemed
Less aged than the hoary trees and rocks
Around them; and there have been holy men,
Who deemed it were not well to pass life thus;
But, let me often to these solitudes
Retire, and in Thy presence, reassure
My feeble virtue. Here, its enemies,
The passions, at Thy plainer footsteps, shrink,
And tremble, and are still.

8.   O God! when Thou
Dost scare the world with tempest, set on fire
The heavens with falling thunderbolts, or fill,
With all the waters of the firmament,
The swift, dark whirlwind, that uproots the woods,
And drowns the villages; when at Thy call,
Uprises the great deep, and throws himself
Upon the continent, and overwhelms
Its cities;—who forgets not, at the sight
Of these tremendous tokens of Thy power,
His pride, and lays his strifes and follies by!
O! from these sterner aspects of Thy face
Spare me and mine; nor let us need the wrath
Of the mad, unchained elements, to teach
Who rules them. Be it ours to meditate,
In these calm shades, Thy milder majesty,
And to the beautiful order of Thy works
Learn to conform the order of our lives.
—*William Cullen Bryant.*

Exercise for Conversation and Study

Who is the author of this poem? Give a brief history of his life and writings. Give scriptural evidence that the groves were used anciently as places of worship. What Bible writer breathes the spirit of this poem into his writings? Read the following passages from the Psalms: 95; 104:24; 143:5-7; 147:1-9. Explain the following rhetorical expressions: "venerable columns," "nestled at his root," "looks so like a smile," "faltering footsteps of decay," "idle hate," "at Thy plainer footsteps," "unchained elements." Commit to memory portions of this poem that have most deeply impressed you.

Syllabication
Divide into syllables the words under "Word Study."

Articulation Drill
Articulate distinctly the words of this poem ending in *d*.

Word Study

1. temples	3. fantastic	6. ancestors
1. architrave	4. tranquillity	7. generation
1. anthems	4. noiselessly	8. continent
2. venerable	5. grandeur	8. overwhelms
2. verdant	5. coronal	

WORSHIP OR SERVICE?

1. I can not choose; I should have liked so much
   To sit at Jesus' feet—to feel the touch
   Of His kind, gentle hand upon my head
   While drinking in the gracious words He said.

2. And yet to serve Him! O divine employ,
   To minister and give the Master joy,
   To bathe in coolest springs His weary feet,
   And wait upon Him while He sat at meat!

3. Worship or service—which? Ah! that is best
   To which He calls me, be it toil or rest,

To labor for Him in life's busy stir,
Or seek His feet a silent worshiper.

4. So let Him choose for us; we are not strong
To make the choice; perhaps we should go wrong,
Mistaking zeal for service, sinful sloth
For loving worship, and so fail of both.
—*Caroline A. Mason.*

THE COUNCIL OF HORSES

> "*Be ye not as the horse, or as the mule, which have no understanding; whose mouth must be held in with bit and bridle, lest they come near unto thee.*"

1. Upon a time a neighing steed,
Who grazed among a numerous breed,
With mutiny had fired the train,
And spread dissension through the plain.
On matters that concerned the state,
The council met in grand debate.
A colt whose eyeballs flamed with ire,
Elate with strength and youthful fire,
In haste stepped forth before the rest,
And thus the listening throng addressed:—

2. "Behold, how abject is our race,
Condemned to slavery and disgrace!
Shall we our servitude retain,
Because our sires have worn the chain?
Consider, friends, your strength and might;
'Tis conquest to assert your right.
How cumbrous is the gilded coach!
The pride of man is our reproach.
Were we designed for daily toil,
To drag the plowshare through the soil,

To sweat in harvest through the road,
   To groan beneath the carrier's load?

3. "How feeble are the two-legg'd kind!
   What force is in our nerves combined!
   Shall then our nobler jaws submit
   To foam and champ the galling bit?
   Shall haughty men my back bestride?
   Shall the sharp spur provoke my side?
   Forbid it, comrades! reject the rein;
   Your shame, your infamy, disdain.
   Let him the lion first control,
   And still the tiger's famished growl.
   Let us, like them, our freedom claim,
   And make him tremble at our name."

4. A general nod approved the cause,
   And all the circle neighed applause.
   When, lo! with grave and solemn pace,
   A steed advanced before the race,
   With age and long experience wise;
   Around he cast his thoughtful eyes,
   And, to the murmurs of the train,
   Thus spoke the Nestor of the plain:—

5. "When I had health and strength like you,
   The toils of servitude I knew;
   Now grateful man rewards my pains,
   And gives me all these wide domains;
   At will I crop the year's increase,
   My later life is rest and peace.
   I grant, to man we lend our pains;
   And aid him to correct the plains;
   But doth not he divide the care,
   Through all the labors of the year?

ENGAGEMENT OF CAVALRY

6. "How many thousand structures rise,
   To fence us from inclement skies!
   For us he bears the sultry day,
   And stores up all our winter's hay.
   He sows, he reaps, the harvest's gain,
   We share the toil and share the grain.
   Since every creature was decreed
   To aid each other's mutual need,
   Appease your discontented mind,
   And act the part by heaven assigned."
   The tumult ceased, the colt submitted,
   And, like his ancestors, was bitted.
   —*John Gay, in "School Speaker and Reader" (adapted).*

THE HORSE IN BATTLE

1. Hast thou given the horse strength?
   Hast thou clothed his neck with thunder?
   Canst thou make him afraid as a grasshopper?
   The glory of his nostrils is terrible.

2. He paweth in the valley, and rejoiceth in his strength:
   He goeth on to meet the armed men.
   He mocketh at fear, and is not affrighted;
   Neither turneth he back from the sword.

3. The quiver rattleth against him,
   The glittering spear and the shield.
   He swalloweth the ground with fierceness and rage:
   Neither believeth he that it is the sound of the trumpet.
   He saith among the trumpets, "Ha, ha;"
   And he smelleth the battle afar off,
   The thunder of the captains, and the shouting.
   —*Job 39:19-25.*

VOCAL PRONUNCIATION

II. ACCENTUATION

Words of more than one syllable have one or more vowels pronounced with greater stress and clearness than the rest. This stress is called *accent*.

The syllabication of a word being known, the next question presented is that of the location of accent.

The sounds of the letters occasion less difficulty. The syllabication and accent being known, the general rules or analogies of the language furnish guidance to the pronunciation of the great mass of English words, notwithstanding all that is said of the anomalous character of our language.

When two accents occur in the same word, they are of unequal force. The heavier one, in such cases, is called the *primary accent;* the lighter is called the *secondary accent.* The secondary accent nearly always precedes the primary. Nearly all words of more than four syllables have a secondary accent. Some very long words have two secondary accents, as in *in-com″ pre-hen″ si-bil′ i-ty;* but no accent ever falls beyond the sixth syllable. A few of the simplest rules only are here given.

Rules for accent

Rule 1. Simple words of two syllables, excepting *a″men′*, never have more than one accent.

It is a very common error to pronounce such words as *combat*, *exile*, etc., with full stress on each syllable. This should be carefully avoided.

A similar error consists in accenting two consecutive syllables in some words of more than two syllables, as in the words *exactly*, *idea*, etc., as sometimes heard.

Rule 2. In compound words each part retains its own accent; as in *morn′ ing-glo′ ry, emp′ ty-hand′ ed.*

When the component words of a compound are monosyllables.

each retains its clear utterance, as when taken alone, but the greater stress is laid on that one which is descriptive or restrictive of the other; as, *wood' wash''*, *home' bred''*. When a compound word has come into such common use, however, as to drop the hyphen, it is often accented like a simple word; as in *cup' board*, *high' land*.

Rule 3. Words which serve as verbs and also as nouns or adjectives, usually have the accent on the last syllable when verbs— in other cases, on the first syllable; as, *con test'*, verb; *con' test*, noun; *com-pound'*, verb; *com' pound*, noun or adjective.

Some words, however, as, *ad-dress'*, *ex-press'*, etc., do not change the accent to denote the part of speech. Many errors in pronunciation come from the failure to note these exceptions to the general rule.

Rule 4. All words ending in *sion* or *tion* have the accent on the syllable next to the last, the penultimate syllable; as in *pre-sen-ta' tion*.

Rule 5. Words ending in *ical* or *acal*, generally have the accent on the syllable next preceding; as in *am-mon' i-cal, fin' i-cal*.

Monosyllables when taken alone, or when at all emphatic, may be treated as if accented syllables. In common composition, however, monosyllabic pronouns, prepositions, conjunctions, auxiliary verbs, and the articles, are usually quite unemphatic, and are then to be treated as unaccented syllables, receiving the same obscuration of the vowel sound.

Exercises in Accent

Note the difference in accent and meaning of the italicised words in the following sentences and give reasons for the difference in accent:—
1. Why does your *absent* friend *absent* himself?
2. Did he *abstract* the *abstract* of your speech from the desk?
3. Note the mark of *accent*, and *accent* the right syllable.
4. Buy some *cement* and *cement* the glass.

5. *Desert* us not in the *desert*.
6. He must *increase*, but I must *decrease*.
7. If they *rebel*, and *overthrow* the government, even the *rebels* can not justify the *overthrow*.
8. In *August*, the *august* writer entered into a *compact* to prepare a *compact* discourse.
9. *Instinct*, not reason, rendered her *instinct* with spirit.
10. Within a *minute* from this time, I will find a *minute* piece of gold.
11. If that *project* fails, he will *project* another.
12. My *increase* is taken to *increase* your wealth.
13. *Perfume* the room with rich *perfume*.

WORK

"My Father worketh hitherto, and I work."

1. There is a perennial nobleness and even sacredness in work. Were he never so benighted, forgetful of his high calling, there is always hope in a man that actually and earnestly works; in idleness alone is there perpetual despair. Work, never so mammonish mean, is in communication with nature. The real desire to get work done will itself lead one more and more to truth, to nature's appointments and regulations, which are truth.

2. Blessed is he who has found his work; let him ask no other blessedness. He has a work, a life purpose; he has found it, and will follow it. How, as a free-flowing channel, dug and torn by noble force through the sour mud-swamp of one's existence, like an ever-deepening river, there it runs and flows!—draining off the sour, festering water gradually from the root of the remotest grass blade; making, instead of pestilential swamp, a green, fruitful meadow with its clear, flowing stream. How blessed for the meadow itself, let the stream and its value be great or small.

3. Labor is life; from the inmost heart of the worker rises his

LABOR

God-given force, the sacred, celestial life essence, breathed into him by the Creator; from his inmost heart awakens him to all nobleness, to all knowledge, "self-knowledge," and much else, as soon as work fitly begins. Knowledge! the knowledge that will hold good in working, cleave thou to that; for nature herself accredits that, says Yea to that. Properly thou hast no other knowledge but what thou hast got by working; the rest is yet all a hypothesis of knowledge, a thing to be argued of in schools, a thing floating in the clouds in endless logic vortices till we try it and fix it. "Doubt of whatever kind, can be ended by action alone."

4. Older than all preached gospels was this unpreached, inarticulate, but ineradicable, forever-enduring gospel: Work and therein have well-being. Man, son of earth and heaven, lies there not in the innermost heart of thee a spirit of active method, a force for work that burns like a painfully smoldering fire, giving thee no rest till thou unfold it, till thou write it down in beneficent facts around thee? What is immethodic waste, thou shalt make methodic, regulated, arable, obedient, and productive to thee. Wheresoever thou findest disorder, there is thy eternal enemy. Attack him swiftly and subdue him. Make order of him, the subject not of chaos, but of intelligence, divinity, and thee! The thistle that grows in thy path, dig it out that a blade of useful grass, a drop of nourishing milk, may grow there instead. The waste cotton shrub, gather its waste white down, spin it, weave it; that in place of idle litter, there may be folded webs, and the naked skin of man be covered.

5. But, above all, where thou findest ignorance, stupidity, brute-mindedness—attack it, I say; smite it wisely, unweariedly, and rest not while thou livest and it lives; but smite, smite in the name of God! The highest God, as I understand it, does audibly so command thee: still audibly, if thou have ears to hear. He, even He, with His unspoken voice, is fuller than any Sinai thunders, or syllabled speech of whirlwinds; for the silence of deep eternities, of worlds

from beyond the morning stars, does it not speak to thee? The unborn ages, the old graves with their long-moldering dust, the very tears that wetted it, now all dry—do not these speak to thee what ear hath not heard? The deep death-kingdoms, the stars in their never-resting courses, all space and all time, proclaim it to thee in continual silent admonition. Thou, too, if ever man should, shalt work while it is called to-day; for the night cometh wherein no man can work.

6. All true work is sacred; in all true work, were it but true hand-labor, there is something of divineness. Labor, wide as the earth, has its summit in heaven. Sweat of the brow; and up from that to sweat of the brain, sweat of the heart; which includes all Kepler calculations, Newton meditations, all sciences, all spoken epics, all acted heroism, martyrdoms—up to that "agony of bloody sweat," which all men have called divine! O brother, if this is not "worship," then I say, the more pity for worship; for this is the noblest thing yet discovered under God's sky.

—*Thomas Carlyle.*

7. You may read the character of men as of nations in their art as in a mirror.

A man may hide himself from you, or misrepresent himself to you, every other way. But he can not in his work; there be sure you have him to the inmost. All that he likes, all that he sees, all that he can do,—his affection, his perseverance, his impatience, his clumsiness, cleverness, everything is there. If the work is a cobweb, you know it was made by a spider; if a honeycomb, by a bee; a worm cast is thrown up by a worm; and a nest wreathed by a bird; and a house built by a man, worthily if he is worthy, and ignobly, if he is ignoble.

—*John Ruskin.*

Exercise for Conversation and Study

Who was Thomas Carlyle? Give a brief description of his life and work. Point out the expressions in this lesson which show that the author had a knowledge of the Scriptures. Is the spirit of labor emphasized in the Bible? John 5:17; Eccl. 9:10; 2 Thess. 3:10-12; 1 Tim. 5:8; 1 Thess. 4:11, 12. Did man work before he sinned? Gen. 2:15. What was God's plan regarding manual labor after man sinned? Gen. 3:17-19. Will man work in the new earth? Isa. 65:22, 23. Who was Newton? Kepler? When did they live? What work did each do that has caused him to be remembered as a benefactor of mankind? Commit to memory:—

And unto Adam He said, . . . "Cursed is the ground for thy sake; in sorrow shalt thou eat of it all the days of thy life; thorns also and thistles shall it bring forth to thee: and thou shalt eat the herb of the field; *in the sweat of thy face* shalt thou eat bread, till thou return unto the ground; for out of it wast thou taken; for dust thou art, and unto dust shalt thou return." Gen. 3:17-20.

Articulation Drill

Give the consonants the full sounds in the words: Elm-lm; milked-lkt; shelves-lvz; call'st-lst; length-ngth; bursts-rsts; nerves-rvz; lisps-sps; rests-sts; where-wh; chasms-zmz.

Pronounce distinctly the following words: Robbed-bd; humbled-bld; ribs-bz; fetched-cht; hedged-djd; width-dth; breadths-dths; wafts-fts; acts-kts.

Word Study

Divide the following into syllables, mark the accent, and spell:—

1. perennial	3. essence	5. audibly
1. mammonish	3. vortices	5. Sinai
2. channel	4. inarticulate	5. syllabled
2. festering	4. ineradicable	6. Kepler
2. pestilential	4. arable	6. Newton
3. celestial	5. stupidity	6. martyrdoms

VOCAL PRONUNCIATION
III. WORDS COMMONLY MISPRONOUNCED

Correctly syllabify, accent, and pronounce the following lists of words.

I	II	III	IV
1. abdomen	1. Calliope	1. facade	1. lath
2. acclimate	2. Canaan	2. February	2. lamentable
3. acoustics	3. carbine	3. finale	3. leisure
4. address	4. Caucasian	4. finance	4. lien
5. Adonis	5. chastisement	5. forgery	5. lyceum
6. albumen	6. coadjutor	6. frontier	6. machination
7. allies	7. combatant	7. franchise	7. maniacal
8. allopathy	8. comparable	8. fugue	8. multiplicand
9. allopathic	9. construe	9. gape	9. naivete
10. almond	10. creek	10. gauntlet	10. national
11. alternate	11. cupola	11. giraffe	11. nomad
12. apparatus	12. cushion	12. glamour	12. obligatory
13. area	13. deficit	13. gladiolus	13. Orion
14. aroma	14. depot	14. granary	14. orotund
15. aspirant	15. discourse	15. homeopathy	15. Palestine
16. banana	16. dishonest	16. hydropathy	16. parent
17. behemoth	17. docile	17. indisputable	17. patriotism
18. benzine	18. donkey	18. inquiry	18. patron
19. blatant	19. envelope	19. integral	19. peremptory
20. bombshell	20. enervate	20. isolate	20. photographer
21. bouquet	21. erring	21. isotherm	21. placard
22. bonnet	22. exemplary	22. italic	22. portent
23. brigand	23. errand	23. jaguar	23. porcelain
24. bronchitis	24. exquisite	24. jaundice	24. precedence
25. brooch	25. extol	25. jugular	25. precedent

V	VI	VII	VIII
1. prelate	1. squalid	1. apricot	1. lethargic
2. presentation	2. squalor	2. accented	2. licorice
3. produce (noun)	3. stalwart	3. balmoral	3. mirage
4. pronunciation	4. talc	4. Belial	4. moccasin
5. pyramidal	5. taunt	5. cochineal	5. molecule
6. rational	6. telegrapher	6. conduit	6. nape
7. raillery	7. Thalia	7. communist	7. nephew
8. raspberry	8. tiny	8. crouch	8. Niger
9. rapine	9. tomato	9. Danish	9. onyx
10. recess	10. tranquil	10. defalcation	10. pall-mall
11. recitative	11. tribune	11. dessert	11. pariah
12. recruit	12. truculent	12. doughty	12. parliament
13. reparable	13. tryst	13. ducat	13. Penelope
14. research	14. vagary	14. dynamite	14. prolix
15. resource	15. valet	15. dyspepsia	15. prophecy
16. respiratory	16. vicar	16. Elihu	16. salmon
17. ribald	17. water	17. epizooty	17. satyr
18. romance	18. won't	18. extant	18. senile
19. root	19. wrath	19. frontispiece	19. simultaneous
20. sacrifice	20. yacht	20. ghoul	20. tableau
21. sagacious	21. yearling	21. Giaour	21. tragacanth
22. salve	22. yolk	22. gibberish	22. trichina
23. scarcely	23. you	23. grimace	23. tenet
24. seine	24. zodiacal	24. incisor	24. Uranus
25. sha'n't	25. zoology	25. intrigue	25. worsted
26. cohort	26. Baal	26. Pleiades	26. mystery
27. nostril	27. Elijah	27. horizon	27. architect
28. Asshur	28. glance	28. Asia	28. permanent
29. Gentile	29. leviathan	29. crimson	29. vague
30. niece	30. hoary	30. fiery	30. stanza

THE DESTRUCTION OF SENNACHERIB

1. The Assyrian came down like a wolf on the fold,
   And his cohorts were gleaming in purple and gold;
   And the sheen of their spears was like stars on the sea,
   When the blue wave rolls nightly on deep Galilee.

2. Like the leaves of the forest when summer is green,
   That host with their banners at sunset were seen;
   Like the leaves of the forest when autumn hath flown,
   That host on the morrow lay withered and strown.

3. For the Angel of Death spread his wings on the blast,
   And breathed in the face of the foe as he passed;
   And the eyes of the sleepers waxed deadly and chill,
   And their hearts but once heaved, and forever grew still!

4. And there lay the steed with his nostril all wide,
   But through it there rolled not the breath of his pride;
   And the foam of his gasping lay white on the turf,
   And cold as the spray of the rock-beating surf.

5. And there lay the rider distorted and pale,
   With the dew on his brow and the rust on his mail;
   And the tents were all silent, the banners alone,
   The lances unlifted, the trumpet unblown.

6. And the widows of Asshur are loud in their wail,
   And their idols are broke in the temple of Baal;
   And the might of the Gentile, unsmote by the sword,
   Hath melted like snow in the glance of the Lord!

   —*Lord Byron.*

LANDING OF THE PILGRIM FATHERS

1. The breaking waves dashed high
    On a stern and rock-bound coast,
   And the woods against the stormy sky
    Their giant branches tossed.

2. And the heavy night hung dark
    The hills and waters o'er,
   When a band of exiles moored their bark
    On the wild New England shore.

3. Not as the conqueror comes,
    They, the true-hearted came;
   Not with the roll of the stirring drums,
    And the trumpet that sings of fame;

4. Not as the flying come;
    In silence and in fear;—
   They shook the depths of the desert gloom
    With their hymns of lofty cheer.

5. Amidst the storm they sang,
    And the stars heard, and the sea;
   And the sounding aisles of the dim woods rang
    To the anthem of the free!

6. The ocean eagle soared
    From his nest by the white wave's foam;
   And the rocking pines of the forest roared—
    This was their welcome home!

7. There were men with hoary hair
    Amidst that pilgrim band:—

LANDING OF THE PILGRIMS

Why had they come to wither there,
Away from their childhood's land?

8. There was a woman's fearless eye,
Lit by her deep love's truth;
There was manhood's brow serenely high,
And the fiery heart of youth.

9. What sought they thus afar?—
Bright jewels of the mine?
The wealth of seas? the spoils of war?—
They sought a faith's pure shrine!

10. Ay, call it holy ground,
The soil where first they trod;
They left unstained what there they found—
Freedom to worship God.

—*Felicia D. Hemans*

Articulation Drill

Articulate distinctly: The helm of elm from a wintry realm, saved a crew from the billow's whelm.

THE DAWN

> *"There was never a night without a day,*
> *Nor an evening without a morning;*
> *And the darkest hour, as the proverb goes,*
> *Is the hour before the dawning."*

1. I had occasion, a few weeks since, to take the early train from Providence to Boston, and for this purpose rose at two o'clock in the morning. Everything around was wrapped in darkness and hushed in silence, broken only by what seemed at that hour the unearthly clank and rush of the train. It was a mild, serene, midsummer's night; the sky was without a cloud, the winds were whist. The moon, then in the last quarter, had just risen, and the stars shone with a spectral luster but little affected by her presence.

2. Jupiter, two hours high, was the herald of the day; the Pleiades, just above the horizon, shed their sweet influence in the east; Lyra sparkled near the zenith; Andromeda veiled her newly-discovered glories from the naked eye in the south; the steady Pointers, far beneath the pole, looked meekly up from their depths of the north to their sovereign. Such was the glorious spectacle as I entered the train.

3. As we proceeded, the timid approach of twilight became more perceptible; the intense blue of the sky began to soften; the smaller stars, like little children, went first to rest; the sister beams of the Pleiades soon melted together; but the bright constellations of the west and north remained unchanged. Steadily the wondrous transfiguration went on. Hands of angels, hidden from mortal eyes, shifted the scenery of the heavens; the glories of the night dissolved into the glories of the dawn.

4. The blue sky now turned more softly gray; the great watch-stars shut their holy eyes; the east began to kindle. Faint streaks of purple soon blushed along the sky; the whole celestial concave was filled with the inflowing tides of the morning light, which came pouring down from above in one great ocean of radiance; till at length, as we reached the Blue Hills, a flash of purple fire

blazed out from above the horizon, and turned the dewy teardrops of flower and leaf into rubies and diamonds. In a few seconds, the everlasting gates of the morning were thrown wide open, and the lord of day, arrayed in glories too severe for the gaze of man, began his state.

5. I do not wonder at the superstition of the ancient Magians, who in the morning of the world went up to the hilltops of Central Asia, and, ignorant of the true God, adored the most glorious work of His hand. But I am filled with amazement, when I am told, that, in this enlightened age and in the heart of the Christian world, there are persons who can witness this daily manifestation of the power and wisdom of the Creator, and yet say in their hearts, "There is no God." —*Edward Everett.*

Exercise for Conversation and Study

Locate on the map the cities mentioned in the lesson. Locate in the sky the constellations spoken of by the writer. What lesson do you learn from the stanza at the head of this selection? Does the Bible refer to the ancient custom of "sun worship"? What does the apostle Paul say about the heathen worshiping the creation instead of the Creator? Rom. 1:22-25. What does nature reveal? Verses 19, 20. Instead of the things of nature saying "There is no God," they say, "Behold your God." Job 12:7-10.

Articulation Drill

Take your hat and put it on your head. He boasts that he twists the texts to suit the sects. His meat was locusts and wild honey. The battle lasts still for the hosts still stand.

Word Study

1. occasion
1. Providence
1. Boston
2. horizon
2. Andromeda
2. spectacle
3. transfiguration
3. scenery
3. dissolved
4. purple
4. concave
4. severe
5. Magians
5. Asia
5. amazement
5. manifestation
5. wisdom
5. Creator

TRUST IN GOD AND DO THE RIGHT

"I will trust in the Lord and not be afraid."

1. Courage, brother! do not stumble,
    Though thy path be dark as night;
   There's a star to guide the humble—
    Trust in God and do the right.

2. Let the road be long and dreary,
    And its ending out of sight;
   Foot it bravely—strong or weary,
    Trust in God and do the right.

3. Perish "policy" and cunning,
    Perish all that fears the light;
   Whether losing, whether winning,
    Trust in God and do the right.

4. Trust no party, trust no faction,
    Trust no leaders in the fight;
   But in every word and action,
    Trust in God and do the right.

5. Trust no forms of guilty passion
    Fiends can look like angels bright;
   Trust no custom, school, or fashion,
    Trust in God and do the right.

6. Some will hate thee, some will love thee,
    Some will flatter, some will slight;
   Turn from man, and look above thee,
    Trust in God and do the right.

7. Simple rule and safest guiding,
Inward peace and inward light;
Star upon our path abiding,
Trust in God and do the right.

—*Selected.*

Articulation Drill

The following drill is given to aid in overcoming the fault of blending the last sounds of one word with the first of another, or suppressing the final sounds of one word when the next begins with a similar sound:—

She keeps pies,	not	She keeps spies.
His small eyes,	not	His small lies.
He had two small eggs,	not	He had two small legs.
Come and see me once more,	not	Command see me once smore.

THE TOWN CHILD AND THE COUNTRY CHILD

"The little children should come especially close to nature. Instead of putting fashion's shackles upon them, let them be free like the lambs, to play in the sweet, fresh sunlight."

(May be read or spoken by two persons in alternation.)

1. Child of the country! free as air
Art thou, and as the sunshine fair;
Born like the lily, where the dew
Lies odorous when the day is new;
Fed mid the May flowers like the bees;
Nursed to sweet music on the knees;
Lulled on the breast to that sweet tune
Which winds make mid the woods in June.
I sing of thee;—'tis sweet to sing
Of such a fair and gladsome thing.

2. Child of the town! for thee I sigh;
   A gilded roof's thy golden sky;
   A carpet is thy daisied sod;
   A narrow street thy boundless wood;
   The rushing deer, the clattering tramp
   Of watchmen; thy best light's a lamp,—
   Through smoke, and not through trellised vine
   And blooming trees, thy sunbeam shines.
   I sing of thee in sadness; where
   Else is wreck wrought in aught so fair?

3. Child of the country! Thy small feet
   Tread on strawberries red and sweet.
   With thee I wander forth to see
   The flowers which most delight the bee;
   The bush o'er which the throstle sung
   In April while she nursed her young;
   The dew beneath the sloe-thorn where
   She bred her twins, the timorous hare;
   The knoll wrought o'er with wild bluebells
   Where brown bees build their balmy cells;
   The greenwood stream, the shady pool
   Where trouts leap when the day is cool;
   The shilfa's nest that seems to be
   A portion of the sheltering tree,
   And other marvels, which my verse
   Can find no language to rehearse.

4. Child of the town! for thee, alas!
   Glad Nature spreads no flowers nor grass;
   Birds build no nests, nor in the sun
   Glad streams come singing as they run.
   A Maypole is thy blossomed tree,

A beetle is thy murmuring bee.
Thy bird is caged, thy dove is where
The poulterer dwells, beside the hare;
Thy fruit is plucked, and by the pound
Hawked, clamorous, o'er the city round;
No roses, twinborn on the stalk,
Perfume thee in thy evening walk.
No voice of birds; but to thee comes
The mingled din of car and drums,
And startling cries, such as are rife
When wine and wassail waken strife.

5. Child of the country! on the lawn
I see thee like the bounding fawn,
Blithe as the bird which tries its wing
The first time on the wings of Spring.
Bright as the sun when from the cloud
He comes as cocks are crowing loud;
Now running, shouting, mid sunbeams,
Now groping trouts in lucid streams;
Now spinning like a mill wheel round,
Now hunting echo's empty sound;
Now climbing up some old tall tree
For climbing's sake. 'Tis sweet to thee
To sit where birds can sit alone,
Or share with thee thy venturous throne.

6. Child of the town and bustling street,
What woes and snares await thy feet!
Thy paths are paved for five long miles,
Thy groves and hills are peaks and stiles;
Thy fragrant air is yon thick smoke,
Which shrouds thee like a mourning cloak.

And thou art cabined and confined
At once from sun and dew and wind,
Or set thy tottering feet but on
Thy lengthened walks of slippery stone.
The coachman there careering reels,
With goaded steeds and maddening wheels;
And commerce pours each prosing son
In pelf's pursuit, and hollos, "Run!"
While flushed with wine, and stung at play,
Men rush from darkness into day.
The stream's too strong for thy small bark;
Where naught can sail save what is stark.

7. Fly from the town, sweet child! for health
Is happiness, and strength, and wealth.
There is a lesson in each flower,
A story in each stream and shower;
On every herb o'er which you tread
Are written words, which, rightly read,
Will lead you from earth's fragrant sod
To hope and holiness and God.

—*Allen Cunningham.*

Exercise for Conversation and Study

Read again the lessons on "Teaching in Parables." Note those passages that speak of the blessings that come to the children and youth who come in close contact with nature. Mention some of the blessings and privileges of the country child. What are the conditions and surroundings of the city child? What style of expression is used when reading of the country child? the city child?

Articulation Drill

Some shun sunshine and some shun shade. She sells seashells. Does she sell seashells? A few fixed facts. Stick six thrifty, thick, thistle sticks.

Word Study

1. country
1. odorous
2. town
2. narrow
2. trellised
3. strawberries
3. throstle
3. timorous
4. poulterer
4. perfume
5. blithe
5. lucid
6. fragrant
6. commerce
7. herb

THE NORTHERN LIGHTS*

"By His Spirit He hath garnished the heavens."

1. A light is troubling heaven! A strange, dull glow
    Hangs like a half-quenched veil of fire between
    The blue sky and the earth; and the shorn stars
    Gleam faint and sickly through it. Day hath left
    No token of its parting, and the blush
    With which it welcomed the embrace of Night
    Has faded from the blue cheek of the West;
    Yet forth from the solemn darkness of the North,
    Stretched o'er the "empty place" by God's own hand,
    Trembles and waves that curtain of pale fire,—
    Tinging with baleful and unnatural hues
    The winter snows beneath. It is as if
    Nature's last curse—the fearful plague of fire—
    Were working in the elements, and the skies
    Even as a scroll consuming.

2.   Lo, a change!
    The fiery wonder sinks, and all along
    A dark, deep crimson rests—a sea of blood,
    Untroubled by a wave. And over all

---
* There was a remarkable display of the aurora borealis in January, 1837, and this poem commemorates the phenomenon. It was printed in the Haverhill *Gazette* at the time, but was never collected.

Bendeth a luminous arch of pale, pure white,
Clearly contrasted with the blue above,
And the dark red beneath it. Glorious!
How like a path for the shining ones,
The pure and beautiful intelligences
Who minister in heaven, and offer up
Their praise as incense; or, like that which rose
Before the pilgrim prophet, when the tread
Of the most holy angels brightened it,
And in his dream the haunted sleeper saw
The ascending and descending of the blest!

3. And yet another change! O'er half the sky
A long, bright flame is trembling, like the sword
Of the great angel of the guarded gate
Of Paradise, when all the holy streams
And beautiful bowers of Eden-land blushed red
Beneath its awful wavering, and the eyes
Of the outcasts quailed before the glare,
As from the immediate questioning of God.

4. O God of mystery! These fires are Thine!
Thy breath hath kindled them, and there they burn
Amid the permanent glory of Thy heavens,
That earliest revelation written out
In starry language, visible to all,
Lifting unto Thyself the heavy eyes
Of the down-looking spirits of the earth!
The Indian leaning on his hunting bow,
Where the ice mountains herd the frozen pole,
And the hoar architect of winter piles
With tireless hand his snowy pyramids,
Looks upward in deep awe,—while all around

The eternal ices kindle with the hues
Which tremble on their gleaming pinnacles
And sharp, cold ridges of enduring frost,—
And points his child to the Great Spirit's fire.

5. Alas for us who boast of deeper lore,
If in the maze of our vague theories,
Our speculations, and our restless aim
To search the secret, and familiarize
The awful things of nature, we forget
To own Thy presence in Thy mysteries!
—*John Greenleaf Whittier.*

Exercise for Conversation and Study

What other name is given to the northern lights? Describe their appearance. How does the poet account for their existence and glory? How does the Creator garnish the heavens? Job 26:13. Point out the beautiful figures of speech in the first stanza. What expressions in this poem indicate that the author had a knowledge of the Scriptures? After noting these expressions, read the following: Job 26:7; Rev. 6:14; Gen. 28:10-14; 4:22-24; Heb. 12:29. What danger in the study of science is pointed out in the last stanza?

Articulation Drill

Amidst the mists and coldest frosts,
With barest wrists, and stoutest boasts,
He thrusts his fists against the posts,
And still insists he sees the ghosts.

Word Study

1. curtain	2. beautiful	4. pyramid
1. plague	2. ascending	4. pinnacles
1. scroll	3. quailed	5. vague
2. crimson	3. questioning	5. theories
2. glorious	4. architect	5. familiarize

THE BIBLE, THE BEST OF CLASSICS

> "*The words of the Lord are pure words: as silver tried in a furnace of earth, purified seven times.*"

1. There is a classic, the best the world has ever seen, the noblest that has ever honored and dignified the language of mortals. If we look into its antiquity, we discover a title to our veneration, unrivaled in the history of literature. If we have respect to its evidences, they are found in the testimony of miracle and prophecy; in the ministry of man, of nature, and of angels, yea, even of "God, manifest in the flesh," of "God blessed forever."

2. If we consider its authenticity, no other pages have survived the lapse of time, that can be compared with it. If we examine its authority (for it speaks as never man spake), we discover that it came from heaven in vision and prophecy, under the sanction of Him who is Creator of all things, and the Giver of every good and perfect gift.

3. If we reflect on its truths, they are lovely and spotless, sublime and holy as God Himself, unchangeable as His nature, durable as His righteous dominion, and versatile as the moral of mankind. If we regard the value of its treasures, we must estimate them, not like the relics of classic antiquity, by the perishable glory and beauty, virtue and happiness, of this world, but by the enduring perfection and supreme felicity of an eternal kingdom.

4. If we inquire who are the men that have recorded its truths, vindicated its rights, and illustrated the excellence of its scheme, from the depth of ages and from the living world, from the populous continent and the isles of the sea, comes forth the answer, "The patriarch and the prophet, the evangelist and the martyr."

5. If we look abroad through the world of men, the victims of folly or vice, the prey of cruelty, of injustice, and inquire what are its benefits even in this temporal state, the great and the humble, the rich and the poor, the powerful and the weak, the learned and

the ignorant, reply as with one voice, that humanity and resignation, purity, order, and peace, faith, hope, and charity, are its blessings upon earth.

6. And if, raising our eyes from time to eternity, from the world of mortals to the world of just men made perfect, from the visible creation, marvelous, beautiful, and glorious as it is, to the invisible creation of angels and seraphs, from the footstool of God to the throne of God Himself, we ask what are the blessings that flow from this single volume, let the question be answered by the pen of the evangelist, the harp of the prophet, and the records of the book of life.

7. Such is the best of classics the world has ever admired; such, the noblest that man has ever adopted as a guide.

—*Grimke.*

Exercise for Conversation and Study

In what sense is the Bible a classical production? What writings are referred to when we speak of the "classics"? Why does the author of this lesson unhesitatingly pronounce the Bible to be the best of the "classics"? How did the Psalmist David regard the Word of God? Ps. 12:6. Give a brief history of the origin of the Bible, and its publication and circulation. Learn the names of the books of the Bible and the author of each.

Articulation Drill

Peter Prangle, the prickly prangly pear picker, picked three pecks of prickly, prangly pears from the prickly prangly pear trees on the pleasant prairies.

Word Study

1. classic
1. antiquity
1. literature
2. authenticity
2. sanction
3. versatile
3. relics
3. felicity
4. scheme
4. evangelist
5. purity
5. resignation
6. seraphs
6. volume
7. admired

THE DARKENING OF THE SUN AND MOON

> "*Immediately after the tribulation of those days shall the sun be darkened, and the moon shall not give her light.*"

1. "The dark day of North America was one of those wonderful phenomena of nature which will always be read of with interest, but which philosophy is at a loss to explain."

2. "In the month of May, 1780, there was a terrific dark day in New England, when 'all faces seemed to gather blackness,' and the people were filled with fear. There was great distress in the village where Edward Lee lived; 'men's hearts failing them for fear' that the judgment day was at hand; and the neighbors all flocked around the holy man, who spent the gloomy hours in earnest prayer for the distressed multitude."

3. "Candles were lighted in many houses. Birds were silent and disappeared. Fowls retired to roost. It was the general opinion that the day of judgment was at hand."

4. "The darkness was such as to occasion farmers to leave their work in the field, and retire to their dwellings. Lights became necessary to the transaction of business within doors. The darkness continued through the day."

5. "The cocks crew as at daybreak, and everything bore the appearance and gloom of night. The alarm produced by this unusual aspect of the heavens was very great."

6. "It was midnight darkness at noonday. . . . Thousands of people who could not account for it from natural causes, were greatly terrified; and, indeed, it cast a universal gloom on the earth. The frogs and nighthawks began their notes."

7. "Similar days have occasionally been known, though inferior in the degree or extent of their darkness. The causes of these phenomena are unknown. They certainly were not the result of eclipses."

8. "Almost, if not altogether alone, as the most mysterious and yet unexplained phenomenon of its kind in nature's diversified range of events during the last century, stands the dark day of May 19, 1780,—a most unaccountable darkening of the whole visible heavens and atmosphere in New England,—which brought intense alarm and distress to multitudes of minds, as well as dismay to the brute creation, the fowls fleeing, bewildered, to their roosts, and the birds to their nests, and the cattle returning to their stalls. Indeed, thousands of the good people of that day became fully convinced that the end of all things terrestrial had come. . . . The extent of this darkness was also very remarkable. It was observed at the most easterly regions of New England; westward to the farthest parts of Connecticut, and at Albany, to the southward, it was observed all along the seacoast; and to the north, as far as the American settlements extended. It probably far exceeded these boundaries, but the exact limits were never positively known."

9. The poet Whittier thus speaks of this event:—

" 'Twas on a May day of the far old year
Seventeen hundred eighty, that there fell
Over the bloom and sweet life of the spring,
Over the fresh earth and the heaven of noon,
A horror of great darkness, like the night
In day of which the Norland sages tell—
The twilight of the gods. The low-hung sky
Was black with ominous clouds, save where its rim
Was fringed with a dull glow, like that which climbs
The crater's sides from the red hell below.
Birds ceased to sing, and all the barnyard fowls
Roosted; the cattle at the pasture bars
Lowed, and looked homeward; bats on leathern wings
Flitted abroad; the sounds of labor died;
Men prayed and women wept; all ears grew sharp

> To hear the doom-blast of the trumpet shatter
> The black sky, that the dreadful face of Christ
> Might look from the rent clouds, not as He looked
> A loving Guest in Bethany, but stern
> As justice and inexorable law."

10. "The darkness of the following night, May 19, 1780, was as unnatural as that of the day had been."

11. "The darkness of the following evening was probably as gross as has ever been observed since the Almighty first gave birth to light. I could not help conceiving at the time that if every luminous body in the universe had been shrouded in impenetrable darkness, or struck out of existence, the darkness could not have been more complete. A sheet of white paper held within a few inches of the eyes, was equally invisible with the blackest velvet."

12. "Almost every one who happened to be out in the evening was lost in going home. The darkness was as uncommon in the night as it was in the day, as the moon had fulled the day before."

13. This statement respecting the phase of the moon proves the impossibility of an eclipse of the sun at that time. And whenever on this memorable night the moon did appear, as at certain times it did, it had, according to this prophecy, the appearance of blood.
—*Thoughts on Daniel and the Revelation.*

Exercise for Conversation and Study

Who uttered the words of prophecy at the beginning of this lesson? On what occasion were these words spoken? Where in the Scriptures is this prophecy recorded? What prophets spoke of the same events? Give Scripture references. When was the prophecy fulfilled? Give Biblical and historical proof. What was the extent of territory affected by the darkening of the sun? Name and locate on the map the places mentioned in the lesson. Describe the effects of this remarkable phenomenon. Who was Whittier? Give a brief sketch of his life and writings.

Articulation Drill

Five wise wives weave withes with which to make knapsack straps. Sysethis and Sysesith say the south wind ceaseth, and that sufficeth us.

Word Study

1. phenomena
1. philosophy
2. terrific
3. opinion
4. transaction
5. unusual
6. thousands
7. similar
7. eclipses
8. mysterious
8. terrestrial
8. Connecticut
8. Albany
9. Whittier
11. Almighty
11. impenetrable
13. impossibility
13. memorable

THE FALLING OF THE STARS

"And the stars of heaven fell unto the earth, even as a fig tree casteth her untimely figs, when she is shaken of a mighty wind."

1. The voice of history still is "Fulfilled!" Being a much later event than the darkening of the sun, there are multitudes in whose memories it is as fresh as though it were yesterday. We refer to the great meteoric shower of November 13, 1833. The following testimonies are from eyewitnesses of this extraordinary event:—

2. "At the cry, 'Look out of the window!' I sprang from a deep sleep, and with wonder saw the east lighted up with the dawn and meteors. . . . I called to my wife to behold; and while robing; she exclaimed, 'See how the stars fall!' I replied, 'That is the wonder;' and we felt in our hearts that it was a sign of the last days. For truly 'the stars of heaven fell unto the earth, even as a fig tree casteth her untimely figs, when she is shaken of a mighty wind.' Rev. 6: 13. This language of the prophet has always been received as metaphorical. Yesterday it was literally fulfilled.

3. "The ancients understood by *aster* in Greek, and *stella* in Latin, the smaller lights of heaven. The refinement of modern

astronomy has made distinction between stars of heaven and meteors of heaven. Therefore the idea of the prophet, as it is expressed in the original Greek, was literally fulfilled in the phenomenon of yesterday, so as no man before yesterday had conceived to be possible that it should be fulfilled. The immense size and distance of the planets and fixed stars forbid the idea of their falling unto the earth. Larger bodies can not fall in myriads unto a smaller body; and most of the planets and all the fixed stars are many times larger than our earth; but these fell toward the earth.

4. "And how did they fall? Neither myself nor one of the family heard any report; and were I to hunt through nature for a simile, I could not find one so apt, to illustrate the appearance of the heavens, as that which St. John uses in the prophecy before quoted: 'The stars of heaven fell unto the earth.' They were not sheets or flakes or drops of fire; but they were what the world understands by falling stars; and one speaking to his fellow, in the midst of the scene, would say, 'See how the stars fall!' And he who heard would not stop to correct the astronomy of the speaker, any more than he would reply, 'The sun does not move,' to one who should tell him, 'The sun is rising.' The stars fell 'even as a fig tree casteth her untimely figs, when she is shaken of a mighty wind.' Here is the exactness of the prophet. The falling stars did not come as if from several trees shaken, but from one. Those which appeared in the east fell toward the east; those which appeared in the north fell toward the north; those which appeared in the west fell toward the west; and those which appeared in the south (for I went out of my residence into the park), fell toward the south. And they fell not as ripe fruit falls; far from it; but they flew, they were cast, like the unripe, which at first refuses to leave the branch, and when, under a violent pressure, it does break its hold, it flies swiftly, straight off, descending; and in the multitude falling, some cross the track of others, as they are

thrown with more or less force, but each one falls on its own side of the tree."

5. "Extensive and magnificent showers of shooting stars have been known to occur at various places in modern times; but the most universal and wonderful which has ever been recorded, is that of the 13th of November, 1833, the whole firmament, over all the United States, being then, for hours, in a fiery commotion. No celestial phenomenon has ever occurred in this country, since its first settlement, which was viewed with such intense admiration by one class in the community, or with so much dread and alarm by another. . . . During the three hours of its continuance, the day of judgment was believed to be only waiting for sunrise."

6. The effect of this phenomenon upon the negro population is described by a Southern planter as follows: "I was suddenly awakened by the most distressing cries that ever fell on my ears. Shrieks of horror and cries for mercy could be heard from most of the negroes of three plantations, amounting in all to some six or eight hundred. While earnestly and breathlessly listening for the cause, I heard a faint voice near the door calling my name. I arose, and taking my sword, stood at the door. At this moment I heard the same voice still beseeching me to rise, and saying, 'O my God! the world is on fire!' I then opened the door, and it is difficult to say which excited me most, the awfulness of the scene or the distressed cries of the negroes. Upward of one hundred lay prostrate on the ground, some speechless, and others uttering the bitterest moans, but with their hands raised, imploring God to save the world and them. The scene was truly awful; for never did rain fall much thicker than the meteors fell toward the earth; east, west, north, and south, it was the same. In a word, the whole heavens seemed in motion."

7. "Argo computes that not less than two hundred forty thousand meteors were at the same time visible above the horizon of

Boston." And of the display at Niagara it is said that "no spectacle so terribly grand and sublime was ever before beheld by man as that of the firmament descending in fiery torrents over the dark and roaring cataract." —*Thoughts on Daniel and the Revelation.*

Exercise for Conversation and Study

What prophets predicted the falling of the stars? Rev. 6:13; Joel 2:10, 11; Isa. 13:9, 10. When did this event occur? Does the Saviour's prophecy indicate when these signs in the sun, moon, and stars were to be fulfilled? Mark 13:24-26. What are meteors, shooting stars, aerolites, planets, and fixed stars? What was the difference between the meteoric shower of 1833 and other meteoric showers that have been witnessed from time to time? What was the extent of this shower? What was the effect upon the people? Of what great event are these signs in the sun, moon, and stars a warning?

Articulation Drill

This specific specific specificates specifically the specificness of the specific of which specific this specific is specific specimen.

Word Study

1. history	4. simile	6. horror
1. meteoric	4. illustrate	6. breathlessly
2. metaphorical	4. midst	6. plantations
3. Greek	5. extensive	7. computes
3. Latin	5. magnificent	7. Niagara
3. yesterday	5. firmament	7. cataract

THE WATER MILL

"The harvest is past, the summer is ended, and we are not saved."

1. O, listen to the water mill, through all the livelong day,
As the clicking of the wheels wears hour by hour away;
How languidly the autumn wind doth stir the withered leaves,
As on the field the reapers sing, while binding up the sheaves!
A solemn proverb strikes my mind, and as a spell is cast,—
"The mill will never grind again with water that is past."

2. O! clasp the proverb to thy soul, dear loving heart and true;
For golden years are fleeting by, and youth is passing, too.
Ah! learn to make the most of life, nor lose one happy day,
For time will ne'er return sweet joys neglected, thrown away;
Nor leave one tender word unsaid, thy kindness sow broadcast,—
"The mill will never grind again with water that is past."

3. O! the wasted hours of life, that have swiftly drifted by,
Alas! the good we might have done, all gone without a sigh;
Love that we might once have saved by a single kindly word,
Thoughts conceived but ne'er expressed, perishing unpenned, unheard.
O, take the lesson to thy soul, forever clasp it fast! —
"The mill will never grind again with water that is past."

4. Work on while yet the sun doth shine, thou man of strength and will,
The streamlet ne'er doth useless glide by clicking water mill;
Nor wait until to-morrow's light beams brightly on thy way;
For all that thou canst call thine own, lies in the phrase "to-day."
Possessions, power, and blooming health, must all be lost at last;—
"The mill will never grind again with water that is past."

WATER WHEEL HOFFEMA, 1638—1709

5. O! love thy God and fellow men, thyself consider last,
For come it will when thou must scan dark errors of the past;
Soon will this fight of life be o'er, and earth recede from view,
And heaven in all its glory shine where all is pure and true.
Ah! then thou'lt see more clearly still the proverb deep and vast:—
"The mill will never grind again with water that is past."
—D. C. McCallum.

Articulation Drill

The flaming fire flashed fearfully in his face.
He drew long lines along the lovely landscape.
Round the rough and rugged rocks the ragged rascal ran.

THE ATMOSPHERE

"He giveth to all life, and breath, and all things."

1. The atmosphere rises above us with its cathedral dome arching toward the heavens, to which it is the most familiar synonym and symbol. It floats around us like that grand object which the apostle John saw in his vision, "a sea of glass like unto crystal." So massive is it, that, when it begins to stir, it tosses about great ships like playthings, and sweeps cities and forests to destruction before it.

2. And yet it is so mobile that we live years in it before we can be persuaded that it exists at all; and the great bulk of mankind never realize the truth that they are bathed in an ocean of air. Its weight is so enormous that iron shivers before it like glass; yet a soap bubble sails through it with impunity, and the tiniest insect waves it aside with its wing.

3. It ministers lavishly to all the senses. We touch it not; but

it touches us. Its warm south wind brings back color to the pale face of the invalid; its cool west winds refresh the fevered brow, and make the blood mantle in our cheeks; even its northern blasts brace into new vigor the hardy children of our rugged clime.

4. The eye is indebted to it for all the magnificence of sunrise, the full brightness of midday, the chastened radiance of the "gloaming," and the "clouds that cradle near the setting sun." But for it, the rainbow would want its "triumphal arch," and the winds would not send their fleecy messengers on errands round the heavens. The cold weather would not shed its snow feathers on the earth, nor drops of dew gather on the flowers. The kindly rain would never fall, nor hailstorm nor fog diversify the face of the sky. Our naked globe would turn its tanned and unshadowed forehead to the sun, and one dreary, monotonous blaze of light and heat dazzle and burn up all things.

5. Were there no atmosphere, the evening sun would in a moment set; and, without warning, plunge the earth in darkness. But the air keeps in her hand a sheaf of his rays and lets them slip slowly through her fingers; so that the shadows gather by degrees, and the flowers have time to bow their heads, and each creature space to find a place of rest, and nestle to repose.

6. In the morning, the garish sun would at once burst from the bosom of night, and blaze above the horizon; but the air watches for his coming, and sends at first one little ray to announce his approach, and then another, and by and by a handful; and so gently draws aside the curtain of night, and slowly lets the light fall on the face of the sleeping earth, till her eyelids open, and, like man, she "goeth forth again to her labor till the evening."

—*Selected.*

Exercise for Conversation and Study

On what day of the creation week was the atmosphere created? Gen. 1: 6-8, 20, 26. For what purpose was it created? How far above the earth does it extend? Of what is it composed? Mention several ways in which air is a blessing to us. Does the air have weight? Prove it. How does it aid in pumping water from a well? Of what are wind and air symbols? John 3:8; 20:22; Acts 2:1, 2. Select the Bible quotations from this lesson. Point out the figures of speech in paragraphs five and six, and note their beauty and appropriateness.

Articulation Drill
Theophilus Thistle, the successful thistle sifter, in sifting a sieve full of unsifted thistles, thrust three thousand thistles through the thick of his thumb; now, if Theophilus Thistle, the successful thistle sifter, in sifting a sieve full of unsifted thistles, thrust three thousand thistles through the thick of *his* thumb, see that *thou*, in sifting a sieve full of unsifted thistles, thrust not three thousand thistles through the thick of *thy* thumb. Success to the successful thistle sifter.

Word Study
1. atmosphere	3. lavishly	5. degrees
1. cathedral	3. invalid	5. nestle
1. destruction	3. mantle	6. garish
2. mobile	4. indebted	6. announce
2. impunity	4. errands	6. approach
2. enormous	4. monotonous	6. handful

THE CREATION

"I have made the earth, and created man upon it: I, even My hands, have stretched out the heavens, and all their host have I commanded."

1. "By the word of the Lord were the heavens made; and all the host of them by the breath of His mouth." "For He spake, and it was; He commanded, and it stood fast." He "laid the foundations of the earth, that it should not be removed forever."

2. As the earth came forth from the hand of its Maker, it was exceedingly beautiful. Its surface was diversified with mountains,

hills, and plains, interspersed with noble rivers and lovely lakes; but the hills and mountains were not abrupt and rugged, abounding in terrific steeps and frightful chasms, as they now do; the sharp, ragged edges of earth's rocky framework were buried beneath the fruitful soil, which everywhere produced a luxuriant growth of verdure. There were no loathsome swamps nor barren deserts. Graceful shrubs and delicate flowers greeted the eye at every turn. The heights were crowned with trees more majestic than any that now exist. The air, untainted by foul miasma, was clear and healthful. The entire landscape outvied in beauty the decorated grounds of the proudest palace. The angelic host viewed the scene with delight, and rejoiced at the wonderful works of God.

3. After the earth, with its teeming animal and vegetable life, had been called into existence, man, the crowning work of the Creator, and the one for whom the beautiful earth had been fitted up, was brought upon the stage of action. To him was given dominion over all that his eye could behold; for "God said, 'Let Us make man in Our image, after Our likeness; and let them have dominion over . . . all the earth.' " "So God created man in His own image; . . . male and female created He them."

4. As man came forth from the hand of his Creator, he was of lofty stature and perfect symmetry. His countenance bore the ruddy tint of health, and glowed with the light of life and joy. Adam's height was much greater than that of men who now inhabit the earth. Eve was somewhat less in stature; yet her form was noble, and full of beauty. The sinless pair wore no artificial garments; they were clothed with a covering of light and glory, such as the angels wear. So long as they lived in obedience to God, this robe of light continued to enshroud them.

5. After the creation of Adam, every living creature was brought before him to receive its name; he saw that to each had been given a companion, but among them "there was not found an

THE CREATION OF LIGHT

help meet for him." Among all the creatures that God had made on the earth, there was not one equal to man. And "God said, 'It is not good that the man should be alone; I will make him an help meet for him.'" Man was not made to dwell in solitude; he was to be a social being. Without companionship, the beautiful scenes and delightful employments of Eden would have failed to yield perfect happiness. Even communion with angels could not have satisfied his desire for sympathy and companionship. There was none of the same nature to love, and to be loved.

6. God Himself gave Adam a companion. He provided "an help meet for him,"—a helper corresponding to him,—one who was fitted to be his companion, and who could be one with him in love and sympathy. Eve was created from a rib taken from the side of Adam, signifying that she was not to control him as the head, nor to be trampled under his feet as an inferior, but to stand by his side as an equal, to be loved and protected by him. A part of man, bone of his bone, and flesh of his flesh, she was his second self; showing the close union and the affectionate attachment that should exist in this relation. "For no man ever yet hated his own flesh, but nourisheth and cherisheth it." "Therefore shall a man leave his father and his mother, and shall cleave unto his wife; and they shall be one."

—*Mrs. E. G. White.*

Exercise for Conversation and Study

Where do we find the only authentic record of the work of creation? What was created on each of the six days of the creation week? How were they created? Ps. 33:6, 9. From what were they made? Heb. 11:3. For what purpose was the earth, and the things therein, created? Isa. 45:18; Rev. 4:11. How are all things upheld? Job 26:7; Heb. 1:3. For what purpose was man created? Isa. 43:7, 21. From what were Adam and Eve created? Gen. 2:7, 21, 22. How did they employ their time? Gen. 1:26-28; 2:15, 19, 20.

Review the articulation drills, taking care to keep your voice instrument in good condition and under perfect control. The breathing exercises, if they have been faithfully continued, ought by this time to have your vocal instrument well prepared for the drill exercises under "Expression" in its several subdivisions.

Word Study

2. diversified	4. symmetry	6. provided
2. interspersed	4. artificial	6. corresponding
2. luxuriant	4. enshroud	6. signifying
2. miasma	5. solitude	6. affectionate
2. angelic	5. sympathy	6. attachment
4. stature	5. companionship	6. nourisheth

EXPRESSION

"So they read in the Book in the law of God distinctly, and *gave the sense,* and *caused them to understand* the reading." Neh. 8: 8. "Even things without life giving sound, whether pipe or harp, except they give a *distinction* in the sounds, how shall it be known what is piped or harped? . . . So likewise ye, except ye utter by the tongue words easy to be understood, how shall it be known what is spoken? for ye shall speak into the air. There are, it may be, so many kinds of voices in the world, and none of them is without signification. Therefore if I know not the meaning of the voice, I shall be unto him that speaketh a barbarian, and he that speaketh shall be a barbarian unto me." 1 Cor. 14:7-11.

Expression of speech is the utterance of thought, feeling, or passion, with due *significance* or force. The following are the main divisions with definitions of each:—

1. *Emphasis* is that peculiar force given to one or more words of a sentence.

2. *Slur* is that smooth, gliding, subdued movement of the voice, by which those parts of a sentence of less comparative importance

are rendered less impressive to the ear, and emphatic words and phrases set in stronger relief.

3. *Inflections* are the bends or slides of the voice, used in reading and speaking.

4. *Modulation* is the act of varying the voice in reading and speaking. Its general divisions are *Pitch, Force, Quality,* and *Rate.*

5. *Monotone* consists of a degree of sameness of sound, or tone, in a number of successive words or syllables.

6. *Personation* consists of those modulations, or changes of the voice necessary to represent two or more persons as speaking.

Each of the above divisions of Expression will be considered in connection with the following lessons, and will be illustrated by clear examples.   —*Adapted from the National Fourth Reader.*

Sounds

Begin a review of "Description of English Sounds."

SOURCE AND AIM OF TRUE EDUCATION

"The knowledge of the Holy is understanding."

1. Our ideas of education take too narrow and too low a range. There is need of a broader scope, a higher aim. True education means more than the pursual of a certain course of study. It means more than a preparation for the life that now is. It has to do with the whole being, and with the whole period of existence possible to man. It is the harmonious development of the physical, the mental, and the spiritual powers. It prepares the student for the joy of service in this world, and for the higher joy of wider service in the world to come.

2. The source of such an education is brought to view in these words of Holy Writ, pointing to the Infinite One: In Him "are hid all the treasures of wisdom." "He hath counsel and understanding."

3. The world has had its great teachers, men of giant intellect and extensive research, men whose utterances have stimulated thought, and opened to view vast fields of knowledge; and these men have been honored as guides and benefactors of their race; but there is One who stands higher than they. We can trace the line of the world's great teachers as far back as human records extend; but the Light was before them. As the moon and the stars of our solar system shine by the reflected light of the sun, so, as far as their teaching is true, do the world's great thinkers reflect the rays of the Sun of Righteousness. Every gleam of thought, every flash of the intellect, is from the Light of the world.

4. In these days much is said concerning the nature and importance of "higher education." The true "higher education" is that imparted by Him with whom "is wisdom and strength;" out of whose mouth "cometh knowledge and understanding."

5. In a knowledge of God, all true knowledge and real development have their source. Wherever we turn, in the physical, the mental, or the spiritual realm; in whatever we behold, apart from the blight of sin, this knowledge is revealed. Whatever line of investigation we pursue with a sincere purpose to arrive at truth, we are brought in touch with the unseen, mighty Intelligence that is working in and through all. The mind of man is brought into communion with the mind of God, the finite with the Infinite. The effect of such communion on body and mind and soul is beyond estimate.

6. In this communion is found the highest education. It is God's own method of development. "Acquaint now thyself with Him," is His message to mankind. The method outlined in these words was the method followed in the education of the father of our race. When in the glory of sinless manhood Adam stood in holy Eden, it was thus that God instructed him.

7. In order to understand what is comprehended in the work of education, we need to consider both the nature of man and the

purpose of God in creating him. We need to consider also the change in man's condition through the coming in of a knowledge of evil, and God's plan for still fulfilling His glorious purpose in the education of the human race.

8. When Adam came from the Creator's hand, he bore, in his physical, mental, and spiritual nature, a likeness to his Maker. "God created man in His own image," and it was His purpose that the longer man lived, the more fully he should reveal this image, —the more fully reflect the glory of the Creator. All his faculties were capable of development; their capacity and vigor were continually to increase. Vast was the scope offered for their exercise; glorious the field opened to their research. The mysteries of the visible universe—the "wondrous works of Him who is perfect in knowledge" — invited man's study. Face-to-face, heart-to-heart communion with his Maker was his high privilege. Had he remained loyal to God, all this would have been his forever. Throughout eternal ages he would have continued to gain new treasures of knowledge, to discover fresh springs of happiness, and to obtain clearer and yet clearer conceptions of the wisdom, the power, and the love of God. More and more fully would he have fulfilled the object of his creation, more and more fully have reflected the Creator's glory.

9. But by disobedience this was forfeited. Through sin the divine likeness was marred, and well-nigh obliterated. Man's physical powers were weakened, his mental capacity was lessened, his spiritual vision dimmed. He had become subject to death. Yet the race was not left without hope. By infinite love and mercy the plan of salvation had been devised, and a life of probation was granted. To restore in man the image of his Maker, to bring him back to the perfection in which he was created, to promote the development of body, mind, and soul, that the divine purpose in his creation might be realized,—this was to be the work of redemption. This is the object of education, the great object of life.

10. Love, the basis of creation and of redemption, is the basis of true education. This is made plain in the law that God has given us as the guide of life. The first and great commandment is, "Thou shalt love the Lord thy God with all thy heart, and with all thy soul, and with all thy strength, and with all thy mind." To love Him, the infinite, the omniscient One, with the whole strength, and mind, and heart, means the highest development of every power. It means that in the whole being—the body, the mind, as well as the soul—the image of God is to be restored.

11. Like the first is the second commandment,—"Thou shalt love thy neighbor as thyself." The law of love calls for the devotion of body, mind, and soul to the service of God and our fellow men. And this service, while making us a blessing to others, brings the greatest blessing to ourselves. Unselfishness underlies all true development. Through unselfish service we receive the highest culture of every faculty. More and more fully do we become partakers of the divine nature. We are fitted for heaven; for we receive heaven into our hearts.

12. Since God is the source of all true knowledge, it is, as we have seen, the first object of education to direct our minds to His own revelation of Himself. Adam and Eve received knowledge through direct communion with God; and they learned of Him through His works. All created things, in their original perfection, were an expression of the thought of God. To Adam and Eve nature was teeming with divine wisdom. But by transgression man was cut off from learning of God through direct communion, and, to a great degree, through His works. The earth, marred and defiled by sin, reflects but dimly the Creator's glory. It is true that His object lessons are not obliterated. Upon every page of the great volume of His created works may still be traced His handwriting. Nature still speaks of her Creator. Yet these revelations are partial and imperfect. And in our fallen state, with weakened powers and restricted vision, we are incapable of in-

terpreting aright. We need the fuller revelation of Himself that God has given in His written Word.

13. The Holy Scriptures are the perfect standard of truth, and as such should be given the highest place in education. To obtain an education worthy of the name, we must receive a knowledge of God, the Creator, and of Christ, the Redeemer, as they are revealed in the sacred Word.

14. Every human being, created in the image of God, is endowed with a power akin to that of the Creator,—individuality, power to think and to do. The men in whom this power is developed are the men who bear responsibilities, who are leaders in enterprise, and who influence character. It is the work of true education to develop this power; to train the youth to be thinkers, and not mere reflectors of other men's thought. Instead of confining their study to that which men have said or written, let the students be directed to the sources of truth, to the vast fields open for research in nature and revelation. Let them contemplate the great facts of duty and destiny, and the mind will expand and strengthen. Instead of educated weaklings, institutions of learning may send forth men strong to think and to act, men who are masters and not slaves of circumstances, men who possess breadth of mind, clearness of thought, and the courage of their convictions.

15. Such an education provides more than mental discipline; it provides more than physical training. It strengthens the character, so that truth and uprightness are not sacrificed to selfish desire or worldly ambition. It fortifies the mind against evil. Instead of some master passion becoming a power to destroy, every motive and desire are brought into conformity to the great principles of right. As the perfection of His character is dwelt upon, the mind is renewed, and the soul is re-created in the image of God.

16. What education can be higher than this? What can equal it in value?

"It can not be gotten for gold,
Neither shall silver be weighed for the price thereof.
It can not be valued with the gold of Ophir,
With the precious onyx, or the sapphire,
The gold and the crystal can not equal it;
And the exchange of it shall not be for jewels of fine gold.
No mention shall be made of coral, or of pearls;
For the price of wisdom is above rubies."

17. Higher than the highest human thought can reach is God's ideal for His children. Godliness—godlikeness—is the goal to be reached. Before the student there is opened a path of continual progress. He has an object to achieve, a standard to attain, that includes everything good, and pure, and noble. He will advance as fast and as far as possible in every branch of true knowledge. But his efforts will be directed to objects as much higher than mere selfish and temporal interests as the heavens are higher than the earth.

18. He who co-operates with the divine purpose in imparting to the youth a knowledge of God, and molding the character into harmony with His, does a high and noble work. As he awakens a desire to reach God's ideal, he presents an education that is as high as heaven and as broad as the universe; an education that can not be completed in this life, but that will be continued in the life to come; an education that secures to the successful student his passport from the preparatory school of earth to the higher grade, the school above. —*Mrs. E. G. White.*

Exercise for Conversation and Study
Commit to memory the following scriptures: Prov. 9:10; Col. 2:

8-10, 3. Who was the wisest man that ever lived? How did he obtain his wisdom and knowledge? 1 Kings 3:5-15; Eccl. 1:13. What was the extent of his knowledge and wisdom? 1 Kings 4:29-34. What two incidents are mentioned in the Bible showing that God answered Solomon's prayer for "a wise and understanding heart"? 1 Kings 3:16-28; 10:1-9.

Sound

Continue the review of the "Description of English Sounds."

Word Study

1. scope	7. comprehend	12. interpreting
1. physical	8. reflect	13. Scriptures
3. utterances	9. disobedience	14. individuality
3. benefactors	9. forfeited	14. institutions
4. knowledge	9. obliterated	15. fortifies
5. investigation	10. omniscient	16. onyx
5. estimate	11. culture	16. Ophir
6. acquaint	12. restricted	16. sapphire

EMPHASIS

1. To give a word emphasis means to pronounce it in a forcible manner. No uncommon tone, however, is necessary, as words may be made emphatic by prolonging sounds, by a pause, or even by a whisper.

2. Emphatic words are often printed in *italics;* those more emphatic in small CAPITALS; and those that receive the greatest force in large CAPITALS.

RULES IN EMPHASIS

1. *Words and phrases peculiarly significant*, or important in meaning, are emphatic; as,—

Whence and *what* art thou, execrable shape?

2. *Words and phrases that contrast*, or point out a difference, are emphatic; as,—

I did not say a *better* soldier, but an *elder*.

3. *The repetition* of an emphatic word or phrase usually requires an *increased* force of utterance; as,—

You injured my child—YOU, sir?

4. A *succession* of important words or phrases usually requires a gradual increase of emphatic force, though emphasis sometimes falls on the last word of a series only; as,—

His *disappointment*, his ANGUISH, his DEATH were caused by your carelessness.

These misfortunes are the same to the poor, the ignorant, and the *weak*, as to the rich, the wise, and the *powerful*.

EXERCISES IN EMPHASIS

In the following exercises require the student to tell which of the above rules is illustrated by each example:—

1. Speak little and well, if you wish to be considered as possessing merit.
2. *Boisterous* in speech, in action *prompt* and *bold*.
3. He buys, he *sells*, he STEALS, he KILLS, for gold.
4. The *young* were slaves to *novelty:* the *old*, to *custom:* the *middle-aged*, to *both:* the *dead*, to *neither*.
5. I shall sing the praises of *October*, as the *loveliest* of months.
6. The GOOD man is *honored*, but the EVIL man is *despised*.
7. The *wicked* flee when no man *pursueth;* but the *righteous* are bold as a lion.
8. A *day*, an HOUR, of *virtuous liberty*, is worth a whole ETERNITY of bondage.
9. None but the *brave*, none but the BRAVE, none but the BRAVE is fair.
10. It is my *living* sentiment, and, by the blessing of God, it shall be my *dying* sentiment—independence NOW and independence FOREVER.
11. In the prosecution of a virtuous enterprise, a *brave* man DESPISES danger and difficulty.
12. Was that country a desert?—No: it was *cultivated* and *fertile; rich* and *populous!* Its sons were men of *genius, spirit,* and *generosity!* Its daughters were *lovely, susceptible,* and *chaste! Friendship* was its inhabitant! *Love* was its inhabitant! *Domestic affection* was its inhabitant! LIBERTY was its inhabitant!

THE EDEN SCHOOL

> "*The Lord giveth wisdom; out of His mouth cometh knowledge and understanding.*"

1. The system of education instituted at the beginning of the world was to be a model for man throughout all after-time. As an illustration of its principles, a model school was established in Eden, the home of our first parents. The garden of Eden was the schoolroom, nature was the lesson-book, the Creator Himself was the instructor, and the parents of the human family were the students.

2. Created to be "the image and glory of God," Adam and Eve had received endowments not unworthy of their high destiny. Graceful and symmetrical in form, regular and beautiful in feature, their countenances glowing with the tint of health and the light of joy and hope, they bore in outward resemblance the likeness of their Maker. Nor was this likeness manifest in the physical nature only. Every faculty of mind and soul reflected the Creator's glory. Endowed with high mental and spiritual gifts, Adam and Eve were made but "little lower than the angels," that they might not only discern the wonders of the visible universe, but comprehend moral responsibilities and obligations.

3. "The Lord God planted a garden eastward in Eden; and there He put the man whom He had formed. And out of the ground made the Lord God to grow every tree that is pleasant to the sight, and good for food; the tree of life also in the midst of the garden." Here, amidst the beautiful scenes of nature untouched by sin, our first parents were to receive their education.

4. In His interest for His children, our heavenly Father personally directed their education. Often they were visited by His messengers, the holy angels, and from them received counsel and instruction. Often, as they walked in the garden in the cool of the day, they heard the voice of God, and face to face held communion

with the Eternal. His thoughts toward them were "thoughts of peace, and not of evil." His every purpose was their highest good.

5. To Adam and Eve was committed the care of the garden, "to dress it and to keep it." Though rich in all that the Owner of the universe could supply, they were not to be idle. Useful occupation was appointed them as a blessing, to strengthen the body, to expand the mind, and to develop the character.

6. The book of nature, which spread its living lessons before them, afforded an exhaustless source of instruction and delight. On every leaf of the forest and stone of the mountains, in every shining star, in earth and sea and sky, God's name was written. With both the animate and inanimate creation,—with leaf and flower and tree, and with every living creature, from the leviathan of the waters to the mote in the sunbeam,—the dwellers in Eden held converse, gathering from each the secrets of its life. God's glory in the heavens, the innumerable worlds in their orderly revolutions, "the balancings of the clouds," the mysteries of light and sound, of day and night—all were objects of study by the pupils of earth's first school.

7. The laws and operations of nature, and the great principles of truth that govern the spiritual universe, were opened to their minds by the infinite Author of all. In "the light of the knowledge of the glory of God," their mental and spiritual powers developed, and they realized the highest pleasures of their holy existence.

8. As it came from the Creator's hand, not only the garden of Eden but the whole earth was exceedingly beautiful. No taint of sin, or shadow of death, marred the fair creation. God's glory "covered the heavens, and the earth was full of His praise." "The morning stars sang together, and all the sons of God shouted for joy." Thus was the earth a fit emblem of Him who is "abundant in goodness and truth;" a fit study for those who were made in His image. The garden of Eden was a representation of what God

desired the whole earth to become, and it was His purpose that, as the human family increased in numbers, they should establish other homes and schools like the one He had given. Thus in course of time the whole earth might be occupied with homes and schools where the words and works of God should be studied, and where the students should thus be fitted more and more fully to reflect throughout endless ages the light of the knowledge of His glory.

—*Mrs. E. G. White.*

Sound and Emphasis

Continue the review of the English sounds. Select emphatic words and phrases from this lesson, and indicate which rule they come under.

Word Study

1. established
1. instructor
2. endowments
2. comprehend
2. visible
3. eastward
4. messengers
4. purpose
5. occupation
6. inanimate
7. existence
7. infinite
8. exceedingly
8. representation
8. occupied

SLUR

1. Emphatic words, or words that express the leading thoughts, are usually pronounced with a louder and more forcible effort of the voice, and are often prolonged. But words that are *slurred* must generally be read in a lower and less forcible tone of voice, more rapidly, and all pronounced nearly alike.

2. In part of the exercises the words which are to be *slurred* are printed in *italic* letters. Pupils will first read the parts of the sentence that appear in Roman, and then the whole sentence, passing lightly and quickly over that which was first omitted. They will also read in like manner the examples that are *unmarked*.

Exercises in Slur

1. Dismiss, *as soon as may be*, all angry thoughts.
2. I am sure, *if you provide for your young brothers and sisters*, that God will bless you.
3. The rich, softened by prosperity, pitied the poor · the poor, disciplined into order, respected the rich.
4. The rivulet sends forth glad sounds, and, *tripping o'er its bed of pebbly sands, or leaping down rocks,* seems, *with continuous laughter,* to rejoice in its own being.
5. Children are wading, *with cheerful cries,*
   In the shoals of the sparkling brook:
   Laughing maidens, *with soft, young eyes,*
   Walk or sit in the shady nook.
6. The moon is at her full, and, riding high,
   Floods the calm fields with light.
   The stars that hover in the summer sky
   Are all asleep to-night.
7. We wish that this column, rising toward heaven among the pointed spires of so many temples dedicated to God, may contribute also to produce, in all minds, a pious feeling of dependence and gratitude.
8. There is a Power above us—*and that there is, all Nature cries aloud through all her works*—He must delight in virtue; and that which He delights in must be happy.
9. A sick man from his chamber looks at the twisted brooks; and feeling the cool breath of each little pool, breathes a blessing on the summer rain.
10. The devout heart, *penetrated with large and affecting views of the immensity of the works of God, the harmony of His laws, and the extent of His beneficence,* bursts into loud and vocal expressions of praise and adoration; and, *from a full and overflowing sensibility,* seeks to expand itself to the utmost limits of creation.

NATURE WORSHIPS GOD

*"All Thy works shall praise
Thee, O Lord."*

1. The harp at Nature's advent strung
    Has never ceased to play;
    The song the stars of morning sung
    Has never died away.

2. And prayer is made, and praise is given,
    By all things near and far;
    The ocean looketh up to heaven,
    And mirrors every star.

3. Its waves are kneeling on the strand,
    As kneels the human knee,
    Their white locks bowing to the sand,—
    The priesthood of the sea!

4. They pour their glittering treasures forth,
    Their gifts of pearl they bring,
    And all the listening hills of earth
    Take up the song and sing.

5. The green earth sends her incense up
    From many a mountain shrine;
    From folded leaf and dewy cup
    She pours her sacred wine.

6. The mists above the morning rills
    Rise white as wings of prayer;
    The altar curtains of the hills
    Are sunset's purple air.

JOHN G. WHITTIER AND HIS HOMES

7. The winds with hymns of praise are loud,
    Or low with sobs of pain,—
    The thunder-organ of the cloud,
    The dropping tears of rain.

8. With drooping head and branches crossed,
    The twilight forest grieves,
    Or speaks with tongues of Pentecost
    From all its sunlit leaves.

9. The blue sky is the temple's arch,
    Its transept, earth and air,
    The music of its starry march,
    The chorus of a prayer.

10. So Nature keeps the reverent frame
    With which her years began,
    And all her signs and voices shame
    The prayerless heart of man.
        —*John Greenleaf Whittier.*

Sound and Slur

Continue the review of English sounds. Point out examples of "slur" that occur in this lesson.

INFLECTION

1. *Inflection*, or the slide, is one of the most important divisions of expression, because all speech is made up of slides, and because the right or wrong formation of these give a pervading character to the whole delivery.

2. A slide consists of two parts; *viz.*, the *radical*, or opening sound, and the *vanish*, or gradual diminution of force, until the sound is lost

in silence. Three things are necessary to the perfect formation of the slide:—

(a) The opening sound must be struck with a *full* and *lively* impulse of the voice.

(b) The diminution of force must be regular and equable—not more rapid in one part than another, but naturally and gracefully declining to the last.

(c) The final *vanish* must be delicately formed, without being abrupt on the one hand, or too much prolonged on the other. Thus a *full opening*, a *gradual decrease*, and a *delicate termination*, are requisite to the perfect formation of a slide.

3. There are three inflections, or slides of the voice:—

(a) The *Rising Inflection* is the upward bend or slide of the voice, indicated thus: ⌒ ; as,—

Do you love your home? ⌒

(b) The *Falling Inflection* is the downward bend or slide of the voice, indicated thus: ⌒ ; as,—

When are you going home? ⌒

(c) The *Circumflex Inflection* is the union of the inflections on the same syllable or word, either beginning with the *rising* and ending with the *falling*, or beginning with the *falling* and ending with the *rising*, thus producing a slight wave of the voice. It is indicated thus: for rising circumflex ᴧ, for falling circumflex v; as,—

You must take me for a *fool*v to think I could do *that*.ᴧ

4. The inflections, or slides, should be placed on the accented syllables or words; as,—

I will *nev*er stay. I said *good*ly not *home*ly.

RULES FOR INFLECTION

1. Direct questions, or those that can be answered by *yes* or *no*, usually require the *rising* inflection; but their answers, the *falling*; as,—

Has any one sailed around the *earth*? ⌒ *Yes*; ⌒ Captain Cook. ⌒

Exceptions.—The falling inflection is required when the direct question becomes an earnest appeal and the answer is anticipated; and when a direct question, not at first understood, is repeated with marked emphasis; as,—

Will⌐ her love survive your *neglect?*⌐ and *may*⌐ not you expect the sneers, both of your *wife,*⌐ and of her *parents?*⌐

Do you reside in the city?⌐ What did you say, *sir?*⌐ Do you reside in the city?⌐

2. Indirect questions, or those that can *not* be answered by yes or no, usually require the *falling* inflection, and their answers the same; as,—

Who said, "A wise man is never less alone than when he is *alone*"?⌐ —*Swift.*⌐

Exceptions.—The *rising* slide is required when an indirect question is used to ask a repetition of what was not at first understood; and when the *answers* to questions, whether direct or indirect, are given in an indifferent or careless manner; as,—

Where⌐ did you *say?*⌐ Shall I tell your *enemy?*⌐ As you please!⌐

3. Questions, words, and clauses, connected by the disjunctive *or*, usually require the *rising* inflection before, and the *falling* after them; though when *or* is used conjunctively, it takes the rising inflection after, as well as before it; as,—

Does he deserve *praise*⌐ or *blame?*⌐

Can *youth,*⌐ or *health,*⌐ or *strength,*⌐ or *honor,*⌐ or *pleasure,*⌐ satisfy the *soul?*⌐

4. When words or clauses are contrasted or compared, the first part usually has the *rising,* and the last the *falling* inflection; though, when one side of the contrast is *affirmed* and the other *denied,* generally the latter has the *rising* inflection, in whatever order they occur; as,—

I have seen the effects of *love*⌐ and *hatred,*⌐ *joy*⌐ and *grief,*⌐ *hope*⌐ and *despair.*⌐

This book is not *mine,*⌐ but *yours.*⌐

5. Familiar address and the pause of suspension, denoting condition, supposition, or incompleteness, usually require the *rising* inflection; as,—

If thine enemy *hunger*,◠ give him bread to eat.

Friends,◠ I come not here to talk.◠

6. The language of concession, politeness, admiration, entreaty, and tender emotions, usually requires the *rising* inflection; as,—

Your remark is *true:*◠ the manners of this country have not all the desirable *ease*◠ and *freedom.*◠

7. The end of a sentence that expresses completeness, conclusion, or result, usually requires the *falling* inflection; as,—

The rose is *beautiful.*◟

8. At each complete termination of thought, before the close of a sentence, the *falling* inflection is usually required; though when several pauses occur, the last but one generally has the *rising* inflection; as,—

Every human being has the idea of *duty;*◟ and to unfold this idea is the end for which life was given him.◟

The rock crumbles;◟ the trees *fall;*◟ the leaves *fade;* ◠ and the grass withers.◟

9. The language of command, rebuke, contempt, exclamation, and terror, usually requires the *falling* inflection; as,—

Thou *slave,*◟ thou *wretch,*◟ thou *coward!*◟ *Away* from my sight!◟

10. The last member of a commencing series, and the last but one of a concluding series, usually require the *rising* inflection; and all others the *falling;* as,—

A good *disposition,*◟ virtuous *principles,*◟ a liberal *education,*◟ and industrious *habits,*◠ are passports to happiness and honor.◟

11. The circumflex is used when the thoughts employed are not sincere or earnest, but are used in jest, irony, or double meaning—in ridicule, sarcasm, or mockery. The circumflex which ends with the *rising* slide should be given to the *negative* ideas, and that which ends with the *falling* slide to the *positive* ideas; as,—

This is your *plain* man,^ if not your *gracious* one.v

They boast^ they come but to *improve*^ our state, *enlarge*^ our thoughts, and *free*^ us from the yoke of *error*.^

Employ the right slides in the sentences that are unmarked, and tell what rule or rules are illustrated by each of the following sentences.

Exercise in Inflection

1. Do you see the beautiful *star?*⸝—Yes; it is *splendid.*⸜
2. Will you forsake us? and will you favor us no more?
3. I said an *elder* soldier,⸜ not a better.⸜ Did I say better?⸝
4. *Are* you, my dear sir, willing to forgive?
5. Why is the *hall*⸜ *crowded?*⸜ What *means*⸜ this *stir*⸜ in town?
6. Does that beautiful lady deserve *praise,*⸝ or *blame?*⸜
7. Will you ride in the carriage, or on horseback?—Neither.
8. Hunting *men,*⸜ not *beasts,*⸝ shall be his game.
9. I said *good,*⸜ not *bad;*⸝ *happy,*⸜ not *miserable.*⸝
10. O *Rome!*⸝ O my *country!*⸝ how art thou fallen!⸜
11. Do men gather grapes from thorns, or figs from thistles?
12. Is a candle bought to be put under a bushel⸝ or under a bed?⸝

—*Adapted from the National Fourth Reader.*

PSALMS OF PRAISE

PSALM CXLVIII

1. Praise ye the Lord.
Praise ye the Lord from the heavens;
Praise Him in the heights.
Praise ye Him, all His angels:
Praise ye Him, all His hosts.
Praise ye Him, sun and moon;
Praise Him, all ye stars of light.

2. Praise Him, ye heavens of heavens,
And ye waters that be above the heavens.

Let them praise the name of the Lord;
For He commanded, and they were created.
He hath also stablished them forever and ever;
He hath made a decree which shall not pass.

3. Praise the Lord from the earth,
Ye dragons, and all deeps:
Fire and hail, snow and vapors,
Stormy wind fulfilling His word,
Mountains and all hills,
Fruitful trees, and all cedars,
Beasts and all cattle,
Creeping things and flying fowl,
Kings of the earth and all people,
Princes and all judges of the earth,
Both young men and maidens,
Old men and children,—
Let them praise the name of the Lord;
For His name alone is excellent;
His glory is above the earth and heaven.

4. He also exalteth the horn of His people,
The praise of all His saints;
Even of the children of Israel, a people near unto Him.
Praise ye the Lord.

PSALM CXLIX

5. Praise ye the Lord.
Sing unto the Lord a new song,
And His praise in the congregation of saints.
Let Israel rejoice in Him that made him;
Let the children of Zion be joyful in their King.
Let them praise His name in the dance;
Let them sing praises unto Him with the timbrel and harp.

6. For the Lord taketh pleasure in His people;
   He will beautify the meek with salvation.
   Let the saints be joyful in glory;
   Let them sing aloud upon their beds.

7. Let the high praises of God be in their mouth,
   And a two-edged sword in their hand;
   To execute vengeance upon the heathen,
   And punishments upon the people;
   To bind their kings with chains,
   And their nobles with fetters of iron;
   To execute upon them the judgment written:
   This honor have all His saints.
   Praise ye the Lord.

PSALM CL

8. Praise ye the Lord.
   Praise God in His sanctuary;
   Praise Him in the firmament of His power;
   Praise Him for His mighty acts;
   Praise Him according to His excellent greatness.

9. Praise Him with the sound of the trumpet;
   Praise Him with the psaltery and harp;
   Praise Him with the timbrel and dance;
   Praise Him with stringed instruments and organs.

10. Praise Him upon the loud cymbals;
    Praise Him upon the high sounding cymbals.
    Let everything that hath breath praise the Lord.
    Praise ye the Lord.

Inflection

Select examples from this lesson that illustrate the different kinds of inflection.

MODULATION

I. PITCH

Modulation is the act of varying the voice in reading and speaking. Its general divisions are *Pitch, Force, Quality,* and *Rate*.

Pitch, the first division of Modulation, refers to the *keynote* of the voice—its general degree of elevation or depression in reading and speaking. There are three general distinctions of pitch: *High, Moderate,* and *Low*.

1. *High Pitch* is that which is heard in calling to a person at a distance. It is used in expressing elevated and joyous feelings and strong emotions; as,—

(*a*) Awake! Awake! put on thy strength, O Zion!
    Put on thy beautiful garments, O Jerusalem, the Holy City!
    Shake thyself from the dust; arise and sit down, O Jerusalem!
    Loose thyself from the bands of thy neck, O captive daughter of
        Zion!

(*b*) Sing, O Heavens! and be joyful, O Earth!
    And break forth into singing, O Mountains!
    For the Lord hath comforted His people,
    And will have mercy upon His afflicted.

2. *Moderate Pitch* is that which is heard in common conversation and description, and in moral reflection, or calm reasoning; as,—

Nature is yours in all her glory; her ever-varying and forever beautiful face smiles peace upon you. Her hills and valleys, fields and flowers, know no desecration in the step of poverty, but welcome ever to their beauty rich and poor alike.

3. *Low Pitch* is that which is heard when the voice falls below the common speaking key. It is used in expressing reverence, awe, sublimity, and tender emotions; as,—

      (*a*) The Lord reigneth;
          Let the people tremble:

He sitteth between the cherubim;
Let the earth be moved.
The Lord is great in Zion;
And He is high above all the people.
Let them praise Thy great and terrible name;
For it is holy.

(b) 'Tis midnight; and on Olives' brow
The star is dimmed that lately shone:
'Tis midnight; in the garden, now,
The suffering Saviour prays alone.

Choose and read other selections which illustrate the three degrees of pitch.

GOD SEES NOT AS MAN SEES

> *"Man looketh on the outward appearance, but the Lord looketh on the heart."*

1. Now David "was ruddy, and withal of a beautiful countenance, and goodly to look to." As Samuel beheld with pleasure the handsome, manly, modest shepherd boy, the voice of the Lord spoke to the prophet, saying, "Arise, anoint him; for this is he." David had proved himself brave and faithful in the humble office of shepherd, and now God had chosen him to be captain of His people. "Then Samuel took the horn of oil, and anointed him in the midst of [from among] his brethren; and the Spirit of the Lord came upon David from that day forward." The prophet had accomplished his appointed work, and with a relieved heart he returned to Ramah.

2. Samuel had not made known his errand, even to the family of Jesse, and the ceremony of anointing David had been performed in secret. It was an intimation to the youth of the high destiny awaiting him, that amid all the varied experiences and perils of

his coming years, this knowledge might inspire him to be true to the purpose of God to be accomplished by his life.

3. The great honor conferred upon David did not serve to elate him. Notwithstanding the high position which he was to occupy, he quietly continued his employment, content to await the development of the Lord's plans in His own time and way. As humble and modest as before his anointing, the shepherd boy returned to the hills, and watched and guarded his flock as tenderly as ever. But with new inspiration he composed his melodies and played upon his harp. Before him spread a landscape of rich and varied beauty. The vines, with their clustering fruit, brightened in the sunshine. The forest trees, with their green foliage, swayed in the breeze. He beheld the sun flooding the heavens with light, coming forth as a bridegroom out of his chamber, and rejoicing as a strong man to run a race. There were the bold summits of the hills, reaching toward the sky; in the far-away distance rose the barren cliffs of the mountain wall of Moab; above all spread the tender blue of the overarching heavens. And beyond was God. He could not see Him, but His works were full of His praise. The light of day, gilding forest and mountain, meadow and stream, carried the mind up to behold the Father of lights, the Author of every good and perfect gift. Daily revelations of the character and majesty of his Creator, filled the young poet's heart with adoration and rejoicing. In contemplation of God and His works, the faculties of David's mind and heart were developing and strengthening for the work of his after-life. He was daily coming into a more intimate communion with God. His mind was constantly penetrating into new depths, for fresh themes to inspire his song, and to wake the music of his harp. The rich melody of his voice poured out upon the air, echoed from the hills as if responsive to the rejoicing of the angels' songs in heaven.

4. Who can measure the results of those years of toil and wandering among the lonely hills? The communion with nature and

with God, the care of his flocks, the perils and deliverances, the griefs and joys, of his lowly lot, were not only to mold the character of David, and to influence his future life, but through the psalms of Israel's sweet singer, they were, in all coming ages, to kindle love and faith in the hearts of God's people, bringing them nearer to the ever-loving heart of Him in whom all His creatures live.

5. David, in the beauty and vigor of his young manhood, was preparing to take a high position with the noblest of earth. His talents, as precious gifts from God, were employed to extol the glory of the divine Giver. His opportunities of contemplation and meditation served to enrich him with that wisdom and piety that made him beloved of God and angels. As he contemplated the perfections of his Creator, clearer conceptions of God opened before his soul. Obscure themes were illuminated, difficulties were made plain, perplexities were harmonized, and each ray of new light called forth fresh bursts of rapture and sweeter anthems of devotion to the glory of God and the Redeemer. The love that moved him, the sorrows that beset him, the triumphs that attended him, were all themes for his active thought; and as he beheld the love of God in all the providences of his life, his heart throbbed with a more fervent adoration and gratitude, his voice rang out in a richer melody, his harp was swept with more exultant joy; and the shepherd boy proceeded from strength to strength, from knowledge to knowledge; for the Spirit of the Lord was upon him.

—*Mrs. E. G. White.*

Modulation

Classify this and the previous lessons as to the degree of pitch to be employed in their proper reading. Bring to the class three selections from the Bible representing the three degrees of pitch.

Word Study

1. ruddy   2. David   3. content   4. griefs   5. manhood
1. Samuel   2. intimation   3. melody   4. Israel's   5. Redeemer
1. Ramah   3. elate   3. depths   5. vigor   5. fervent

MODULATION

II. FORCE

Force is the volume or loudness of voice, used on the same key or pitch, when reading or speaking. Though the degrees of force are numerous, varying from a soft whisper to a shout, yet they are divided into three main divisions; *Loud, Moderate,* and *Gentle.*

1. *Loud Force* is used in strong but suppressed passions, and in emotions of sorrow, grief, respect, veneration, dignity, apathy, and contrition; as,—

(*a*) VIRTUE takes the place of *all* things. It is the *nobility* of ANGELS! It is the MAJESTY of GOD!

(*b*) Roll on, thou deep and dark-blue ocean,—roll!
Ten thousand fleets sweep over thee in vain.

2. *Moderate Force,* or medium degree of loudness, is used in ordinary assertion, narration, and description; as,—

Remember now thy Creator in the days of thy youth, while the evil days come not, nor the years draw nigh, when thou shalt say, "I have no pleasure in them."

3. *Gentle Force,* or a slight degree of loudness, is used to express caution, fear, secrecy, and tender emotions; as,—

(*a*) How shall I give thee up, Ephraim?
How shall I deliver thee, Israel?
How shall I make thee as Admah?
How shall I set thee as Zeboim?
Mine heart is turned within Me,
My repentings are kindled together.
I will not execute the fierceness of Mine anger,
I will not return to destroy Ephraim:
For I am God, and not man;
The Holy One in the midst of thee:
And I will not enter into the city.

NOTE.—For a general exercise on force, select a sentence, and deliver it on a given key, with voice just sufficient to be heard; then gradually increase the quantity, until the whole power of the voice is brought into play. Reverse the process without change of key, ending with a whisper. This exercise can not be too frequently repeated. Read other selections to illustrate different degrees of force.

(b) Take her up tenderly, lift her with care;
Fashioned so slenderly, young and so fair.
—*Adapted from the National Fourth Reader.*

THE LABORER

1. Stand up—erect! Thou hast the form
    And likeness of thy God! Who more?
   A soul as dauntless mid the storm
   Of daily life, a heart as warm
    And pure as breast e'er wore.

2. What then? Thou art as true a man
    As moves the human mass among;
   As much a part of the great plan
   That with creation's dawn began,
    As any of the throng.

3. Who is thine enemy? The high
    In station, or in wealth the chief?
   The great, who coldly pass thee by,
   With proud step and averted eye?
    Nay, muse not such belief.

4. If true unto thyself thou wast,
    What were the proud one's scorn to thee?
   A feather which thou mightest cast
   Aside, as idly as the blast
    The light leaf from the tree.

5. No. Uncurbed passions, low desires,
    Absence of noble self-respect,
   Death in the breast's consuming fires,
   To that high nature which aspires
    Forever, till thus checked;—

6. These are thine enemies—thy worst:
   They chain thee to thy lowly lot;
   Thy labor and thy life accursed.
   O, stand erect, and from them burst,
   And longer suffer not.

7. Thou art thyself thine enemy;
   The great—what better then than thou?
   As theirs is not thy will as free?
   Has God with equal favors thee
   Neglected to endow?

8. True, wealth thou hast not—'tis but dust;
   Nor place—uncertain as the wind;
   But that thou hast, which, with thy crust
   And water may despise the lust
   Of both—a noble mind.

9. With this, and passions under ban,
   True faith, and holy trust in God,
   Thou art the peer of any man.
   Look up then, that thy little span
   Of life may be well trod.
                               —*William D. Gallagher.*

Modulation
Read this lesson with the proper degree of force. Classify the previous lessons as to the degree of force to be employed in reading them. Make selections from the Bible that represent the three degrees of force.

Word Study
1. dauntless	5. absence	8. uncertain
3. averted	5. aspires	9. ban
3. belief	6. accursed	9. peer
5. uncurbed	7. endow	9. span

MODULATION

III. QUALITY

Quality has reference to the kinds of tone used in reading and speaking. The qualities of tone are as follows:—

1. *The Pure Tone.* It is a clear, smooth, round, flowing sound, accompanied with moderate pitch; and is used to express peace, cheerfulness, joy, and love; as,—

   (*a*) O come, let us sing unto Jehovah;
   Let us make a joyful noise to the Rock of our salvation,
   Let us come before His presence with thanksgiving,
   Let us make a joyful noise unto Him with psalms.

   (*b*) Lo, the winter is past,
   The rain is over and gone;
   The flowers appear on the earth;
   The time of the singing of birds is come,
   And the voice of the turtledove is heard in our land.

   (*c*) Why art thou cast down, O my soul?
   And why art thou disquieted within me?
   Hope thou in God;
   For I shall yet praise Him,
   Who is the health of my countenance,
   And my God.

   (*d*) Methinks I love all common things—
   The common air, the common flower;
   The dear, kind, common thought that springs
   From hearts that have no other dower,
   No other wealth, no other power,
   Save love; and will not that repay
   For all else fortune tears away?

2. *The Orotund* is the pure tone deepened, enlarged, and intensified. It is used in all energetic and vehement forms of expression, and in giving utterance to grand and sublime emotions; as,—

(*a*) O that my words were now written!
O that they were printed in a book!
That they were graven with an iron pen
And lead in the rock forever!
For I know that my Redeemer liveth,
And that He shall stand at the latter day upon the earth:
And though after my skin worms destroy this body
Yet in my flesh shall I see God:
Whom I shall see for myself;
And mine eyes shall behold, and not another;
Though my reins be consumed within me.

(*b*) O Zion, that bringest *good tidings*,
Get *thee up* into the high mountain!
O JERUSALEM, that bringest *good tidings*,
Lift up thy voice with *strength!*
LIFT IT UP, be not afraid!
Say unto the cities of Judah,
"BEHOLD YOUR GOD!"

(*c*) *Strike*—till the last armed foe *expires:*
STRIKE—for your *altars* and your fires;
STRIKE—for the green graves of your sires,
GOD, and your *native land*.

3. *The Aspirated Tone* is an expulsion of the breath more or less strong,—the words, or some of them, being spoken in a whisper. It is used to express amazement, fear, terror, horror, revenge, and remorse; as,—

(*a*) How ill this taper burns!
(*b*) *Ha! Who comes here?*

(c) Cold drops of sweat hang on my trembling flesh,
My blood grows *chilly,* and *I freeze with horror!*

(d) While thronged the citizens with terror dumb,
Or whispering with white lips, *"The foe, they come, they come!"*

4. *The Guttural* is a deep undertone, used to express hatred, contempt, and loathing. It usually occurs on the emphatic words; as,—

(a) O full of all subtilty and all mischief,
Thou child of the devil, thou enemy of all righteousness,
Wilt thou not cease to pervert the right ways of the Lord?

(b) Thou *slave,* thou *wretch,* thou *coward!*
Thou cold-blooded *slave!*
Thou wear a lion's hide?
Doff it, for *shame,* and hang
A *calf skin* on those recreant limbs.

5. *A Tremulous Tone or Tremor,* consists in a tremulous iteration, or a number of impulses of sound of the least assignable duration. It is used in excessive grief, pity, plaintiveness, and tenderness; in an intense degree of suppressed excitement, or satisfaction; and when the voice is enfeebled by age.

The tremulous tone should not be applied throughout the whole of an extended passage, but only on selected emphatic words, as otherwise the effect would be monotonous. In the third of the following examples, where the tremor of age is supposed to be joined to that of supplicating distress, the tremulous tone may be applied to every emphatic syllable capable of prolongation, which is the case with all except the words *pity* and *shortest;* but even these may receive it in a limited degree.

(a) O that my head were waters,
And mine *eyes* a *fountain* of *tears,*
That I might *weep day and night*
For the *slain* of the daughter of my people!

(b) O *love, remain!* It is not yet *near day!*
It was the *nightingale,* and not the *lark,*

That pierced the fearful hollow of thine ear;
Nightly she sings in yon pomegranate tree,
Believe me, love, it was the nightingale.

(c) *Pity the sorrows of a poor old man,*
Whose trembling limbs have borne him to your door,
Whose days are dwindled to the shortest span:
O give relief, and Heaven will bless your store.

(d) O that my grief were thoroughly weighed,
And my calamity laid in the balances together!
For now it would be heavier than the sand of the sea:
Therefore my words are swallowed up. . . .
O that I might have my request;
And that God would grant me the thing that I long for!
Even that it would please God to destroy me;
That He would let loose His hand and cut me off!
—*Adapted from the National Fourth Reader.*

IMMENSITY OF GOD'S WORKS

"Lift up your eyes on high,
And behold who hath created these things,
That bringeth out their host by number:
He calleth them all by names
By the greatness of His might,
For that He is strong in power;
Not one faileth."

1. I was yesterday about sunset walking in the open fields, until the night insensibly fell upon me. I at first amused myself with all the richness and variety of colors which appeared in the western parts of heaven. In proportion as they faded away and went out, several stars and planets appeared, one after another, until the whole firmament was in a glow. The blueness of the ether was exceedingly heightened and enlivened by the season of the

year, and by the rays of all those luminaries that passed through it. The galaxy appeared in its most beautiful white. To complete the scene, the full moon rose at length in that clouded majesty which Milton takes notice of, and opened to the eyes a new picture of nature, which was more finely shaded, and disposed among softer lights, than that which the sun had before discovered to us.

2. As I was surveying the moon walking in her brightness, and taking her progress among the constellations, a thought rose in me which I believe very often perplexes and disturbs men of serious and contemplative natures. David himself fell into it in that reflection: "When I consider Thy heavens, the work of Thy fingers, the moon and the stars, which Thou hast ordained; what is man, that Thou art mindful of him? and the son of man, that Thou visitest him?" In the same manner, when I considered that infinite host of stars, or, to speak more philosophically, of suns, which were then shining upon me, with those innumerable sets of planets or worlds which were moving around their respective suns—when I still enlarged the idea, and supposed another heaven of suns and worlds rising still above this which we have discovered, and these still enlightened by a superior firmament of luminaries, which are planted at so great a distance that they may appear to the inhabitants of the former as the stars do to us!—in short, while I pursued this thought, I could not but reflect on that little, insignificant figure which I myself bore amidst the immensity of God's works.

3. Were the sun which enlightens this part of the creation, were all the host of planetary worlds that move about him, utterly extinguished and annihilated, they would not be missed more than a grain of sand upon the seashore. The space they possess is so exceedingly little in comparison with the whole, that it would scarce make a blank in creation. The chasm would be imperceptible to an eye that could take in the whole compass of nature, and pass from one end of the creation to the other; and it is

possible there may be such a sense in ourselves hereafter, or in creatures which are at present more exalted than ourselves. We see many stars by the help of glasses which we do not discover with our naked eyes; and the finer our telescopes are, the more still our discoveries. Huyghens carries this thought so far that he does not think it impossible that there may be stars whose light has not yet traveled down to us since their first creation. There is no question that the universe has certain bounds set to it; but when we consider that it is the work of infinite power prompted by infinite goodness, with an infinite space to exert itself in, how can our imagination set any bounds to it? —*Joseph Addison.*

Modulation

Classify this selection as to pitch, force, and quality. Bring to the class short selections from the Bible that illustrate the different qualities of voice.

Word Study

1. Milton
1. luminaries
1. galaxy
1. ether
1. insensibly

2. insignificant
2. firmament
2. respective
2. philosophically
2. surveying

3. exert
3. Huyghens
3. imperceptible
3. annihilated
3. planetary

MODULATION

IV. RATE

Rate refers to movement in reading and speaking, and is *quick*, *moderate*, or *slow*.

1. *Quick Rate* is used to express joy, mirth, confusion, violent anger, and sudden fear; as,—

   (a) The lake has burst! The lake has burst!
   Down through the chasm the wild waves flee:
   They gallop along, with roaring and song,
   Away to the eager awaiting sea!

(*b*) There was mounting in hot haste: the steed,
  The mustering squadron, and the clattering car
  Went pouring forward with impetuous speed,
  And swiftly forming in the ranks of war.

2. *Moderate Rate* is used in ordinary assertion, narration, and description; in cheerfulness, and the gentler forms of the emotions; as,—

  The heavens declare the glory of God;
  And the firmament showeth His handiwork.
  Day unto day uttereth speech,
  And night unto night showeth knowledge.
  There is no speech nor language
  Where their voice is not heard.
  Their line is gone out through all the earth,
  And their words to the end of the world.
  In them hath He set a tabernacle for the sun,
  Which is as a bridegroom coming out of his chamber,
  And rejoiceth as a strong man to run a race.
  His going forth is from the end of the heaven,
  And his circuit unto the ends of it:
  And there is nothing hid from the heat thereof.

3. *Slow Rate* is used to express grandeur, vastness, pathos, solemnity, adoration, horror, and consternation; as,—

  (*a*) Canst thou by searching find out God?
  Canst thou find out the Almighty unto perfection?
  It is as high as heaven; what canst thou do?
  Deeper than hell; what canst thou know?
  The measure thereof is longer than the earth,
  And broader than the sea.

  (*b*) O the depth of the riches
  Both of the wisdom and knowledge of God!
  How unsearchable are His judgments,
  And His ways past finding out!

(*c*) And they rest not day and night, saying,
Holy! Holy! Holy! Lord God Almighty!
Which was, and is, and is to come.

(*d*) O Thou Eternal One! whose presence bright
   All space doth occupy, all motion guide;
Unchanged through Time's all-devastating flight;
   Thou only God! There is no god beside!
Being above all beings! Mighty One!
   Whom none can comprehend and none explore!
Who fill'st existence with Thyself alone—
   Embracing all, supporting, ruling o'er—
Being whom we call God, and know no more.

(*e*) The curfew tolls the knell of parting day;
   The lowing herd winds slowly o'er the lea;
The plowman homeward plods his weary way,
   And leaves the world to darkness and to me.

(*f*) The merchants of these things, which were made rich by her, shall stand afar off for the fear of her torment, weeping and wailing, and saying, "Alas, alas that great city, that was clothed in fine linen, and purple, and scarlet, and decked with gold, and precious stones, and pearls! For in one hour so great riches is come to naught." And every shipmaster, and all the company in ships, and sailors, and as many as trade by sea, stood afar off, and cried when they saw the smoke of her burning, saying, "What city is like unto this city!" And they cast dust on their heads, and cried, weeping and wailing, saying, "Alas, alas that great city, wherein were made rich all that had ships in the sea by reason of her costliness! for in one hour is she made desolate." Rejoice over her, thou Heaven, and ye holy apostles and prophets; for God hath avenged you on her.

LONGFELLOW'S STUDY

FAITH, HOPE, AND LOVE

"God is love."

1. Love is the root of creation,—God's essence; worlds without number
Lie in His bosom like children: He made them for this purpose only:
Only to love and be loved again; He breathed forth His spirit
Into the slumbering dust, and upright standing, it laid its
Hand on its heart, and felt it was warm with a flame out of heaven.
Quench, O quench not that flame! it is the breath of your being.
Love is life, but hatred is death.

2.   Not father nor mother
Loved you as God has loved you; for 'twas that you may be happy
Gave He His only Son. When He bowed down His head in the death-hour,
Solemnized Love its triumph: the sacrifice then was completed.
Lo! then was rent on a sudden the veil of the temple, dividing
Earth and heaven apart, and the dead from their sepulchers rising,
Whispered with pallid lips and low in the ears of each other
The answer—but dreamed of before—to creation's enigma—Atonement!
Depths of Love are Atonement's depths, for Love is Atonement.

3. Therefore, child of mortality, love thou the merciful Father;
Wish what the Holy One wishes, and not from fear, but affection;
Fear is the virtue of slaves; but the heart that loveth is willing;
Perfect was before God, and perfect is Love, and Love only.

4. Lovest thou God as thou oughtest, then lovest thou likewise thy
    brethren;
  One is the sun in heaven,—and one, only one, is Love also.
  Bears not each human figure the godlike stamp on his forehead?
  Readest thou not in his face thine origin? Is he not sailing—
  Lost like thyself on an ocean unknown? and is he not guided
  By the same stars that guide thee? Why should'st thou hate,
    then, thy brother?
  Hateth he thee, forgive! For 'tis sweet to stammer one letter
  Of the Eternal's language;—on earth it is called Forgiveness!

5. Knowest thou Him who forgave with the crown of thorns on
    His temples?
  Earnestly prayed for His foes, for His murderers? Say, dost
    thou know Him?
  Ah! thou confessest His name; so follow likewise His example;
  Think of thy brother no ill, but throw a veil over his failings;
  Guide the erring aright; for the good, the heavenly Shepherd
  Took the lost lamb in His arms, and bore it back to its mother.

6. This is the fruit of Love, and it is by its fruits that we know it.
  Love is the creature's welfare, with God; but Love among mortals
  Is but an endless sigh! He longs, and endures, and stands
    waiting;
  Suffers and yet rejoices, and smiles with tears on his eyelids.
  Hope,—so is called upon earth his recompense,—Hope, the befriending,
  Does what she can; for she points evermore up to heaven, and
    faithful
  Plunges her anchor's peak in the depths of the grave, and beneath it
  Paints a more beautiful world,—a dim, but a sweet play of
    shadows!

Races, better than we, have leaned on her wavering promise,
Having naught else but Hope.

7. Then praise we our Father in heaven,
Him who has given us more; for to us has Hope been transfigured,
Groping no longer in night she is Faith, she is living assurance.
Faith is enlightened Hope; she is light, is the eye of affection,
Dreams of the longing interprets, and carves their visions in marble.
Faith is the sun of life; and her countenance shines like the Hebrew's,
For she has looked upon God; the heaven on its stable foundation
Draws she with chains down to earth, and the New Jerusalem sinketh,
Splendid, with portals twelve in golden vapors descending.
—*"Children of the Lord's Supper," translated from the Swedish by Longfellow.*

Modulation

Classify this selection as to pitch, force, quality, and rate, and read in harmony with your classification. Select from previous lessons one which requires the pure-tone quality of voice. Determine the pitch, force, and rate.

MONOTONE

1. *Monotone* consists of a degree of sameness of sound, or tone, in a number of successive words or syllables.

2. It is very seldom the case that a perfect sameness is to be observed in reading any passage or sentence. But very little variety of tone is to be used in reading either prose or verse that contains elevated descriptions, or emotions of solemnity, sublimity, or reverence.

3. The monotone usually requires a low tone of voice, loud or

prolonged force, and a slow rate of utterance. It is this tone only that can present the conditions of the supernatural and the ghostly.

4. The words to be read in monotone are in italics and must be spoken evenly, or without inflection.

EXERCISES IN MONOTONE

1. I heard a voice saying, "*Shall mortal man be more just than God? Shall a man be more pure than his Maker?*"

2. *Lord, Thou hast been our dwelling-place* in all generations. Before the *mountains were brought forth, or ever Thou hadst formed* the *earth* and the *world, even from everlasting to everlasting, Thou art God.*

3. *Man dieth* and *wasteth* away; *yea, man giveth up the ghost, and where* is he? As the *waters fail* from the *sea,* and the *flood decayeth,* and *drieth* up, so *man lieth down,* and *riseth* not; *till the heavens be no more, they shall not* awake, *nor be raised out* of their sleep.

4. The *cloud-capped towers,* the *gorgeous palaces,*
The *solemn temples,* the *great globe* itself—
Yea, all which it inherit, *shall* dissolve,
And, *like this unsubstantial pageant,* faded—
Leave not a rack behind.

THE SKY

"*Hast thou with Him spread out the sky, which is strong, and as a molten looking-glass?*"

1. It is a strange thing how little, in general, people know about the sky. It is the part of creation in which Nature has done more for the sake of pleasing man, more for the sole and evident purpose of talking to him and teaching him, than in any other of her works; and it is just the part in which we least attend to her. There are not many of her other works in which some more material or essential purpose than the mere pleasing of man is not answered by every part of their organization; but every essential purpose of

the sky might, so far as we know, be answered if, once in three days or thereabouts, a great, ugly, black rain-cloud were brought up over the blue, and everything well watered, and so all left blue again till next time, with, perhaps, a film of morning and evening mist for dew.

2. Instead of this, there is not a moment of any day of our lives when Nature is not producing scene after scene, picture after picture, glory after glory, and working still upon such exquisite and constant principles of the most perfect beauty, that it is quite certain that it is all done for us, and intended for our perpetual pleasure. And every man, wherever placed, however far from other sources of interest or of beauty, has this doing for him constantly.

3. The noblest scenes of the earth can be seen and known but by few; it is not intended that man should live always in the midst of them; he injures them by his presence, he ceases to feel them if he be always with them. But the sky is for all; bright as it is, it is not "too bright nor good for human nature's daily food;" it is fitted, in all its functions, for the perpetual comfort and exalting of the heart; for the soothing it, and purifying it from its dross and dust. Sometimes gentle, sometimes capricious, sometimes awful; never the same for two moments together; almost human in its passions, almost spiritual in its tenderness, almost divine in its infinity, its appeal to what is immortal in us is as distinct as its ministry of chastisement or of blessing to what is mortal is essential.

4. Yet we never attend to it; we never make it a subject of thought, but as it has to do with our animal sensations. We look upon all by which it speaks to us more clearly than to brutes,— upon all which bears witness to the intention of the Supreme that we are to receive more from the covering vault than the light and the dew which we share with the weed and the worm,—only as a succession of meaningless and monotonous accidents, too common

and too vain to be worthy of a moment of watchfulness or a glance of admiration.

5. If, in our moments of utter idleness and insipidity, we turn to the sky as a last resource, which of its phenomena do we speak of? One says it has been wet, and another it has been windy, and another it has been warm. Who, among the whole chattering crowd, can tell me of the forms and precipices of the chain of tall white mountains that gilded the horizon at noon yesterday? Who saw the narrow sunbeam that came out of the south, and smote upon their summits, until they melted and moldered away in a dust of blue rain? Who saw the dance of the dead clouds, when the sunlight left them last night, and the west wind blew them before it like withered leaves?

6. All has passed unregretted or unseen; or, if the apathy be ever shaken off, even for an instant, it is only by what is gross or what is extraordinary; and yet it is not in the broad and fierce manifestations of the elemental energies, not in the clash of the hail, nor the drift of the whirlwind, that the highest characters of the sublime are developed. God is not in the earthquake nor in the fire, but in the "still, small voice." They are but the blunt and the low faculties of our nature which can only be addressed through lampblack and lightning. It is in quiet and subdued passages of unobtrusive majesty; the deep, and the calm, and the perpetual; that which must be sought ere it is seen, and loved ere it is understood; things which the angels work out for us daily, and yet vary eternally, which are never wanting, and never repeated; which are to be found always, yet each found but once—it is through these that the lesson of devotion is chiefly taught and the blessing of beauty given. —*Ruskin.*

Monotone and Modulation

Drill thoroughly on the examples given under "Monotone." Name the quality of voice, pitch, force, and rate to be employed in reading this lesson.

Word Study
1. evident
1. thereabouts
1. film
2. exquisite
2. constantly
3. function
3. chastisement
4. animal
5. insipidity
5. precipices
6. apathy
6. unobtrusive

PERSONATION

1. *Personation* consists of those modulations or changes of the voice necessary to represent two or more persons speaking.

2. This principle of expression upon the correct application of which much of the beauty and efficiency of delivery depends, is employed in reading dialogues and other pieces of a conversational nature.

3. The student should exercise his discrimination and ingenuity in studying the character of persons to be represented,—fully informing himself with regard to their temperament and peculiarities, as well as their condition and feelings at the time,—and so modulate his voice as best to personate them.

EXERCISE IN PERSONATION

He. Dost thou love wandering? Whither would'st thou go?
    Dream'st thou, sweet daughter, of a land more fair?
    Dost thou not love these age-blue streams that flow?
    The spicy forests? and the golden air?

She. O, yes, I love the woods, and streams so gay;
    And more than all, O father, I love *thee;*
    Yet would I fain be wandering—far away,
    Where such things never were, nor e'er shall be.

He. Speak, mine own daughter with the sun-bright locks!
    To what pale, banished region would'st thou roam?

She. O father, let us find our frozen rocks!
    Let's seek that country of all countries—HOME!

He. Seest thou these orange flowers? this palm that rears
    Its head up toward heaven's blue and cloudless dome?

She. I dream, I dream; mine eyes are hid in tears;
    My heart is wandering round our ancient home.

He. Why, then, we'll go. Farewell, ye tender skies,
    Who sheltered us when we were forced to roam!

She. On, on! Let's pass the swallow as he flies!
    Farewell, kind land! Now, father, *now* FOR HOME!

INSCRIPTION FOR THE ENTRANCE INTO A WOOD

"O Lord, how manifold are Thy works!
In wisdom hast Thou made them all."

(Pure Tone.)

Expression; Standard Formula.—Quality, *pure;* pitch, *moderate;* force, *moderate;* rate, *moderate.*

1. Stranger, if thou hast learned a truth which needs
No school of long experience, that the world
Is full of guilt and misery; and hast known
Enough of all its sorrows, crimes, and cares
To tire thee of it, enter this wild wood
And view the haunts of Nature.

2.   The calm shade
Shall bring a kindred calm, and the sweet breeze
That makes the green leaves dance, shall waft a balm
To thy sick heart. Thou wilt find nothing here
Of all that pained thee in the haunts of men,
And made thee loathe thy life.

3.   The primal curse
Fell, it is true, upon the unsinning earth,
But not in vengeance. God hath yoked to guilt
Her pale tormentor, misery. Hence these shades
Are still the abodes of gladness; the thick roof
Of green and stirring branches is alive
And musical with birds that sing and sport
In wantonness of spirit; while, below,
The squirrel with raised paws and form erect,
Chirps merrily.

4.   Throngs of insects in the glade
Try their thin wings, and dance in the warm beam
That waked them into life. Even the green trees
Partake the deep contentment; as they bend
To the soft winds, the sun from the blue sky
Looks in, and sheds a blessing on the scene.
Scarce less the cleft-born wild flower seems to enjoy
Existence than the winged plunderer
That sucks its sweets.

5.   The massy rocks themselves
And the old and ponderous trunks of prostrate trees,
That lead from knoll to knoll, a causey rude,
Or bridge the sunken brook, and their dark roots
With all their earth upon them, twisting high,
Breathe fixed tranquillity. The rivulet
Sends forth glad sounds, and tripping o'er its bed
Of pebbly sands, or leaping down the rocks,
Seems with continuous laughter to rejoice
In its own being.

6.   Softly tread the marge,
Lest from her midway perch thou scare the wren

That dips her bill in water. The cool wind,
That stirs the stream in play, shall come to thee,
Like one that loves thee, nor will let thee pass
Ungreeted, and shall give its light embrace.
—*William Cullen Bryant*.

Review

What are the names of the different qualities of voice? What are the three degrees of pitch? of force? of rate? What should be the pitch, force, and rate of this selection? Why? Pure quality of tone is used in what kinds of expression?

If you have drilled thoroughly on the expression drills given under "Pitch," "Force," "Quality," and "Rate," you will see that it is necessary to develop the organs of voice, which can be done only by their proper exercise.

Drill on the examples given under "Pure Tone." Select other pieces requiring the pure-tone quality of voice.

Word Study

1. inscription	3. primal	4. plunderer
1. entrance	3. musical	5. ponderous
1. haunts	3. wantonness	5. tranquillity
2. kindred	3. squirrel	6. midway

PATERNAL INSTRUCTION

> "*My son, hear the instruction of thy father,
> And forsake not the law of thy mother.*"

Expression; Standard Formula.—Quality, *pure;* pitch, *moderate;* force, *moderate;* rate, *moderate.*

1. Paternus had but one son, whom he educated himself. As they were sitting together in the garden, when the child was ten years old, Paternus thus addressed him: "Though you now think yourself so happy because you have hold of my hand, you are in the hands and under the tender care of a much greater Father and Friend than I am, whose love to you is far greater than mine, and from whom you receive such blessings as no mortal can give.

2. "That God whom you see me daily worship; whom I daily call upon to bless both you and me, and all mankind; whose wondrous acts are recorded in those Scriptures which you constantly read,—that God who created the heavens and the earth; who was the God of Abraham, Isaac, and Jacob, whom God blessed and praised in the greatest afflictions; who delivered the Israelites out of the hands of the Egyptians; who was the protector of Joseph, Moses, and Daniel; who sent so many prophets into the world; who appointed His Son to redeem mankind;—this God, who has done all these great things, who has created so many millions of men, with whom the good of all ages will be happy forever;—this great God, the Creator of the worlds, of angels, and men, is your Father and Friend.

3. "I myself am not half the age of this shady oak, under which we sit; many of our fathers have sat under its boughs; we have all called it ours in our turn, though it stands, and drops its masters as it drops its leaves.

4. "You see, my son, this wide and large firmament over our heads, where the sun and moon and all the stars appear in their turns. If you were to be carried to any of these bodies, at this vast distance from you, you would still discover others as much

above you as the stars which you see here are above the earth. Were you to go up or down, east or west, north or south, you would find the same height without any top, and the same depth without any bottom.

5. "Yet, so great is God, that all these bodies added together are only as a grain of sand in His sight. But you are as much the care of this great God and Father of all the worlds and all spirits, as if He had no son but you, or there were no creature for Him to love and protect but you alone. He numbers the hairs of your head, watches over you sleeping and waking, and has preserved you from a thousand dangers, unknown both to you and to me.

6. "Therefore, my child, fear and worship and love God. Your eyes indeed can not yet see Him, but all things which you see are so many marks of His power and presence, and He is nearer to you than anything which you can see.

7. "Take Him for your Lord, and Father, and Friend; look up unto Him as the fountain and cause of all the good that you have received from me, and reverence me only as the bearer and minister of God's good things to you. He that blessed my father before I was born, will bless you when I am dead.

8. "As you have been used to look to me in all your actions, and have been afraid to do anything unless you first knew my will; so let it now be a rule of your life to look up to God in all your actions, to do everything in His fear, and to abstain from everything which is not according to His will.

9. "Next to this, love all mankind with such tenderness and affection as you love yourself. Think how God loves all mankind, how merciful He is to them, how tender He is of them, how carefully He preserves them, and then strive to love the world as God loves it.

10. "Do good, my son, first of all to those who most deserve it, but remember to do good to all. The greatest sinners receive daily instances of God's goodness toward them; He nourishes and preserves them, that they may repent and return to Him; do you there-

fore imitate God, and think no one too bad to receive your relief and kindness, when you see that he wants it.

11. "Let your dress be sober, clean, and modest; not to set off the beauty of your person, but to declare the sobriety of your mind; that your outward garb may resemble the inward plainness and simplicity of your heart. For it is highly reasonable that you should be one man, and appear outwardly such as you are inwardly.

12. "In meat and drink, observe the rules of Christian temperance and sobriety. Consider your body only as the servant and minister of your soul; and only so nourish it as it may best perform a humble and obedient service.

13. "Love humility in all its instances; practice it in all its parts; for it is the noblest state of the soul of man; it will set your heart and affections right toward God, and fill you with whatever temper is tender and affectionate toward men.

14. "Let every day therefore be a day of humility; condescend to all the weakness and infirmities of your fellow creatures; cover their frailties; love their excellences; encourage their virtues; relieve their wants; rejoice in their prosperity; compassionate their distress; receive their friendship; overlook their unkindness; forgive their malice; be a servant of servants; and condescend to do the lowest offices of the lowest of mankind.

15. "It seems but the other day since I received from my dear father the same instructions which I am now leaving with you. And the God who gave me ears to hear, and a heart to receive, what my father enjoined on me, will, I hope, give you the grace to love and follow the same instructions." —*Law.*

Exercise for Conversation and Study

Where in the Scriptures do we find paternal instruction given? Who is the author of the quotation at the beginning of the lesson? What quality of tone should be employed in reading this lesson? What pitch? force? rate? Select from the Bible portions of scripture that require the same quality of voice as does this lesson. Mark the lessons thus far studied that require the pure tone of voice.

Word Study

1. Paternus
2. Abraham
3. boughs
4. discover
5. thousand
6. worship
7. reverence
8. abstain
9. merciful
10. relief
11. garb
12. nourish
13. humility
14. frailties
14. condescend

A KNOWLEDGE OF GOD

> "*O the depth of the riches both of the wisdom and knowledge of God! how unsearchable are His judgments, and His ways past finding out!*"

1. Many are the ways in which God is seeking to make Himself known to us and to bring us into communion with Him. Nature speaks to our senses without ceasing. The open heart will be impressed with the love and glory of God as revealed through the works of His hands. The listening ear can hear and understand the communications of God through the things of nature. The green fields, the lofty trees, the buds and flowers, the passing cloud, the falling rain, the babbling brook, the glories of the heavens, speak to our hearts, and invite us to become acquainted with Him who made them all.

2. Our Saviour bound up His precious lessons with the things of nature. The trees, the birds, the flowers of the valley, the hills, the lake, and the beautiful heavens, as well as the incidents and surroundings of daily life, were all linked with words of truth, that His lessons might thus be often recalled to mind, even amid the busy cares of man's life of toil.

3. God would have His children appreciate His works, and delight in the simple, quiet beauty with which He has adorned our earthly home. He is a lover of the beautiful, and above all

that is outwardly attractive, He loves beauty of character; He would have us cultivate purity and simplicity, the quiet graces of the flowers.

4. If we will but listen, God's created works will teach us precious lessons of obedience and trust. From the stars that in their trackless course through space follow from age to age their appointed path, down to the minutest atom, the things of nature obey the Creator's will. And God cares for everything and sustains everything that He has created. He who upholds the unnumbered worlds throughout immensity, at the same time cares for the wants of the little brown sparrow that sings its humble song without a fear. When men go forth to their daily toil, as when they engage in prayer; when they lie down at night, and when they rise in the morning; when the rich man feasts in his palace, or when the poor man gathers his children about the scanty board, each is tenderly watched by the heavenly Father. No tears are shed that God does not notice. There is no smile that He does not mark.

5. If we would but fully believe this, all undue anxiety would be dismissed. Our lives would not be so filled with disappointment as now; for everything, whether great or small, would be left in the hands of God, who is not perplexed by the multiplicity of cares, or overwhelmed by their weight. We should then enjoy a rest of soul to which many have long been strangers.

6. As your senses delight in the attractive loveliness of the earth, think of the world that is to come, that shall never know the blight of sin and death; where the face of nature will no more wear the shadow of the curse. Let your imagination picture the home of the saved, and remember that it will be more glorious than your brightest imagination can portray. In the varied gifts of God in nature we see but the faintest gleaming of His glory. It is written, "Eye hath not seen, nor ear heard, neither have entered into the heart of man, the things which God hath prepared for them that love Him."

7. The poet and the naturalist have many things to say about nature, but it is the Christian who enjoys the beauty of the earth with the highest appreciation, because he recognizes his Father's handiwork, and perceives His love in flower and shrub and tree. No one can fully appreciate the significance of hill and vale, river and sea, who does not look upon them as an expression of God's love to man.

8. God speaks to us through His providential workings, and through the influence of His Spirit upon the heart. In our circumstances and surroundings, in the changes daily taking place around us, we may find precious lessons, if our hearts are but open to discern them. The psalmist, tracing the work of God's providence, says, "The earth is full of the goodness of the Lord." "Whoso is wise and will observe these things, even they shall understand the loving-kindness of Jehovah."

9. God speaks to us in His word. Here we have in clearer lines the revelation of His character, of His dealings with men, and the great work of redemption. Here is open before us the history of patriarchs and prophets and other holy men of old. They were men "subject to like passions as we are." We see how they struggled through discouragements like our own, how they fell under temptation as we have done, and yet took heart again and conquered through the grace of God; and beholding, we are encouraged in our striving after righteousness. As we read of the precious experiences granted them, of the light and love and blessing it was theirs to enjoy, and of the work they wrought through the grace given them, the Spirit that inspired them kindles a flame of holy emulation in our hearts, and a desire to be like them in character—like them to walk with God.

10. Jesus said of the Old Testament Scriptures,—and how much more is it true of the New,—"These are they which testify of Me," the Redeemer, Him in whom our hopes of eternal life are centered. Yes, the whole Bible tells of Christ. From the first record

of creation—"for without Him was not anything made that was made"—to the closing promise, "Behold, I come quickly," we are reading of His works and listening to His voice. If you would become acquainted with the Saviour, study the Holy Scriptures.

11. Never should the Bible be studied without prayer. Before opening its pages we should ask for the enlightenment of the Holy Spirit, and it will be given. When Nathanael came to Jesus, the Saviour exclaimed, "Behold an Israelite indeed, in whom is no guile." Nathanael said, "Whence knowest Thou me?" Jesus answered, "Before that Philip called thee, when thou wast under the fig tree, I saw thee." And Jesus will see us also in the secret places of prayer, if we will seek Him for light, that we may know what is truth. Angels from the world of light will be with those who in humility of heart seek for divine guidance.

12. The Holy Spirit exalts and glorifies the Saviour. It is His office to present Christ, the purity of His righteousness, and the great salvation that we have through Him. Jesus says, "He shall receive of Mine, and shall show it unto you." The spirit of truth is the only effectual teacher of divine truth. How must God esteem the human race, since He gave His Son to die for them, and appoints His Spirit to be man's teacher and continual Guide.

—*Mrs. E. G. White.*

Exercise for Conversation and Study

In how many ways does God reveal Himself to His children? What ways are mentioned in the first paragraph of this lesson? What things in nature speak to our hearts? What do they invite us to do? What must be our attitude if we shall hear and understand the communications of God through the things of nature? Ps. 46:10, first clause. What lessons will God's created works teach us? What in His creation teaches obedience? What teaches trust? How does the Creator desire us to regard His wonderful handiwork? Who can enjoy the beauties of nature even more than the naturalist and the poet? Why? How does God

speak to us through His providences? through His word? through
His Holy Spirit? What is the advantage of being instructed through
the various ways mentioned in this lesson, over being limited to any
one way?

Word Study

1. communion	3. appreciate	5. weight
1. acquainted	3. attractive	5. anxiety
1. babbling	4. obedience	6. portray
2. precious	4. immensity	7. poet
2. surroundings	5. multiplicity	7. significance

GOD

*"Canst thou by searching find out God?
Canst thou find out the Almighty unto
perfection?"*

Expression; Standard Formula.—Quality, *orotund;* pitch, *moderate;* force, *moderate;* rate, *slow.*

1. O Thou eternal One! whose presence bright
   All space doth occupy, all motion guide
   Unchanged through time's all-devastating flight;
   Thou only God! There is no god beside!
   Being above all beings! Mighty One!
   Whom none can comprehend and none explore;
   Who fill'st existence with Thyself alone;
   Embracing all,—supporting,—ruling o'er,—
   Being whom we call God—and know no more!

2. In its sublime research, philosophy
   May measure out the ocean deep—may count
   The sands or the sun's rays;—but, God! for Thee
   There is no weight nor measure:—none can mount

Up to Thy mysteries. Reason's brightest spark,
   Though kindled by Thy light, in vain would try
To trace Thy counsels, infinite and dark;
   And thought is lost ere thought can soar so high,
   Even like past moments in eternity.

3. Thou from primeval nothingness didst call
      First chaos, then existence:—Lord! on Thee
   Eternity had its foundation;—all
      Sprung forth from Thee:—of light, joy, harmony,
      Sole origin:—all life, all beauty Thine.
   Thy word created all, and doth create;
   Thy splendor fills all space with rays divine.
      Thou art, and wert, and shalt be! glorious! great!
      Light-giving, life-sustaining Potentate!

4. Thy chains the unmeasured universe surround,
      Upheld by Thee, by Thee inspired with breath!
   Thou the beginning with the end hast bound. . . .
   As sparks mount upward from the fiery blaze,
      So suns are born, so worlds spring forth from Thee:
      And as the spangles in the sunny rays
      Shine round the silver snow, the pageantry
   Of heaven's bright army glitters in Thy praise.

5. A million torches lighted by Thy hand
      Wander unwearied through the blue abyss;
   They own Thy power, accomplish Thy command,
      All gay with life, all eloquent with bliss.
   What shall we call them? Piles of crystal light—
      A glorious company of golden streams—
   Lamps of celestial ether burning bright—

Suns lighting systems with their joyous beams?
But Thou to these art as the noon to night.

6. Yes! as a drop of water in the sea,
　　All this magnificence in Thee is lost:—
　What are ten thousand worlds compared to Thee?
　　And what am I then? Heaven's unnumbered host,
　Though multiplied by myriads, and arrayed
　　In all the glory of sublimest thought,
　Is but an atom in the balance; weighed
　　Against Thy greatness, is a cipher brought
　　Against infinity! O, what am I then?—Naught!

7. Naught! yet the effluence of Thy light divine,
　　Pervading worlds, hath reached my bosom, too;
　Yes! in my spirit doth Thy Spirit shine,
　　As shines the sunbeam in a drop of dew.
　Naught! yet I live, and on Hope's pinions fly
　　Eager toward Thy presence; for in Thee
　I live, and breathe, and dwell; aspiring high,
　　Even to the throne of Thy divinity.
　　I am, O God! and surely *Thou* must be!

8. Thou art! directing, guiding all, Thou art!
　　Direct my understanding, then, to Thee;
　Control my spirit, guide my wandering heart.
　　Though but an atom midst immensity,
　Still I am something, fashioned by Thy hand!
　　I hold a middle rank 'twixt heaven and earth,
　On the last verge of mortal being stand,
　　Close to the realms where angels have their birth,
　Just on the boundaries of the spirit land!

9. O thoughts ineffable! O visions blest!
   Though worthless our conceptions all of Thee,
   Yet shall Thy shadowed image fill our breast,
   And waft its homage to Thy Deity.
   God! thus alone my lonely thoughts can soar;
   Thus seek Thy presence, Being wise and good!
   Midst Thy vast works admire, obey, adore.
                                          —*Derzhavin.*

Modulation

What quality of tone is employed in the correct reading of this lesson? Why? What kinds of expression require this quality of voice? Where is the orotund voice produced? How does it differ from the pure tone in quality?

Drill on the examples given under "Orotund Tone." Select other pieces requiring the orotund quality of voice.

Word Study

1. unchanged	3. splendor	7. effluence
2. research	3. Potentate	8. immensity
2. weight	4. spangles	9. conceptions
3. primeval	4. pageantry	9. ineffable
3. origin	5. eloquent	9. homage
3. existence	6. magnificence	

CONVERSATION

> "*Let your speech be alway with grace, seasoned with salt, that ye may know how ye ought to answer every man.*"

1. Never speak anything for a truth which you know or believe to be false. Lying is a great sin against God, who gave us a tongue to speak the truth and not falsehood. It is a great offense against humanity itself; for, where there is no regard to truth, there can be no safe society between man and man. And it is an injury to the speaker; for, besides the disgrace which it brings upon him, it occasions so much baseness of mind that he can scarcely tell truth, or avoid lying, even when he has no color of necessity for it; and, in time, he comes to such a pass that as other people can not believe he speaks truth, so he himself scarcely knows when he tells a falsehood.

2. As you must be careful not to lie, so you must avoid coming near it. You must not equivocate, nor speak anything positively for which you have no authority but report, or conjecture, or opinion.

3. Let your words be few, especially when your superiors or strangers are present, lest you betray your weakness, and rob yourselves of the opportunity which you might otherwise have had to gain knowledge, wisdom, and experience, by hearing those whom you silence by your impertinent talking.

4. Be not too earnest, loud, or violent in your conversation. Silence your opponent with reason, not with noise. Be careful not to interrupt another when he is speaking; hear him out, and you will understand him better, and be able to give him the better answer.

5. Consider before you speak, especially when the business is of moment; weigh the sense of what you mean to utter, and the expressions you intend to use, that they may be significant, perti-

nent, and inoffensive. Inconsiderate persons do not think till they speak; or they speak, and then think.

6. Some men excel in husbandry, some in gardening, some in mathematics. In conversation, learn as near as you can where the skill or excellence of any person lies; put him upon talking on that subject, observe what he says, keep it in your memory, or commit it to writing. By this means you will glean the worth and knowledge of everybody you converse with; and at an easy rate acquire what may be of use to you on many occasions.

7. When you are in company with light, vain, impertinent persons, let the observing of their failings make you the more cautious, both in your conversation with them and in your general behavior, that you may avoid their errors. If any one, whom you do not know to be a person of truth, sobriety, and weight, relates strange stories, be not too ready to believe or report them; and yet (unless he is one of your family acquaintances) be not too forward to contradict him. If the occasion requires you to declare your opinion, do it modestly and gently, not bluntly nor coarsely; by this means you will avoid giving offense, or being abused for too much credulity.

8. If a man, whose integrity you do not very well know, makes you great and extraordinary professions, do not give much credit to him. Probably you will find that he aims at something besides kindness to you, and that when he has served his turn, or been disappointed, his regard for you will grow cool. Beware also of him who flatters you, and commends you to your face, or to one who he thinks will tell you of it; most probably he has either deceived and abused you, or means to do so. Remember the fable of the fox commending the singing of the crow that had something in her mouth which the fox wanted.

9. Be careful that you do not commend yourselves. It is a sign that your reputation is small and sinking, if your own tongue must praise you; and it is fulsome and unpleasing to others to hear such commendations. Speak well of the absent whenever you have

a suitable opportunity. Never speak ill of them, or of anybody, unless you are sure they deserve it, and unless it is necessary for their amendment, or for the safety and benefit of others.

10. Avoid, in your ordinary communications, not only oaths, but all imprecations and earnest protestations. Forbear scoffing and jesting at the condition or natural defects of any person. Such offenses leave a deep impression; and they often cost a man dear.

11. Be very careful that you give no reproachful, menacing, or spiteful words to any person. Good words make friends; bad words make enemies. It is great prudence to gain as many friends as we honestly can, especially when it may be done at so easy a rate as a good word; and it is great folly to make an enemy by ill words, which are of no advantage to the party who uses them. When faults are committed, they may, and by a superior they must, be reproved; but let it be done without reproach or bitterness; otherwise it will lose its due end and use, and, instead of reforming the offense, it will exasperate the offender, and lay the reprover justly open to reproof.

12. If a person be passionate, and give you ill language, rather pity him than be moved to anger. You will find that silence, or very gentle words, are the most exquisite revenge for reproaches; they will either cure the distemper in the angry man, and make him sorry for his passion, or they will be a severe reproof and punishment to him. But at any rate, they will preserve your innocence, give you the deserved reputation of wisdom and moderation, and keep up the serenity and composure of your mind. Passion and anger make a man unfit for everything that becomes him as a man or as a Christian.

13. Never utter any profane speeches, nor make a jest of any scripture expressions. When you pronounce the name of God or of Christ, or repeat any passages or words of Holy Scripture, do it with reverence and seriousness, and not lightly, for that is "taking the name of God in vain." If you hear of any unseemly ex-

pressions used in religious exercises, do not publish them, endeavor to forget them; or, if you mention them at all, let it be with pity and sorrow, not with derision or reproach.

—*Sir Matthew Hale.*

Exercise for Conversation and Study

Select from the proverbs of Solomon those that emphasize the principles of conversation brought out in this reading lesson. What instruction did Christ give regarding conversation? Matt. 5:33-37. What advice did the apostle Paul give on this subject? Eph. 4:29; Col. 3:8; 4:6; Titus 2:6-8. What does the apostle James say about the tongue? James 3:2-10. What account is taken of the words that we speak? Matt. 12:37. What, then, should be our constant petition to God? Ps. 19:14. What will be the condition of the redeemed? Rev. 14:4, 5.

Modulation—Pitch

Review the expression exercises under "Pitch."

Word Study

1. falsehood
2. equivocate
2. conjecture
3. impertinent
4. conversation
5. inconsiderate
6. husbandry
7. behavior
7. sobriety
7. credulity
8. extraordinary
9. amendment
10. imprecations
10. protestations
11. menacing
11. exasperate
12. passionate
13. derision

CLEAR THE WAY

Expression; Standard Formula.—Quality, *pure tone;* pitch. *high;* force, *loud;* rate, *moderate to quick.*

1. Men of thought! be up and stirring night and day:
   Sow the seed—withdraw the curtain—CLEAR THE WAY!
   Men of action, aid and cheer them, as ye may!
      There's a fount about to stream,
      There's a light about to beam,
      There's a warmth about to glow,
      There's a flower about to blow;
   There's a midnight blackness changing into gray.
   Men of thought and men of action, CLEAR THE WAY!

2. Once the welcome light has broken, who shall say
   What the unimagined glories of the day?
   What the evil that shall perish in its ray?
      Aid the dawning, tongue and pen;
      Aid it, hopes of honest men;
      Aid it, paper; aid it, type;
      Aid it, for the hour is ripe,
   And our earnest must not slacken into play.
   Men of thought and men of action, CLEAR THE WAY!

3. Lo! a cloud's about to vanish from the day;
   And a brazen wrong to crumble into clay.
   Lo! the right's about to conquer: CLEAR THE WAY!
      With the right shall many more
      Enter smiling at the door;
      With the giant wrong shall fall
      Many others, great and small,
   That for ages long have held us for their prey.
   Men of thought and men of action, CLEAR THE WAY!
                                   —*Charles Mackay.*

Exercise for Conversation and Study

What "brazen wrong" is referred to in the third stanza? What style of expression is required in reading this lesson? What quality of tone? What pitch? force? rate? Commit the poem to memory so that you can speak it with good expression.

Modulation

Review the expression exercises under "Force." Read "Man the Lifeboat," and compare the style of expression with this lesson.

THE BURIAL OF MOSES

"No man knoweth of his sepulcher unto this day."

Expression; Standard Formula.—Quality, *orotund;* pitch, *low;* force, *gentle,* rate, *slow.*

1. By Nebo's lonely mountain,
   On this side Jordan's wave,
   In a vale in the land of Moab,
   There lies a lonely grave;
   But no man dug that sepulcher,
   And no man saw it e'er,
   For the angels of God upturned the sod,
   And laid the dead man there.

2. That was the grandest funeral
   That ever passed on earth;
   Yet no man heard the tramping,
   Or saw the train go forth;
   Noiselessly as the daylight
   Comes when the night is done,
   And the crimson streak on ocean's cheek
   Grows into the great sun—

3. Noiselessly as the springtime
    Her crown of verdure weaves,
   And all the trees on all the hills
    Unfold their thousand leaves—
   So, without sound of music,
    Or voice of them that wept,
   Silently down from the mountain's crown
    The great procession swept.

4. Perchance the bald old eagle,
    On gray Beth-peor's height,
   Out of his rocky eyrie,
    Looked on the wondrous sight.
   Perchance the lion, stalking,
    Still shuns the hallowed spot,
   For beast and bird have seen and heard
    That which man knoweth not.

5. Lo! when the warrior dieth,
    His comrades in the war,
   With arms reversed, and muffled drum,
    Follow the funeral car.
   They show the banners taken,
    They tell his battles won,
   And after him lead his masterless steed,
    While peals the minute gun.

6. Amid the noblest of the land
    Men lay the sage to rest,
   And give the bard an honored place,
    With costly marble drest,
   In the great minster transept,
    Where lights like glories fall,
   And the sweet choir sings, and the organ rings
    Along the emblazoned hall.

7. This was the bravest warrior
    That ever buckled sword;
  This the most gifted poet
    That ever breathed a word;
  And never earth's philosopher
    Traced with his golden pen,
  On the deathless page, truths half so sage
    As he wrote down for men.

8. And had he not high honor?—
    The hillside for his pall;
  To lie in state while angels wait,
    With stars for tapers tall;
  And the dark rock pines, like tossing plumes,
    Over his bier to wave,
  And God's own hand, in that lonely land,
    To lay him in his grave—

9. In that strange grave, without a name,
    Whence his uncoffined clay
  Shall break again—O wondrous thought!—
    Before the judgment day,
  And stand, with glory wrapped around,
    On the hills he never trod,
  And speak of the strife that won our life,
    With the incarnate Son of God.

10. O lonely tomb in Moab's land!
    O dark Beth-peor's hill!
  Speak to these curious hearts of ours,
    And teach them to be still.
  God hath His mysteries of grace—
    Ways that we can not tell;
  He hides them deep, like the secret sleep
    Of him He loved so well.

—*Cecil Frances Alexander.*

Exercise for Conversation and Study

Where was Moses buried? How old was he when he died? What was his physical condition just before his death? Is Moses' body still in the grave? What stanzas or portions of stanzas deviate in style of expression from the standard formula for this piece?

Modulation

Commit to memory the following verses, and speak them with proper expression. The style of expression is the same as the above, but with deeper feeling.

MIDNIGHT

1. 'Tis midnight; and on Olives' brow
    The star is dimmed that lately shone:
   'Tis midnight; in the garden now
    The suffering Saviour prays alone.

2. 'Tis midnight; and from all removed,
    The Saviour wrestles lone with fears;
   E'en that disciple whom He loved
    Heeds not his Master's grief and tears.

3. 'Tis midnight; and for others' guilt
    The Man of Sorrows weeps in blood;
   Yet He who hath in anguish knelt,
    Is not forsaken by His God.

4. 'Tis midnight; and from other plains
    Is borne the song that angels know;
   Unheard by mortals are the strains
    That sweetly soothe the Saviour's woe.

—*William B. Tappan.*

THE SEASONS

"I solitary court
The inspiring breeze and meditate upon
the book
Of nature, ever open; aiming thence
Warm from the heart to learn the moral
song."

1. Persons of reflection and sensibility contemplate with interest the scenes of nature. The changes of the year impart a color and character to their thoughts and feelings. When the seasons walk their round, when the earth buds, the corn ripens, and the leaf falls, not only are the senses impressed, but the mind is instructed, the heart is touched with sentiment, the fancy amused with visions. To a lover of nature and of wisdom, the vicissitude of seasons conveys a proof and exhibition of the wise and benevolent contrivance of the Author of all things.

2. When suffering the inconveniences of the ruder parts of the year, we may be tempted to wonder why this rotation is necessary; —why we could not be constantly gratified with vernal bloom and fragrance, or summer beauty and profusion. We imagine that in a world of our creation there would always be a blessing in the air, and flowers and fruits on the earth. The chilling blast and driving snow, the desolated field, withered foliage, and naked trees, should make no part of the scenery which we would produce. A little thought, however, is sufficient to show the folly, if not impiety, of such distrust in the appointments of the great Creator.

3. The succession and contrast of the seasons give scope to that care and foresight, diligence and industry, which are essential to the dignity and enjoyment of human beings, whose happiness is connected with the exertion of their faculties. With our present constitution and state, in which impressions on the senses enter so much into our pleasures and pains, and the vivacity of our sensations is affected by comparison, the uniformity and continuance of a perpetual spring would greatly impair its pleasing effect upon our feelings.

4. The present distribution of the several parts of the year is evidently connected with the welfare of the whole, and the production of the greatest sum of being and enjoyments. That motion in the earth, and change of place in the sun, which cause one region of the globe to be consigned to cold, decay, and barrenness, impart to another heat and life, fertility and beauty. Whilst in our climate the earth is bound with frost, and the "chilly, smothering snows" are falling, the inhabitants of another behold the earth first planted with vegetation and appareled in verdure, and those of a third are rejoicing in the appointed weeks of harvest.

5. Each season comes, attended with its benefits, and beauties, and pleasures. All are sensible of the charms of spring. Then the senses are delighted with the feast that is furnished on every field and on every hill. The eye is sweetly delayed on every object to which it turns. It is grateful to perceive how widely, yet chastely, Nature hath mixed her colors and painted her robe; how bountifully she hath scattered her blossoms and flung her odors. We listen with joy to the melody she hath awakened in the groves, and catch health from the pure and tepid gales that blow from the mountains.

6. When the summer exhibits the whole force of active nature, and shines in full beauty and splendor; when the succeeding season offers its purple stores and golden grain, or displays its blended and softened tints; when the winter puts on its sullen aspect, and brings stillness and repose, affording a respite from the labors that have occupied the preceding months, inviting us to reflection, and compensating for the want of attractions abroad by fireside delights and home-felt joys; in all this interchange and variety we find reason to acknowledge the wise and benevolent care of the God of seasons.

7. We are passing from the finer to the ruder portions of the year. The sun emits a fainter beam, and the sky is frequently overcast. The gardens and fields have become a waste, and the

forests have shed their verdant honors. The hills are no more enlivened with the bleating of flocks, and the woodland no longer resounds with the song of birds. In these changes we see evidences of our instability, and images of our transitory state.

"So flourishes and fades majestic man."

8. Our life is compared to a falling leaf. When we are disposed to count on protracted years, to defer any serious thoughts of futurity, and to extend our plans through a long succession of seasons, the spectacle of the "fading, many-colored woods" and the naked trees affords a salutary admonition of our frailty. It should teach us to fill the short year of life, or that portion of it which may be allotted to us, with useful employments and harmless pleasures; to practice that industry, activity, and order which the course of the natural world is constantly preaching.

9. Let not the passions blight the intellect in the spring of its advancement; nor indolence nor vice canker the promise of the heart in the blossom. Then shall the summer of life be adorned with moral beauty; the autumn yield a harvest of wisdom and virtue; and the winter of age be cheered with pleasing reflections on the past, and bright hopes of the future.

—*Monthly Anthology.*

LOAVES AND FISHES

1. A voice amid the desert.
                        Not of him
Who in rough garments clad and locust-fed
Cried to the sinful multitude, and claimed
Fruits of repentance, with the lifted scourge
Of terror and reproof. A milder guide,
With gentler tones, doth teach the listening throng.
Benignant pity moved Him as he saw
The shepherdless and poor. He knew to touch
The springs of every nature. The high lore
Of heaven He humbled to the simplest child,
And in the guise of parable allured
The sluggish mind to follow truth and live.
They whom the thunders of the law had stunned
Woke to the gospel's melody with tears;
And the glad Jewish mother held her babe
High in her arms, that its young eye might meet
Jesus of Nazareth.

2.   It was so still,
Though thousands clustered there, that not a sound
Brake the long spell of eloquence which held
The wilderness in chains, save now and then,
As the gale freshened, came the murmured speech
Of distant billows, chafing with the shores
Of the Tiberian sea.

3.   Day wore apace,
Noon hasted, and the lengthening shadows brought
The unexpected eve. They lingered still,
Eyes fixed and lips apart; the very breath
Constrained, lest some escaping sigh might break

The tide of knowledge sweeping o'er their souls
Like a strange, raptured dream. They heeded not
The spent sun, closing at the curtained west
His burning journey. What was time to them,
Who heard entranced the eternal Word of life?
But the weak flesh grew weary. Hunger came,
Sharpening each feature, and to faintness drained
Life's vigorous fount. The holy Saviour felt
Compassion for them. His disciples press,
Care-stricken, to His side: "Where shall we find
Bread in this desert?"

4.   Then, with lifted eye,
He blessed and brake the slender store of food,
And fed the famished thousands. Wondering awe
With renovated strength inspired their souls,
As, gazing on the miracle, they marked
The gathered fragments of their feast, and heard
Such heavenly words as lip of mortal man
Had never uttered.

5.   Thou, whose pitying heart
Yearned over the countless miseries of those
Whom Thou didst die to save, touch Thou our souls
With the same spirit of untiring love.
Divine Redeemer! may our fellow man,
Howe'er by rank or circumstance disjoined,
Be as a brother in his hour of need.
            —L. H. Sigourney.

Exercise for Conversation and Study

What style of expression should be used in reading this lesson? Give the standard formula of expression. What besides proper expression gives power and beauty to language? *Answer.*—The figures of speech. The following are some of the figures that occur in this selection: "the lifted scourge of terror and reproof," "the shepherdless," "the thunders of the law," "the gospel's melody," "the spell of eloquence which held the wilderness in chains," "the murmured speech of distant billows," "the tide of knowledge sweeping o'er their souls like a strange, raptured dream," "the curtained west," "his burning journey," "hunger . . . drained life's vigorous fount."

Modulation

Other selections having the same style of expression as the above lesson are, "God's First Temples," page 145; "The Northern Lights," page 175. Read these selections and determine the standard formula of expression for each.

DEPORTMENT

> "Be ye kind one to another, tender hearted, forgiving one another, even as God for Christ's sake hath forgiven you."

1. The value of courtesy is too little appreciated. Many who are kind at heart lack kindness of manner. Many who command respect by their sincerity and uprightness are sadly deficient in geniality. This lack mars their own happiness, and detracts from their service to others. Many of life's sweetest and most helpful experiences are, often for mere want of thought, sacrificed by the uncourteous.

2. Cheerfulness and courtesy should especially be cultivated by parents and teachers. All may possess a cheerful countenance, a gentle voice, a courteous manner, and these are elements of power. Children are attracted by a cheerful, sunny demeanor.

Show them kindness and courtesy, and they will manifest the same spirit toward you and toward one another.

3. True courtesy is not learned by the mere practice of rules of etiquette. Propriety of deportment is at all times to be observed; wherever principle is not compromised, consideration of others will lead to compliance with accepted customs; but true courtesy requires no sacrifice of principle to conventionality. It ignores caste. It teaches self-respect, respect for the dignity of man as man, a regard for every member of the great human brotherhood.

4. There is danger of placing too high a value upon mere manner and form, and devoting too much time to education in these lines. The life of strenuous effort demanded of every youth, the hard, often uncongenial work required even for life's ordinary duties, and much more for lightening the world's heavy burden of ignorance and wretchedness,—these give little place for conventionalities.

5. Many who lay great stress upon etiquette show little respect for anything, however excellent, that fails of meeting their artificial standard. This is false education. It fosters critical pride and narrow exclusiveness.

6. The essence of true politeness is consideration for others. The essential, enduring education is that which broadens the sympathies and encourages universal kindliness. That so-called culture which does not make a youth deferential toward his parents, appreciative of their excellences, forbearing toward their defects, and helpful to their necessities; which does not make him considerate and tender, generous and helpful, toward the young, the old, and the unfortunate, and courteous toward all, is a failure.

7. Real refinement of thought and manner is better learned in the school of the divine Teacher than by any observance of set rules. His love pervading the heart gives to the character those refining touches that fashion it in the semblance of His own. This

education imparts a heaven-born dignity and sense of propriety. It gives a sweetness of disposition and a gentleness of manner that can never be equaled by the superficial polish of fashionable society.

8. The Bible enjoins courtesy, and it presents many illustrations of the unselfish spirit, the gentle grace, the winsome temper, that characterize true politeness. These are but reflections of the character of Christ. All the real tenderness and courtesy in the world, even among those who do not acknowledge His name, is from Him. And He desires these characteristics to be perfectly reflected in His children. It is His purpose that in us men shall behold His beauty.

9. The most valuable treatise on etiquette ever penned is the precious instruction given by the Saviour, with the utterance of the Holy Spirit through the apostle Paul,—words that should be ineffaceably written in the memory of every human being, young or old:—

"As I have loved you, that ye also love one another."

> "Love suffereth long and is kind;
> Love envieth not;
> Love vaunteth not itself,
> Is not puffed up,
> Doth not behave itself unseemly,
> Seeketh not its own,
> Is not provoked,
> Taketh not account of evil;
> Rejoiceth not in unrighteousness,
> But rejoiceth with the truth;
> Beareth all things,
> Believeth all things,
> Hopeth all things,
> Endureth all things.
> Love never faileth."

10. Another precious grace that should be carefully cherished is reverence. True reverence for God is inspired by a sense of His infinite greatness and a realization of His presence. With this sense of the Unseen the heart of every child should be deeply impressed. The hour and place of prayer and the services of public worship the child should be taught to regard as sacred because God is there. And as reverence is manifested in attitude and demeanor, the feeling that inspires it will be deepened.

11. Well would it be for young and old to study and ponder and often repeat those words of Holy Writ that show how the place marked by God's special presence should be regarded.

"Put off thy shoes from off thy feet," He commanded Moses at the burning bush; "for the place whereon thou standest is holy ground."

Jacob, after beholding the vision of the angels, exclaimed, "The Lord is in this place; and I knew it not. . . . This is none other but the house of God, and this is the gate of heaven."

"The Lord is in His holy temple; let all the earth keep silence before Him."

> "The Lord is a great God,
> And a great King above all gods. . . .
> O, come, let us worship and bow down;
> Let us kneel before the Lord our Maker."
> "It is He who hath made us and not we ourselves;
> We are His people, and the sheep of His pasture.
> Enter into His gates with thanksgiving,
> And into His courts with praise;
> Be thankful unto Him and bless His name."

12. Reverence should be shown also for the name of God. Never should that name be spoken lightly or thoughtlessly. Even in prayer its frequent or needless repetition should be avoided. "Holy and reverend is His name." Angels, as they speak it, veil

their faces. With what reverence should we, who are fallen and sinful, take it upon our lips!

13. We should reverence God's Word. For the printed volume we should show respect, never putting it to common uses, or handling it carelessly. And never should Scripture be quoted in a jest, or paraphrased to point a witty saying. "Every word of God is pure;" "as silver tried in a furnace of earth, purified seven times."

14. Above all, let children be taught that true reverence is shown by obedience. God has commanded nothing that is unessential, and there is no other way of manifesting reverence so pleasing to Him as obedience to that which He has spoken.

15. Reverence should be shown for God's representatives,—for ministers, teachers, and parents who are called to speak and act in His stead. In the respect shown to them He is honored.

16. And God has especially enjoined tender respect toward the aged. He says, "The hoary head is a crown of glory, if it be found in the way of righteousness." It tells of battles fought, and victories gained; of burdens borne, and temptations resisted. It tells of weary feet nearing their rest, of places soon to be vacant. Help the children to think of this, and they will smooth the path of the aged by their courtesy and respect, and will bring grace and beauty into their young lives as they heed the command to "rise up before the hoary head, and honor the face of the old man."

—Mrs. E. G. White.

Exercise for Conversation and Study

What is the most valuable treatise on etiquette ever penned? 1 Cor. 13:4-8. Commit these verses of Scripture to memory. Read the following scriptures, and give the principal thoughts contained in each: Eph. 4:29-32; Phil. 2:1-5. What style of expression have we in this lesson? Why? Give the standard formula.

Modulation

"The Bells," page 115, is a good example of the use of pure tone. Determine the pitch, rate, and force to be used in reading this poem.

Word Study

1. geniality	5. critical	9. ineffaceably
1. courtesy	6. essence	9. vaunteth
2. demeanor	7. semblance	10. reverence
3. conventionality	7. observance	12. repetition
3. etiquette	8. winsome	13. paraphrased
4. strenuous	9. treatise	16. hoary

FIGURES OF SPEECH
I. FIGURES BASED ON RESEMBLANCE

Value and Use of Figures.—Among their chief uses are these:—

1. They are both an ornament and a strength to any language.

2. They give variety by affording an entirely different way of expressing a thought.

3. They enable us to present ideas so that they may be more easily grasped. This is especially true of abstract ideas, as they are made easier of comprehension by being associated with concrete objects.

4. They add force to language.

5. They enable us to express our thoughts in a more attractive form.

6. They increase the capabilities of language by giving the same word the power of presenting different ideas. For example, in the sentence, "He is a fox," the word "fox," which usually denotes an animal, is here employed to designate a characteristic of the animal—that of craftiness.

7. They give elevation, dignity, and grace to language.

8. In general terms it may be said that figures of speech intensify all the qualities of style and expression.

Kinds of Figures.—The figures of speech most commonly used may be classified thus:—

1. Those based on the idea of resemblance—the Simile, Metaphor, Allegory, Personification.

2. Those based on contiguity or the law of association—Synecdoche, Metonymy, Hyperbole, Apostrophe, Vision.

3. Those based on the idea of contrast—Antithesis, Euphemism, Irony.

I. *The Simile.*—It is a figure which expresses the likeness one object bears to another. The objects compared must differ in kind. The likeness is generally expressed by some word such as, *like, as, compared to.*

Examples of Simile:—
1. I will make thy seed as the dust of the earth.
2. Unstable as water, thou shalt not excel.
3. His voice was like the sound of many waters.
4. Their eyes were like embers.
5. He fell as falls the thunder-riven oak.

Value of the Simile.—The simile aids the understanding in illustrating the thought by comparison to something already known; it impresses the feelings by the surprise of finding a likeness where none was expected, and it pleases by the beauty of the comparison.

II. *The Metaphor.*—It is a figure of speech in which likeness between two objects is implied. Of the two objects, one is well known, and the other is unknown; and the former is applied to explain the latter; thus, "The French Revolution was the whirlwind of the universe." Here the well-known power and effects of the "whirlwind" are used to give a vivid idea of the terribly destructive effects of the French Revolution.

Difference between a Metaphor and a Simile.—The metaphor and the simile both contain a comparison, but in the latter the resemblance between the things compared is formally expressed, while in the former it is only implied. If we say, "He upholds the state as the pillars uphold the edifice," we make a comparison by a simile; but if we say, "He is the pillar of state," we make a comparison by a metaphor.

Examples of Metaphor:—
1. He is my rock.
2. The Lord hath made bare His mighty arm.
3. The schoolroom is a hive of industry.
4. Procrastination is the thief of time.
5. The class is taking rapid steps in knowledge.

Value of the Metaphor.—It is often of great value in explaining the unknown. For example, the Scriptures, in attempting to describe to us the abode of the blest, speak of it as a "city" (Revelation 21). We know what a city is and our knowledge is at once transferred to explain the unknown.

2. It is also employed to deepen the impression on our feelings by adding a force and energy that could not be secured by plain language; as, "The news was a dagger to my heart."

3. Again, it may give an agreeable surprise and enable us to clothe abstract ideas with life, form, color, and motion.

III. *The Allegory.*—It consists of a series of metaphors so connected as to form a story, each step of which is symbolic of something else. A well-known example is the "Pilgrim's Progress." In it the difficulties of the Christian's life are symbolized and simplified by being depicted under the figure of the difficulties of a journey from the City of Destruction to the Celestial City. A Scriptural allegory is found in Gal. 4:21-31.

A *Parable* is a short allegory in which some religious or moral truth is taught or illustrated. The incident or event may be real or supposed, and is usually drawn from nature or human life. This was Christ's method of teaching. Read the parables of "The Sower" and the "Ten Talents."

A *Fable* is a kind of allegory in which the story or incident that points or illustrates a moral, is supposed to be spoken by some animal or inanimate object. *Example:* Read Judges 9:8-15.

Value of Allegory.—As these figures contain an incident, or story, each possesses, in addition to the usual advantages of a metaphor, the clearness of the concrete and the interest of a plot.

IV. *Personification.*—It consists in attributing life and mind to inanimate objects. It has three degrees of gradation.

1. The lowest degree of personification is produced with adjectives, and consists in ascribing the qualities of living beings to inanimate objects, as, "living stones," "the raging storm," "the angry sea," "wandering stars," "the smiling land."

2. The next higher degree of personification is produced with verbs and consists in making inanimate objects perform the actions of living

beings, as, "The stones would immediately cry out;" "The stone shall cry out of the wall, and the beam out of the timber shall answer it."

3. The highest degree consists in ascribing to the objects human feeling and purposes, as, "Earth felt the wound." This degree of personification is sometimes combined with the apostrophe, as, "Put on thy beautiful garments, O Jerusalem, the holy city."

All Metaphors.—All degrees of personification are metaphors, but they are called personifications because objects are raised to or toward persons.

Examples of Personification:—
1. The mountains saw Thee, and they trembled.
2. The depth saith, "It is not in me;" and the sea saith, "It is not with me."
3. What ailed thee, O thou Sea, that thou fleddest? thou Jordan, that thou wast driven back?
4. The earth was laughing after the shower passed by.
5. Morning looked on the dreadful scene.

Value of Personification.—The rhetorical value of the figure arises from the fact that inanimate things are invested with a greater interest as they rise in dignity and become endowed with personal qualities that lead us to have a fellow-feeling with them.

—*William's "Composition and Rhetoric" (adapted), published by D. C. Heath and Company, Boston, Mass.*

THE RAINBOW

"I do set My bow in the cloud."

1. The evening was glorious, and light through the trees
   Played the sunshine and raindrops, the birds and the breeze;
   The landscape, outstretching in loveliness, lay
   On the lap of the year, in the beauty of May.

2. For the Queen of the Spring, as she passed down the vale,
   Left her robe on the trees, and her breath on the gale;
   And the smile of her promise gave joy to the hours,
   And flush in her footsteps sprang herbage and flowers.

3. The skies like a banner in sunset unrolled,
   O'er the waste threw their splendor of azure and gold;
   But one cloud at a distance rose dense, and increased,
   Till its margin of black touched the zenith and east.

4. We gazed on the scenes, while around us they glowed,
   When a vision of beauty appeared on the cloud;
   'Twas not like the sun, as at midday we view,
   Nor the moon, that rolls nightly through starlight and blue.

5. Like a spirit it came in van of a storm!
   The eye and the heart hailed its beautiful form.
   For it looked not severe, like an angel of wrath,
   But its garments of brightness illumed its dark path.

6. In the hues of its grandeur, sublimely it stood,
   O'er the river, the village, the field, and the wood;
   And river, field, village, and woodland grew bright,
   As conscious they gave and afforded delight.

7. 'Twas the bow of Omnipotence; bent in His hand
   Whose grasp at Creation the universe spanned;

278

THE RAINBOW

MILLET 1814—1875

'Twas the presence of God, in a symbol sublime,
His vow from the Flood to the exit of time!

8. Not dreadful, as when in the whirlwind He pleads,
When storms are His chariots, and lightnings His steeds,
The black clouds His banner of vengeance unfurled,
And thunder His voice to a guilt-stricken world.

9. In the breath of His presence when thousands expire,
And seas boil with fury, and rocks burn with fire,
And the sword and the plague-spot with dead strew the plain,
And vultures and wolves are the graves of the slain;

10. Not such was the rainbow, that beautiful one!
Whose arch was refraction, its keystone the sun.
A pavilion it seemed which the Deity graced,
And Justice and Mercy met there and embraced.

11. Awhile, and it sweetly bent over the gloom,
Like Love o'er a death couch, or Hope o'er the tomb,
Then left the dark scene; whence it slowly retired,
As Love had just vanished, or Hope had expired.

12. I gazed not alone on the source of my song;
To all who beheld it these verses belong;
Its presence to all was the path of the Lord!
Each full heart expanded, grew warmer, adored.

13. Like a visit—the converse of friends—or a day,
That bow from my sight passed forever away;
Like that visit, that converse, that day—to my heart,
That bow from remembrance can never depart.

14. 'Tis a picture in memory distinctly defined,
With the strong and unperishing colors of mind;

A part of my being beyond my control,
Beheld on that cloud and transcribed on my soul.

—*Baldwin's London Magazine.*

Exercise for Conversation and Study

What Scriptures are strongly inferred in stanzas 5, 7, 8, 9, and 10? What causes the rainbow to appear? How many colors does it have? Name them. What is the style of expression in this lesson? Determine the standard formula. Write out the similes that occur in stanzas 3, 5, 11, and 13; and the metaphors in stanzas 1, 2, 4, 10, and 11. Explain the value of the simile and metaphor, illustrating the same by the similes and metaphors found in the lesson.

LITTLE HAL

Expression.—Varied and impassioned.

1. Old Ironsides at anchor lay,
    In the harbor of Mahon;
   A dead c-a-l-m rested on the bay—
    The w-a-v-e-s to s-l-e-e-p had gone—
   When little *Hal*, the captain's son,
    A lad both b-r-a-v-e and g-o-o-d,
   In *sport* up *shroud* and *rigging* ran,
    And on the m-a-i-n truck stood!

2. A *shudder* shot through every *vein;*
    All eyes were turned on *high;*
   There stood the boy with *dizzy* brain,
    Between the s-e-a and s-k-y.
   No h-o-l-d had he *above, below;*
    A-l-o-n-e he stood in *air;*
   To that f-a-r height none d-a-r-e-d to go—
    No a-i-d could r-e-a-c-h him there.

(The word "shudder" is *very* abrupt in emphasis; it expresses sudden pain and fear. The first syllable is short, and time can not be given to it. Sound sharply the "sh" with a little prolongation to aspirate it, and bring out thus the shock and terror.)

   3. We g-a-z-e-d, but not a *man* could *speak!*
      With horror a-l-l aghast,
   In groups, with *pallid* brow and cheek,
      We *watched* the quivering *mast.*
   The atmosphere grew *thick* and *hot*
      And of a l-u-r-i-d hue,
   As, *riveted* to the spot,
      Stood officers and crew.

(Half whisper the word "horror," to suit the quality of voice to the spirit—on the general principle that all painful, disagreeable ideas require aspiration; all pure and pleasing ideas require a clear, pure tone, to suit the *sound* to the *sense*.)

   4. The f-a-t-h-e-r came on deck. He gasped,
      "O God! *Thy* will be done!"
   Then suddenly a *rifle* grasped,
      And aimed it at his *son;*
   "*Jump*—f-a-r out, boy, into the *wave!*
      JUMP, or I f-i-r-e!" he said;
   "That o-n-l-y chance your l-i-f-e can s-a-v-e!
      JUMP, JUMP, boy!"—He obeyed.

   5. He *sank*—he r-o-s-e—he *lived*—he m-o-v-e-d,
      And for the ship struck out;
   On *board* we h-a-l-e-d the lad beloved,
      With many a *manly shout.*
   The f-a-t-h-e-r drew, in s-i-l-e-n-t j-o-y,
      Those wet a-r-m-s round his *neck,*
   And folded to his h-e-a-r-t his boy—
      Then f-a-i-n-t-e-d on the deck.

("*Jump*" should be shouted louder and *louder* as it is repeated. "He sank—he rose—he lived—he moved," should be read with very *long pauses* between the ideas, and with very long quantity on "rose" and "moved," so as to give *time enough* for all this to take place. You must *see* it all, *imagine* it, and speak it very *earnestly*. In the third and fourth lines, *smooth*, *loud*, and *pure* tones should shout with joy that little Hal is safe. But the *father* is too deeply moved to shout, or even to *speak;* his *silent* joy we should read with subdued tenderness.) —*George P. Morris.*

Modulation

How many different styles of expression are required in the reading of this lesson? What is the style of expression in the first stanza? in the second? in the third? in the first four lines of the fourth? the last four lines of the same stanza? How does the expression of the first half of stanza five compare with the latter half? The *italicized* words are to be *emphasized*, and the words with separate letters are to be prolonged in speaking them.

Practice thoroughly on this lesson. Be free and natural in your expression. Here you will be able to use all the voice power that you have developed by the breathing exercises. Read "The Town Child and the Country Child," on page 171, noting the change of the style of expression in alternate stanzas.

Figures of Speech

In all your future reading, look for the similes and metaphors. Write out those contained in this lesson. How can a *shudder* shoot, as stated in the second stanza?

FIGURES OF SPEECH

II. FIGURES BASED ON THE LAW OF ASSOCIATION

I. *Metonymy.*—Owing to the varied relations by which things may be connected, there are many kinds of this figure. The most common relations that give rise to metonymy are:—

1. Cause and effect; as, "He writes a beautiful hand" (handwriting).
2. Effect and cause; as, "There is death [something that causes death] in the pot."
3. Container and the thing contained; as, "The kettle [the water] boils."
4. Sign and the thing signified; as, "The bullet [war] is giving place to the ballot" (the organizations of peace).
5. Instrument and agent; as, "He scattered parliaments with the breath of his mouth" (powerful influence). "By the breath of God [mighty power], frost is given."
6. Material and thing made out of it; as, "The marble [monument] speaks."
7. An author and his work; as, "They have Moses and the prophets" (their writings).
8. Abstract and concrete; as, "Youth and beauty [the young and the beautiful] shall be laid in the dust."
9. Progenitor and posterity; as, "Hear, O Israel" (descendants of Israel).
10. Name of an object, and the object that inspires it; as, "That is my delight" (the cause of my delight).

Value of Metonymy.—Metonymy presents an object, not by naming it, but by suggesting it through some relation, and thus adds vividness, variety, and beauty, to style.

Examples of Metonymy:—

1. He drank only one bottle.
2. He addressed the chair.
3. The grave mingles the dust of enemies.
4. The cottage exceeds the palace for piety.

5. Lift your thoughts from earth to heaven.
6. His gray hair saved him from death.
7. Youth should always reverence age.

II. *The Synecdoche.*—It is a figure of speech by which the name of a part is applied to the whole, or that of the whole to a part. The most common and useful kinds of synecdoche consist in putting,—

1. The part for the whole; as, "She has seen sixteen summers" (years).
2. The species for the genus; as, "He is a cutthroat" (murderer).
3. An individual for the species; as, "He is a Crœsus" (a very rich man).
4. One of the characteristics of a person for the person named; as, "The covenants of the Almighty."
5. The whole for the part; as, "The arrow struck me" (my arm).
6. The genus for the species; as, "He is a wretched creature" (man).
7. A definite number for an indefinite; as, "Ten thousand fleets sweep over thee in vain."

Examples of Synecdoche:—
1. A hundred head of sheep.
2. A thousand bosoms throbbed with delight.
3. The hand of the diligent maketh rich.
4. She had seen but six winters when she died.
5. Thousands of thousands ministered unto Him.

Value of the Synecdoche.—As we grasp a part of a thing more easily than the whole, this figure enables us to put something that we are familiar with for something that we do not know so well, and thereby adds vividness, clearness, and force to the expression.

Metonymy and Synecdoche.—In metonymy, an object is suggested by mentioning some prominent property, quality, or characteristic; in the synecdoche, by naming some part.

Metonymy and Metaphor.—Each of these figures presents an object to the mind by naming something else; but the metaphor implies a comparison between what is said and what is meant, while the metonymy does not, but mentions something which is so related as readily to suggest the idea intended.

Hyperbole is exaggeration. It represents things as greater or less, better or worse, than they really are; thus, "The waves ran mountain high."

Apostrophe is a figure of speech in which the speaker turns away from his object to address some object he imagines to be present. If the object is something inanimate it is personified by the address.

Personification and Apostrophe.—When inanimate objects are addressed, they are, of course, personified; but the difference between these two figures consists in the address. Objects personified are carried up toward, or to the rank of, persons, but they are not addressed; objects apostrophized, whether persons or personified things, are addressed.

Value of the Apostrophe.—The rhetorical value of the figure consists in giving variety and surprise by the unexpected form, and animation by the vivid conception of the presence of something known to be absent.

—*Adapted from William's "Composition and Rhetoric."*

THE MORE EXCELLENT WAY

"Covet earnestly the best gifts, and yet show I unto you a more excellent way."

Expression; Standard Formula.—Quality, *orotund;* pitch, *moderate;* force, *moderate;* rate, *moderate.*

If I speak with the tongues of men and of angels,
>But have not love,

I am become sounding brass, or a clanging cymbal.
And if I have the gift of prophecy,
And know all mysteries and all knowledge;
And if I have all faith so as to remove mountains,
>But have not love,
>I am nothing.

And if I bestow all my goods to feed the poor,
And if I give my body to be burned,
>But have not love,
>It profiteth me nothing.
>Love suffereth long, and is kind;
>>Love envieth not;
>>Love vaunteth not itself,
>>>Is not puffed up,
>>Doth not behave itself unseemly,
>>>Seeketh not its own,
>>>Is not provoked,
>>>Taketh not account of evil;
>>Rejoiceth not in unrighteousness,
>>But rejoiceth with the truth;
>>>Beareth all things,
>>>Believeth all things,
>>>Hopeth all things,
>>>Endureth all things.
>>>Love never faileth:

But whether there be prophecies, they shall be done away.

Whether there be tongues, they shall cease;
Whether there be knowledge, it shall be done away.
        For we know in part,
        And we prophesy in part;
        But when that which is perfect is come,
        That which is in part shall be done away.
            When I was a child,
            I spake as a child,
            I felt as a child,
            I thought as a child;
        Now that I am become a man,
        I have put away childish things.
        For now we see in a mirror darkly,
            But then face to face;
            Now I know in part,
But then shall I know fully, even as also I was fully known.
            But now abideth
            FAITH, HOPE, LOVE.
            These three;
            And the greatest of these is
            LOVE.
        —*1 Corinthians 13, American Standard Revised Version.*

Exercise for Conversation and Study

This selection from the writings of the apostle Paul is worthy of careful study both as to thought and style of expression. It would be well to memorize it; and above all to practice its principles. The language is simple and direct. It does not abound with beautiful figures, for like love itself, it needs no adornment. Drill carefully on this selection until you can read it with the spirit and the understanding also.

THE CHARMS OF THE MOUNTAINS

> "*They that trust in the Lord shall be as Mount Zion, Which can not be removed, but abideth forever.*"

1. There is a charm connected with mountains, so powerful that the merest mention of them, the merest sketch of their magnificent features, kindles the imagination, and carries the spirit at once into the bosom of their enchanted regions. How the mind is filled with their vast solitude! How the inward eye is fixed on their silent, their sublime, their everlasting peaks! How our hearts bound to the music of their solitary cries, to the tinkle of their gushing rills, to the sound of their cataracts! How inspiriting are the odors that breathe from the upland turf, from the rock-hung flower, from the hoary and solemn pine! How beautiful are those lights and shadows thrown abroad, and that fine, transparent haze which is diffused over the valleys and lower slopes, as over a vast, inimitable picture!

2. At this season of the year [autumn] the ascents of our mountains are most practicable. The heat of summer has dried up the moisture with which winter rains saturate the spongy turf of the hollows; and the atmosphere, clear and settled, admits of the most extensive prospects. Whoever has not ascended our mountains knows little of the beauties of this beautiful island. Whoever has not climbed their long and healthy ascents, and seen the trembling mountain flowers, and glowing moss, the richly-tinted lichens at his feet; and scented the fresh aroma of the uncultivated sod, and of spicy shrubs; and heard the bleat of the flock across their solitary expanses, and the wild cry of the mountain plover, the raven, or the eagle; and seen the rich and russet hues of distant slopes and eminences, the livid gashes of ravines and precipices, the white, glittering line of falling waters, and the cloud tumultuously whirling round the lofty summit; and then stood panting on

YOSEMITE VALLEY, CALIFORNIA

that summit, and beheld the clouds alternately gather and break over a thousand giant peaks and ridges of every varied hue, but all silent as images of eternity; and cast his gaze over lakes and forests, and smoking towns, and wide lands, to the very ocean, in all their gleaming and reposing beauty—knows nothing of the treasures of pictorial wealth which his own country possesses.

3. But when we let loose the imagination from even these splendid scenes, and give it free charter to range through the far more glorious ridges of continental mountains,—through Alps, Apennines, or Andes,—how is it possessed and absorbed by all the awful magnificence of their scenery and character! The skyward and inaccessible pinnacles, the

> "Palaces where Nature thrones
> Sublimity in icy halls,"

the dark Alpine forests, the savage rocks and precipices, the fearful and unfathomable chasms filled with the sound of ever-precipitating waters; the cloud, the silence, the avalanche, the cavernous gloom, the terrible visitations of heaven's concentrated lightning, darkness, and thunder; or the sweeter features of living, rushing streams, spicy odors of flowers and shrub, fresh, spirit-elating breezes sounding through the dark pine grove; the ever-varying lights and shadows and aerial hues; the wide prospects, and, above all, the simple inhabitants!

4. We delight to think of the people of mountainous regions; we please our imagination with their picturesque and quiet abodes; with their peaceful, secluded lives, striking and unvarying costumes, and primitive manners. We involuntarily give to the mountaineer heroic and elevated qualities. He lives amongst noble objects, and must imbibe some of their nobility; he lives amongst the elements of poetry, and must be poetical; he lives where his fellow beings are far, far separated from their kind, and surrounded by the sternness and the perils of savage nature; his social affec-

tions must therefore be proportionately concentrated, his home ties lively and strong; but, more than all, he lives within the barriers, the strongholds, the very last refuge which Nature herself has reared to preserve alive liberty in the earth, to preserve to man his highest hopes, his noblest emotions, his dearest treasures, his faith, his freedom, his health, and his home. How glorious do those mountain ridges appear when we look upon them as the unconquerable abodes of free hearts; as the stern, heaven-built walls from which the few, the feeble, the persecuted, the despised, the helpless child, the delicate woman, have from age to age, in their last perils, in all their weaknesses and emergencies, when power and cruelty were ready to swallow them up, looked down and beheld the million waves of despotism break at their feet; have seen the rage of murderous armies and tyrants, the blasting spirit of ambition, fanaticism, and crushing domination recoil from their bases in despair. "Thanks be to God for mountains!" is often the exclamation of my heart as I trace the history of the world. From age to age they have been the last friends of man. In a thousand extremities they have saved him. What great hearts have throbbed in their defiles from the days of Leonidas to those of Andreas Hofer! What lofty souls, what tender hearts, what poor and persecuted creatures have they sheltered in their stony bosoms from the weapons and tortures of their fellow men!

"Avenge, O Lord, Thy slaughtered saints, whose bones
Lie scattered on the Alpine mountains cold!"

was the burning exclamation of Milton's agonized and indignant spirit, as he beheld those sacred bulwarks of freedom for once violated by the disturbing demons of the earth; and the sound of his fiery and lamenting appeal to Heaven will be echoed in every generous soul to the end of time.

5. Thanks be to God for mountains! The variety which they impart to the glorious bosom of our planet were no small advan-

tage; the beauty which they spread out to our vision in their woods and waters, their crags and slopes, their clouds and atmospheric hues, were a splendid gift; the sublimity which they pour into our deepest souls from their majestic aspects; the poetry which breathes from their streams, and dells, and airy heights, from the sweet abodes, the garb and manners of their inhabitants, the songs and legends which have awaked in them, were a proud heritage to imaginative minds;—but what are all these when the thought comes that without mountains the spirit of man must have bowed to the brutal and the base, and probably have sunk to the monotonous level of the unvaried plain.

6. When I turn my eyes upon the map of the world, and behold how wonderfully the countries where our faith was nurtured, where our liberties were generated, where our philosophy and literature, the fountains of our intellectual grace and beauty, sprang up, were as distinctly walled out by God's hand with mountain ramparts from the eruptions and interruptions of barbarism, as if at the especial prayer of the early fathers of man's destinies,—I am lost in an exulting admiration. Look at the bold barriers of Palestine! See how the infant liberties of Greece were sheltered from the vast tribes of the uncivilized North by the heights of Hæmus and Rhodope! Behold how the Alps describe their magnificent crescent, inclining their opposite extremities to the Adriatic and Tyrrhene Seas, locking up Italy from the Gallic and Teutonic hordes till the power and spirit of Rome had reached their maturity, and she had opened the wide forest of Europe to the light, spread far her laws and language, and planted the seeds of many mighty nations!

7. Thanks be to God for mountains! Their colossal firmness seems almost to break the current of time itself. The geologist in them searches for traces of the earlier world; and it is there, too, that man, resisting the revolutions of lower regions, retains through innumerable years his habits and his rights. While a multitude of changes has remolded the people of Europe, while languages,

and laws, and dynasties, and creeds have passed over it, like shadows over the landscape, the children of the Kelt and the Goth, who fled to the mountains a thousand years ago, are found there now, and show us in face and figure, in language and garb, what their fathers were,—show us a fine contrast with the modern tribes dwelling below and around them; and show us, moreover, how adverse is the spirit of the mountain to mutability, and that there the fiery heart of freedom is found forever.

—*William Howitt.*

Exercise for Conversation and Study

Where are the mountains situated that are spoken of in this lesson? Were religious exercises and worship connected with mountains in Bible times? Give examples. What is the standard formula of expression for this lesson? Point out any deviations. Are there many figures of speech in the lesson? What kinds of figures?

Modulation

Drill on the expression for stanzas 6 and 7; especially on the oft-repeated exclamation, "Thanks be to God for mountains!"

Figures of Speech

Make a list of the figures previously studied, which are contained in this lesson, and also indicate their rhetorical value.

Word Study

1. cataracts
1. inimitable
2. autumn
2. saturate
2. tumultously
3. Apennines
3. inaccessible
3. pinnacles
4. picturesque
4. proportionately
4. agonized
4. bulwark
5. atmospheric
5. imaginative
6. eruptions
6. Adriatic
7. geologist
7. dynasties

THE MOUNTAINS

> *"As the mountains are round about Jerusalem,*
> *So the Lord is round about His people from henceforth,*
> *Even forever."*

1. God loves the mountains. Since earth's primal days,
   When puny man awoke to light and life,
   His steps have haunted all their mystic ways,
   Above, remote from petty human strife.
   Man's monuments endure but for a day,
   But these eternal in their strength alway.

2. How little all things human builded seem!
   The marble pomp of proud, imperial Rome;
   The Tower of Babel, but a madman's dream;
   The boast of Grecian art, St. Peter's dome,
   The pigmy pyramids, the Pharaoh's pride,
   How like to motes our mighty peaks beside!

3. We proudly choose some fondly cherished spot,
   And rear our shafts for future eyes to see.
   A little time, and lo! our works are not;
   They perish as the leaves that fall, but ye
   Have stood in strength since immemorial time,
   And still shall stand, forever more sublime.

4. Beloved by Nature fond, the sun's first rays
   Bask on each crown in ecstasy of bliss,
   With soft caress, and his last lingering blaze
   The towering purple summits softly kiss,
   Ere yet he sinks within the golden west
   And leaves the world to solitude and rest.

5. The mountains have been Freedom's safe retreat
    From tyranny since time's first early dawn;
   Here Liberty has fled with bleeding feet
    When in the plain all light and hope had flown;
   And standing proudly on the towering height
   Has bid defiance to the tyrant's might.

6. O mighty peaks, so all supremely grand!
    Springing to meet the azure vault above,
   Warding from storm the slumbering, peaceful land,
    Bending o'er all with tender, ceaseless love;
   Watch still, mute sentries, set by Him on high
   To guard us during life and point us to the sky.
   —*Howard T. Lee.*

Modulation

Determine the style and standard formula for this poem.

Figures of Speech

Point out the figures and classify them.

FIGURES OF SPEECH
III. FIGURES BASED ON CONTRAST

I. *Antithesis.*—It consists in putting in juxtaposition two things unlike so that each will appear more striking by the contrast.

Examples.—"To be a blessing, and not a curse." "The prodigal robs his heir, the miser robs himself."

Rule.—In antithesis the contrasted ideas should be expressed by similar constructions; nouns should be contrasted with nouns, adjectives with adjectives, verbs with verbs, and so on; and the arrangement of the words in the contrasted clauses should be as nearly alike as possible; as,—

1. "Flattery brings friends; truth brings foes."
2. "Enemies in war; in peace, friends."

3. "Forewarned; forearmed."

Value of Antithesis.—The effect of this figure arises chiefly from the fact that an object or idea appears more striking when it stands side by side with its opposite. White appears whiter when bordered with black; sound seems louder when followed by silence. If, therefore, we wish to give a thought special emphasis, we can employ no more effective method than to place it in contrast with its opposite.

Examples of Antithesis:—
1. Sink or swim, live or die, survive or perish.
2. She is a help, not a hindrance.
3. The rich man complains aloud; the poor man repines in secret.
4. They that sow in tears shall reap in joy.
5. He loves the whole human family, and hates to see the least member of it injured.
6. As we wax hot in faction, in battle we grow cold.

II. *Euphemism.*—It is a softened way of saying what would be disagreeable or offensive if told in plain language. It is usually based on some other figure; as, synecdoche, metonymy, metaphor. Thus, "Our friend Lazarus sleepeth," instead of saying plainly, "Lazarus is dead."

III. *Irony.*—It is language which, taken literally, expresses the contrary of what is meant. The real drift of the speaker is seen in his tone or manner. Thus, Elijah said to the prophets of Baal, "Cry aloud, for he is a god."

Value of Irony.—These figures by stating not what is meant, but something else which suggests it, produce a livelier impression than does the direct statement. Moreover, the surprise, arising from finding that words may convey a meaning so different from that which they literally bear, or one so skillfully interwoven with it, interests and delights the reader.

—*Adapted from William's "Composition and Rhetoric."*

THE LAUNCHING OF THE SHIP

Expression; Standard Formula.—Quality, *pure tone;* pitch, *moderate to high;* force, *moderate to loud;* rate, *moderate.*

1. All is finished, and at length
     Has come the bridal day
   Of beauty and of strength.
   To-day the vessel shall be launched!
   With fleecy clouds the sky is blanched,
     And o'er the bay,
   Slowly, in all his splendors bright,
   The great sun rises to behold the sight.

2. The ocean old,
   Centuries old,
   Strong as youth and as uncontrolled,
     Paces restless to and fro,
   Up and down the sands of gold.
   His beating heart is not at rest;
   And far and wide
     With ceaseless flow
     His beard of snow
   Heaves with the heaving of his breast.

3. He waits impatient for his bride.
   There she stands,
   With her foot upon the sands,
   Decked with flags and streamers gay,
   In honor of her marriage day,
   Her snow-white signals fluttering, blending,
   Round her like a veil descending,
   Ready to be
   The bride of the gray old sea.

4. Then the master,
   With a gesture of command,
   Waved his hand.
   And at the word,
   Loud and sudden there was heard,
   All around them and below,
   The sound of hammers, blow on blow,
   Knocking away the shores and spurs.
   And see! she stirs!
   She starts! she moves! she seems to feel
   The thrill of life along her keel!
   And, spurning with her foot the ground,
   With one exulting, joyous bound,
   She leaps into the ocean's arms!

5. And lo, from the assembled crowd
   There rose a shout, prolonged and loud,
   That to the ocean seemed to say,
   "Take her, O Bridegroom, old and gray,
   Take her to thy protecting arms,
   With all her youth and all her charms!"
   How beautiful she is! How fair
   She lies within those arms, that press
   Her form with many a soft caress
   Of tenderness and watchful care!
   Sail forth into the sea, O Ship!
   Through wind and wave, right onward steer;
   The moistened eye, the trembling lip,
   Are not the signs of doubt and fear.

6. Thou, too, sail on, O Ship of State!
   Sail on, O Union, strong and great!
   Humanity, with all its fears,
   With all the hopes of future years,

Is hanging breathless on thy fate.
We know what Master laid thy keel—
What Workman wrought thy ribs of steel—
Who made each mast and sail and rope;
What anvils rang, what hammers beat;
In what a forge, and what a heat,
Were shaped the anchors of thy hope.

7. Fear not each sound and shock—
'Tis of the wave, and not the rock;
'Tis but the flapping of the sail,
And not a rent made by the gale.
In spite of false lights on the shore,
Sail on, nor fear to breast the sea.
Our hearts, our hopes, are all with thee;
Our hearts, our hopes, our prayers, our tears,
Our faith triumphant o'er our fears,
Are all with thee—are all with thee!
—*Henry Wadsworth Longfellow.*

Modulation

The above poem furnishes an excellent opportunity for *pure-tone* expression, ranging from moderate to high pitch; and from moderate to a loud force. The rate for the most part is moderate. Drill thoroughly. Imagine that you behold the scene.

Figures of Speech

This lesson abounds with figures. Review the lessons on figures of speech. Write a list of figures contained in this lesson and classify them. In the second stanza we are told that the ocean "paces restless to and fro," and has a "beating heart" and "beard of snow" which "heaves with the heaving of his breast." What did the poet see that caused him to speak thus? Do these affirmed comparisons make the scene described more vivid?

FIGURES OF SPEECH
IV. GENERAL EXERCISES ON FIGURES

Name the figure or figures in each of the following sentences, and then express the meaning in plain language. Also point out and correct any errors in the use or form of the figures.
1. The heavens are veined with fire.
2. The Lord is my Rock.
3. Nothing succeeds like success.
4. He could scarcely earn enough to keep body and soul together.
5. She thought of her child as a flower of the field cut down and withered in the midst of its sweetness.
6. The old man leaned his silver head against the breast of youth.
7. The keen morning air bites our faces and hands.
8. A cloud lay cradled near the setting sun.
9. The mountains and the valleys their joyous voices raise.
10. The sun smiled far over the summer sea.
11. Fair laughs the morn and soft the zephyr blows.
12. His feet are nearing the grave.
13. I saw their thousand years of snow.
14. Solitude sometimes is best society.
15. There is a tide in the affairs of men, which, taken at the flood, leads on to fortune.
16. A friend can not be known in prosperity, and an enemy can not be hidden in adversity.
17. This noble passion, child of integrity, hath from my soul wiped the black scruples.
18. I think our country sinks beneath the yoke.
19. Uneasy lies the head that wears a crown.
20. What saw the winter moon that night as its beams struggled through the rain?
21. Till Love and Joy look round and call the earth their own.
22. A yell that rent the firmament from all the town arose.
23. That heart never melted at the concourse of sweet sounds.
24. The world is the chessboard, the pieces are the phenomena of the universe, the rules of the game are the laws of nature.

25. Love, though deep as the sea, will wither as the rose.
26. Choose and eat; there is life in the one and death in the other.
27. France was torn by internal strife.
28. Words were given us to conceal our thoughts.
29. The spring sun was setting, and it flung a crimson flush over the blue waters and white houses.
30. These boys will grow to be men, and will drag the heavy artillery along the dusty roads of life.
31. Their souls rose on the ardor of prayer like Elijah ascending to heaven.
32. Smiles are the channels of future tears.
33. The soft snow came; it seemed as if nature had let fall its handkerchief to hide the earth.
34. Diligence is the mother of good luck, and God gives all things to industry.
35. We may be sure that confidence sat undisturbed upon his brow.
36. Time writes no wrinkles on thine azure brow.

—*Adapted from William's "Composition and Rhetoric."*

A VIRTUOUS WOMAN

"A prudent wife is from the Lord."

1. Who can find a virtuous woman?
   For her price is far above rubies.
   The heart of her husband doth safely trust in her,
   So that he shall have no need of spoil.
   She will do him good and not evil
   All the days of her life.

2. She seeketh wool and flax,
   And worketh willingly with her hands.
   She is like the merchants' ships;
   She bringeth her food from afar.
   She riseth also while it is yet night,
   And giveth meat to her household,
   And a portion to her maidens.

3. She considereth a field and buyeth it;
   With the fruit of her hands she planteth a vineyard.
   She girdeth her loins with strength,
   And strengtheneth her arms.
   She perceiveth that her merchandise is good:
   Her candle goeth not out by night.

4. She layeth her hand to the spindle,
   And her hands hold the distaff.
   She stretcheth out her hand to the poor;
   Yea, she reacheth forth her hands to the needy,
   She is not afraid of the snow for her household,
   For all her household are clothed with scarlet.
   She maketh herself coverings of tapestry;
   Her clothing is silk and purple.

5. Her husband is known in the gates,
   When he sitteth among the elders of the land.

She maketh fine linen and selleth it;
And delivereth girdles unto the merchant.
Strength and honor are her clothing;
And she shall rejoice in time to come.

6. She openeth her mouth with wisdom;
And in her tongue is the law of kindness.
She looketh well to the ways of her household,
And eateth not the bread of idleness.
Her children rise up, and call her blessed;
Her husband also, and he praiseth her:
"Many daughters have done virtuously,
But thou excellest them all."

7. Favor is deceitful, and beauty is vain:
But a woman that feareth the Lord, she shall be praised.
Give her of the fruit of her hands,
And let her works praise her in the gates.
—*Solomon.*

Exercise for Conversation and Study

For what purpose was Eve created? Is there a distinct sphere for woman's activities as well as for man's? Enumerate the virtues and activities of a virtuous woman as described by Solomon. Name some of the virtuous women of Bible times; of modern times.

Modulation and Figures of Speech

Read with proper expression "The Winged Worshipers," page 48, and the "Ode to a Waterfowl," page 63.

Point out the figures of speech found in these poems and classify them.

THE TRUE DIGNITY OF LABOR

"Six days shalt thou labor and do all thy work."
"The sleep of a laboring man is sweet."

1. From the foundation of the world there has been a tendency to look down upon labor, and upon those who live by it, with contempt as though it were something mean and ignoble. This is one of those vulgar prejudices which have arisen from considering everything vulgar that is peculiar to the multitude.

2. Because the multitude have been suffered to remain too long rude and ignorant, everything associated with their condition has been confounded with the circumstances of this condition. The multitude were, in their rudeness and ignorance, mean in the public estimation, and the labor of their hands was held to be mean, too.

3. Nay, it has been said that labor is the result of God's primary curse pronounced on man for his disobedience. But that is a great mistake. God told Adam that the ground was cursed for his sake; but not that his labor was cursed. He told him that in the sweat of his face he should eat his bread till he returned to the ground. But so far from labor partaking of the curse, it was given him as the means of triumphing over the curse.

4. The ground was to produce thorns and thistles, but labor was to extirpate these thorns and thistles, and to cover the face of the earth with fruit trees and bounteous harvests. And labor has done this: labor has already converted the earth, so far as its surface is concerned, from a wilderness into a paradise.

5. Man eats his bread in the sweat of his face; but is there any bread so sweet as that, when he has only nature to contend with, and not the false arrangements of his fellow men? So far is labor from being a curse—so far is it from being a disgrace—it is the very principle which, like the winds of the air, or the agitation of the sea, keeps the world in health. It is the very lifeblood of so-

ciety, stirring in all its veins, and diffusing vigor and enjoyment through the whole system.

6. Without man's labor, God had created the world in vain! Without our labor, all life, except that of the rudest and most savage kind, must perish. Arts, civilization, refinement, and religion must perish. Labor is the grand pedestal of God's blessings upon earth; it is more—like man and the world itself—it is the offspring and the work of God.

7. All honor then to labor, the offspring of Deity; the most ancient of ancients, sent forth by the Almighty into these nether worlds as the most noble of nobles! Honor to that divine principle which has filled the earth with all the comforts, and joys, and affluence that it possesses, and is undoubtedly the instrument of happiness wherever life is found.

8. Without labor, what is there? Without it, there were no world itself. Whatever we see or perceive—in heaven or on the earth—is the product of labor. The sky above us, the ground beneath us, the air we breathe, the sun, the moon, the stars—what are they?—The product of labor. They are the labors of the Omnipotent, and all our labors are but a continuance of His. Our work is a divine work. We carry on what God began.

9. What a glorious spectacle is that of the labor of man upon the earth! It includes everything in it that *is* glorious. Look round, my friends, and tell me what you see that is worth seeing that is not the work of your hands, and the hands of your fellows —the multitude of all ages?

10. What is it that felled the ancient forests and cleared vast morasses of other ages? that makes green fields smile in the sun, and corn, rustling in the breezes of heaven, whisper of plenty and domestic joy? What raised first the hut, and then the cottage, and then the palace? What filled all these with food and furniture —with food simple and also costly; with furniture of infinite variety, from the three-legged stool to the most magnificent cabinet

and the regal throne? What made glass, and dyed it with all the hues of rainbows or of summer sunsets? What constructed presses and books, and filled up the walls of libraries, every inch of which contained a mass of latent light hoarded for the use of ages?

11. What took the hint from the split walnut-shell which some boy floated on the brook, and set on the flood the first boat, and then the ship, and has scattered these glorious children of man, the water-walking ships, over all the oceans of the world, and filled them with the produce of all lands, and the machinery of profoundest inventions? What has made the wide sea like a great city street, where merchants are going to and fro full of eager thoughts of self-accumulation, but not the less full of international blessings?

12. What has made the land like one great garden, laid down its roads that run like veins to every portion of the system of life, cut its canals, cast up its lines of railways, and driven along them, in fire and vapor, the awful but beneficial dragons of modern enterprise? What has piled up all our cities with their glittering and exhaustless wealth, their splendid utensils, their paintings, their mechanic wonders, all serving domestic life, and its beloved fireside delights. Labor! labor! labor! It is labor, and your labor, men of the multitude, that has done it all!

13. True, the wise ones tell us that it is intellect that has done it. And all honor to intellect! It is not you nor I, fellow workers, who will attempt to rob the royal power of intellect of one iota of his renown. Intellect is also a glorious gift of the Divinity—a divine principle in the earth. We set intellect at the head of labor, and bid it lead the way to all wonders and discoveries; but we know that intellect can not go alone. Intellect can not separate itself from labor.

14. Intellect has also its labor; and in its most abstract and ethereal form can not develop itself without the co-operation of its twin brother, labor. When intellect exerts itself—when it thinks, and invents, and discovers—it then labors. Through the medium

of labor it does all that it does; and upon labor it is perfectly dependent to carry out all its mechanical operations. Intellect is the head—labor, the right hand. Take away the hand, and the head is a magazine of knowledge and fire that is sealed up in eternal darkness. Such are the relationships of labor and intellect.
—*William Howitt.*

Exercise for Conversation and Study

Which of the Ten Commandments enjoins labor upon man? Commit to memory this commandment, and tell where in the Scriptures it is recorded. Did Christ while on earth set man an example in the matter of physical labor? What trade did He learn? What trade did the apostle Paul work at while he was preaching the gospel? What advantage is it to a minister of the gospel to have the knowledge of a trade? What was Adam's occupation before he sinned? What did he do after he had sinned? What did his two sons, Cain and Abel, do? Gen. 4:1, 2.

Modulation

Compare this piece with the one entitled "Work," found on page 157, as regards its style of expression. Determine the standard formula of expression of both. Drill on "Work" until you can give it good expression.

Figures of Speech

Select and classify the figures in both pieces.

Word Study

1. foundation
1. prejudices
2. associated
2. estimation
3. triumphing
4. extirpate
5. agitation
5. system
6. civilization
6. pedestal
7. nether
8. Omnipotent
9. spectacle
10. morasses
11. international
12. canals
13. discoveries
14. ethereal

A HUMAN BEING WITH NOTHING TO DO

"Why stand ye here all the day idle?"

1. Most miserable, worthy of most profound pity, is such a being! The most insignificant object in nature becomes a source of envy; the birds warble on every tree in ecstasy of joy; the tiny flower, hidden from all eyes, sends forth its fragrance of full happiness; the mountain stream dashes along with a sparkle and murmur of pure delight. The object of their creation is accomplished, and their life gushes forth in harmonic work.

2. O plant! O stream! worthy of admiration to the wretched idler! Here are powers ye never dreamed of—faculties divine, eternal; a head to think, but nothing to concentrate the thoughts; a heart to love, but no object to bathe with the living tide of affection; a hand to do, but no work to be done; talents unexercised, capacities undeveloped, a human life thrown away—wasted as water poured forth in the desert.

3. Who can describe the fearful void of such an existence, the yearnings for object, the self-reproach for wasted powers, the weariness of daily life, the loathing of pleasure, of frivolity, and the fearful consciousness of deadening life—of spiritual paralysis which hinders all response to human interest—when enthusiasm ceases to arouse, and noble deeds no longer call forth the tear of joy; when the world becomes a blank, humanity a far sound, and no life is left but the heavy, benumbing weight of personal hopelessness and desolation.

4. Happier far is the toiling drudge who coins body and soul into the few poor shillings that can only keep his family in a long starvation. He has hope unceasingly to lighten him, a duty to perform, a spark of love within that can not die; and wretched, weary, and unhuman as his life may be, it is of royal worth—it is separated by the immeasurable distance of life and death, from the poor wretch who is cursed for having no work to do.

—*Selected.*

Word Study

1. miserable	2. talents	3. enthusiasm
1. profound	2. unexercised	3. humanity
1. insignificant	2. capacities	3. benumbing
1. ecstasy	3. existence	3. personal
1. accomplished	3. yearnings	3. desolation
1. harmonic	3. frivolity	4. starvation
2. admiration	3. consciousness	4. unceasingly
2. faculties	3. spiritual	4. immeasurable
2. concentrate	3. paralysis	4. separated

LABOR

Expression; Standard Formula.—Quality, *pure tone*; pitch, *moderate* to *high*; force, *moderate* to *loud*; rate, *moderate*.

1. Labor is rest from the sorrows that greet us;
Rest from all petty vexations that meet us,
Rest from the sin-promptings that ever entreat us,
Rest from world-sirens that lure us to ill.
Work—and pure slumbers shall wait on thy pillow,
Work—thou shalt ride over Care's coming billow;
Lie not down wearied 'neath Woe's weeping willow!
Work with a stout heart and resolute will!

2. Labor is health! Lo, the husbandman reaping,
How through his veins goes the life-current leaping;
How his strong arm, in its stalwart pride sweeping,
True as a sunbeam the swift sickle guides.
Labor is wealth:—in the sea the pearl groweth,
Rich the queen's robe from the frail cocoon floweth,
From the fine acorn the strong forest bloweth,
Temple and statue the marble block hides.

3. Droop not, though shame, sin, and anguish are round thee,
Bravely fling off the cold chain that hath bound thee;
Look to yon pure heaven smiling beyond thee;
   Rest not content in thy darkness—a clod!
Work for some good, be it ever so slowly;
Cherish some flower, be it ever so lowly;
Labor!—all labor is noble and holy;
   Let thy great deeds be thy prayer to thy God.

4. Pause not to dream of the future before us;
Pause not to weep the wild cares that come o'er us:
Hark, how Creation's deep, musical chorus,
   Unintermitting goes up into heaven!
Never the ocean wave falters in flowing;
Never the little seed stops in its growing;
More and more richly the rose heart keeps glowing,
   Till from its nourishing stem it is riven.

5. "Labor is worship!" the robin is singing,
"Labor is worship!" the wild bee is ringing.
Listen! that eloquent whisper upspringing,
   Speaks to thy soul from out Nature's great heart.
From the dark cloud flows the life-giving shower;
From the rough sod blows the soft-breathing flower;
From the small insect, the rich coral bower:
   Only man, in the plan, ever shrinks from his part.

6. Labor is life!—'tis the still water faileth;
Idleness ever despaireth, bewaileth;
Keep the watch wound, for the dark rust assaileth!
   Flowers droop and die in the stillness of noon.
Labor is glory!—the flying cloud lightens;
Only the waving wing changes and brightens;
Idle hearts only the dark future frightens;
   Play the sweet keys would'st thou keep them in tune!

                        —*Frances S. Osgood.*

THANATOPSIS

"The last enemy that shall be destroyed is death."

1. To him who, in the love of Nature, holds
Communion with her visible forms, she speaks
A various language; for his gayer hours
She has a voice of gladness, and a smile
And eloquence of beauty; and she glides
Into his darker musings with a mild
And healing sympathy, that steals away
Their sharpness ere he is aware.

2.   When thoughts
Of the last bitter hour come like a blight
Over thy spirit, and sad images
Of the stern agony, and shroud, and pall,
And breathless darkness, and the narrow house,
Make thee to shudder, and grow sick at heart;—
Go forth under the open sky, and list
To Nature's teachings, while from all around—
Earth and her waters, and the depths of air—
Comes a still voice—Yet a few days, and thee
The all-beholding sun shall see no more
In all his course; nor yet in the cold ground,
Where thy pale form was laid, with many tears,
Nor in the embrace of ocean shall exist
Thy image.

3.   Earth, that nourished thee, shall claim
Thy growth, to be resolved to earth again;
And, lost each human trace, surrendering up
Thine individual being shalt thou go
To mix forever with the elements,
To be a brother to the insensible rock

And to the sluggish clod, which the rude swain
Turns with his share and treads upon. The oak
Shall send his roots abroad, and pierce thy mold.

4.   Yet not to thy eternal resting place
Shalt thou retire alone—nor could'st thou wish
Couch more magnificent. Thou shalt lie down
With patriarchs of the infant world—with kings,
The powerful of the earth—the wise, the good,
Fair forms, and hoary seers of ages past,
All in one mighty sepulcher.

5.   The hills,
Rock-ribbed and ancient as the sun,—the vales,
Stretching in pensive quietness between;
The venerable woods; rivers that move
In majesty, and the complaining brooks,
That make the meadows green; and, poured round all,
Old ocean's gray and melancholy waste,—
Are but the solemn decorations all
Of the great tomb of man.

6.   The golden sun,
The planets, all the infinite host of heaven,
Are shining on the sad abodes of death,
Through the still lapse of ages. All that tread
The globe are but a handful to the tribes
That slumber in its bosom. Take the wings
Of morning, pierce the Barcan wilderness,
Or lose thyself in the continuous woods
Where rolls the Oregon, and hears no sound
Save his own dashings—yet—the dead are there;
And millions in those solitudes, since first
The flight of years began, have laid them down
In their last sleep—the dead reign there alone.

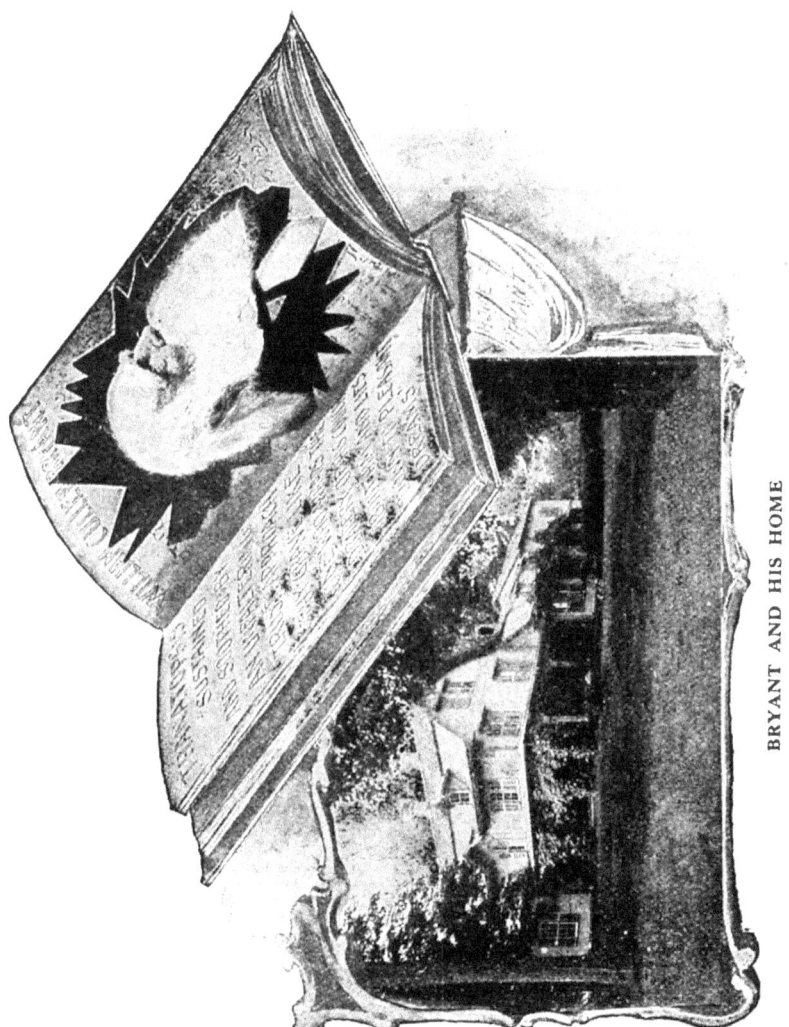

BRYANT AND HIS HOME

7. So shalt thou rest; and what if thou withdraw
In silence from the living, and no friend
Take note of thy departure? All that breathe
Will share thy destiny. The gay will laugh
When thou art gone, the solemn brood of care
Plod on, and each one as before will chase
His favorite phantom; yet all these shall leave
Their mirth and their employments, and shall come
And make their bed with thee. As the long train
Of ages glides away, the sons of men,
The youth in life's green spring, and he who goes
In the full strength of years, matron and maid,
The speechless babe, and the gray-headed man,—
Shall, one by one, be gathered to thy side,
By those who in their turn shall follow them.

8. So live, that when thy summons comes to join
The innumerable caravan which moves
To that mysterious realm where each shall take
His chamber in the silent halls of death,
Thou go not, like the quarry slave at night,
Scourged to his dungeon; but, sustained and soothed
By an unfaltering trust, approach thy grave
Like one who wraps the drapery of his couch
About him, and lies down to pleasant dreams.

—*William Cullen Bryant.*

Figures of Speech

Explain the following expressions:—

1. Stern agony.
2. Sluggish clod.
3. Venerable woods.
4. Complaining brooks.
5. Melancholy waste.
6. Solemn brood of care.
7. Life's green spring.
8. Pale realms of shade.
9. Silent halls of death.

315

THE LOVING-KINDNESS OF JEHOVAH

"Yea, I have loved thee with an everlasting love: therefore with loving-kindness have I drawn thee."

Expression; Standard Formula.—Quality, *pure tone;* pitch, *moderate;* force, *moderate;* rate, *moderate.*

1. The earth is full of the loving-kindness of Jehovah.
    All His work is done in faithfulness.
    He loveth righteousness and justice. . . .
    Blessed is the nation whose God is Jehovah,
    The people whom He hath chosen for His own inheritance.

2. Behold, the eye of Jehovah is upon them that fear Him,
    Upon them that hope in His loving-kindness;
    To deliver their soul from death,
    And to keep them alive in famine.

3. Our soul hath waited for Jehovah;
    He is our help and our shield.
    For our heart shall rejoice in Him,
    Because we have trusted in His holy name.

4. I sought Jehovah, and He answered me,
    And delivered me from all my fears.
    They looked unto Him, and were radiant;
    And their faces shall never be confounded.
    This poor man cried, and Jehovah heard him,
    And saved him out of all his troubles.

5. The angel of the Lord encampeth round about them that fear Him,
    And delivereth them.
    O, taste and see that Jehovah is good:
    Blessed is the man that taketh refuge in Him.

6. O, fear Jehovah, ye His saints;
   For there is no want to them that fear Him.
   The young lions do lack, and suffer hunger;
   But they that seek Jehovah shall not want any good thing.

7. The righteous cried, and Jehovah heard,
   And delivered them out of all their troubles.
   Jehovah is nigh unto them that are of a broken heart,
   And saveth such as are of a contrite spirit.
   The Lord redeemeth the soul of His servants;
   And none of them that trust in Him shall be desolate.
   —*Selections from the Psalms.*

Figures of Speech

Bring to class a list of similes and metaphors selected from the Bible.

TIME

"Redeeming the time, because the days are evil."

1. Our time belongs to God. Every moment is His, and we are under the most solemn obligation to improve it to His glory. Of no talent He has given will He require a more strict account than of our time.

2. The value of time is beyond computation. Christ regarded every moment as precious, and it is thus that we should regard it. Life is too short to be trifled away. We have but a few days of probation in which to prepare for eternity. We have no time to waste, no time to devote to selfish pleasure, no time for the indulgence of sin. It is now that we are to form characters for the future, immortal life. It is now that we are to prepare for the searching judgment.

3. The human family have scarcely begun to live when they begin to die, and the world's incessant labor ends in nothingness unless a true knowledge in regard to eternal life is gained. The man who appreciates time as his working day will fit himself for a mansion and for a life that is immortal. It is well that he was born.

4. We are admonished to redeem the time. But time squandered can never be recovered. We can not call back even one moment. The only way in which we can redeem our time is by making the most of that which remains, by being co-workers with God in His great plan of redemption.

5. In him who does this, a transformation of character takes place. He becomes a son of God, a member of the royal family, a child of the heavenly King. He is fitted to be the companion of the angels.

6. Now is our time to labor for the salvation of our fellow men. There are some who think that if they give money to the cause of Christ, this is all they are required to do; the precious time in which they might do personal service for Him passes unimproved. But it is the privilege and duty of all who have health and strength to render to God active service. All are to labor in winning souls to Christ. Donations of money can not take the place of this.

7. Every moment is freighted with eternal consequences. We are to stand as minute men, ready for service at a moment's notice. The opportunity that is now ours to speak to some needy soul the word of life may never offer again. God may say to that one, "This night thy soul shall be required of thee," and through our neglect he may not be ready. In the great judgment day, how shall we render our account to God?

8. Life is too solemn to be absorbed in temporal and earthly matters, in a treadmill of care and anxiety for the things that are but an atom in comparison with the things of eternal interest.

Yet God has called us to serve Him in the temporal affairs of life. Diligence in this work is as much a part of true religion as is devotion. The Bible gives no indorsement of idleness. It is the greatest curse that afflicts our world. Every man and woman who is truly converted will be a diligent worker.

9. Upon the right improvement of our time depends our success in acquiring knowledge and mental culture. The cultivation of the intellect need not be prevented by poverty, humble origin, or unfavorable surroundings. Only let the moments be treasured. A few moments here and a few there, that might be frittered away in aimless talk; the morning hours so often wasted in bed; the time spent in traveling on trams or railway cars, or waiting at the station; the moments of waiting for meals, waiting for those who are tardy in keeping an appointment,—if a book were kept at hand, and these fragments of time were improved in study, reading, or careful thought, what might not be accomplished. A resolute purpose, persistent industry, and careful economy of time, will enable men to acquire knowledge and mental discipline which will qualify them for almost any position of influence and usefulness.

10. It is the duty of every Christian to acquire habits of order, thoroughness, and despatch. There is no excuse for slow bungling at work of any character. When one is always at work, and the work is never done, it is because mind and heart are not put into the labor. The one who is slow, and who works at a disadvantage, should realize that these are faults to be corrected. He needs to exercise his mind in planning how to use the time so as to secure the best results. By tact and method, some will accomplish as much work in five hours as another does in ten. Some who are engaged in domestic labor are always at work, not because they have so much to do, but because they do not plan so as to save time. By their slow, dilatory ways, they make much work out of very little. But all who will, may overcome these fussy, lingering habits.

In their work let them have a definite aim. Decide how long a time is required for a given task, and then bend every effort toward accomplishing the work in the given time. The exercise of the will power will make the hands move deftly.

11. Through lack of determination to take themselves in hand and reform, persons can become stereotyped in a wrong course of action; or by cultivating their powers they may acquire ability to do the very best of service. Then they will find themselves in demand anywhere and everywhere. They will be appreciated for all that they are worth.

12. By many children and youth, time is wasted that might be spent in carrying home burdens, and thus showing a loving interest in father and mother. The youth might take upon their strong young shoulders many responsibilities which some one must bear.

13. The life of Christ from His earliest years was a life of earnest activity. He lived not to please Himself. He was the Son of the infinite God, yet He worked at the carpenter's trade with His father Joseph. His trade was significant. He had come into the world as a character builder, and as such all His work was perfect. Into all His secular labor He brought the same perfection as into the characters He was transforming by His divine power. He is our pattern.

14. Parents should teach their children the value and right use of time. Teach them that to do something which will honor God and bless humanity is worth striving for. Even in their early years they can be missionaries for God.

15. Parents can not commit a greater sin than by allowing their children to have nothing to do. The children soon learn to love idleness, and they grow up shiftless, useless men and women. When they are old enough to earn their living, and find employment, they work in a lazy, droning way, yet expect to be paid as much as if they were faithful. There is a world-wide difference between this

class of workers and those who realize that they must be faithful stewards.

16. Indolent, careless habits, indulged in secular work, will be brought into the religious life, and will unfit one to do any efficient service for God. Many who through diligent labor might have been a blessing to the world, have been ruined through idleness. Lack of employment and of steadfast purpose opens the door to a thousand temptations. Evil companions and vicious habits deprave mind and soul, and the result is ruin for this life and for the life to come.

17. Whatever the line of work in which we engage, the word of God teaches us to be "not slothful in business; fervent in spirit; serving the Lord." "Whatsoever thy hand findeth to do, do it with thy might," "knowing that of the Lord ye shall receive the reward of the inheritance; for ye serve the Lord Christ."

—*Mrs. E. G. White.*

Figures of Speech

Find, in the Bible, illustrations of the following figures: allegory, parable, and the three degrees of personification. Explain the value of each.

Word Study

1. obligation
2. eternity
3. incessant
4. admonished
4. squandered
5. transformation
6. donations
7. freighted
8. indorsement
9. resolute
9. discipline
10. dilatory
10. decide
10. deftly
11. stereotyped
12. responsibilities
13. significant
14. missionaries
16. indolent
16. efficient
16. vicious

PAUL'S DEFENSE BEFORE KING AGRIPPA

"It shall be given you in that same hour what ye shall speak."

1. Then Agrippa said unto Paul, "Thou art permitted to speak for thyself." Then Paul stretched forth the hand, and answered for himself: "I think myself happy, King Agrippa, because I shall answer for myself this day before thee touching all the things whereof I am accused of the Jews: especially because I know thee to be expert in all customs and questions which are among the Jews: wherefore I beseech thee to hear me patiently.

2. "My manner of life from my youth, which was at the first among my own nation at Jerusalem, know all the Jews which knew me from the beginning, if they would testify, that after the most straitest sect of our religion I lived a Pharisee.

3. "And now I stand and am judged for the hope of the promise made of God unto our fathers: unto which promise our twelve tribes, instantly serving God day and night, hope to come. For which hope's sake, King Agrippa, I am accused of the Jews. Why should it be thought a thing incredible with you, that God should raise the dead?

4. "I verily thought with myself, that I ought to do many things contrary to the name of Jesus of Nazareth. Which thing I also did in Jerusalem; and many of the saints did I shut up in prison, having received authority from the chief priests; and when they were put to death, I gave my voice against them.

5. "And I punished them oft in every synagogue, and compelled them to blaspheme; and being exceedingly mad against them, I persecuted them even unto strange cities. Whereupon as I went to Damascus with authority and commission from the chief priests, at midday, O king, I saw in the way a light from heaven, above the brightness of the sun, shining round about me and them which journeyed with me.

6. "And when we were all fallen to the earth, I heard a voice

speaking unto me, and saying in the Hebrew tongue, 'Saul, Saul, why persecutest thou Me? It is hard for thee to kick against the pricks.' And I said, 'Who art Thou, Lord?'

7. "And He said, 'I am Jesus, whom thou persecutest. But rise, and stand upon thy feet: for I have appeared unto thee for this purpose, to make thee a minister and a witness both of these things which thou hast seen, and of those things in the which I will appear unto thee; delivering thee from the people, and from the Gentiles, unto whom now I send thee, to open their eyes, and to turn them from darkness to light, and from the power of Satan unto God, that they may receive forgiveness of sins, and inheritance among them which are sanctified by faith that is in Me.'

8. "Whereupon, O King Agrippa, I was not disobedient unto the heavenly vision: but showed first unto them of Damascus, and at Jerusalem, and throughout all the coasts of Judea, and then to the Gentiles, that they should repent and turn to God, and do works meet for repentance. For these causes the Jews caught me in the temple, and went about to kill me.

9. "Having therefore obtained help of God, I continue unto this day, witnessing both to small and great, saying none other things than those which the prophets and Moses did say should come; that Christ should suffer, and that He should be the first that should rise from the dead, and should show light unto the people, and to the Gentiles."

10. And as he thus spake for himself, Festus said with a loud voice, "Paul, thou art beside thyself; much learning doth make thee mad." But he said, "I am not mad, most noble Festus; but speak forth the words of truth and soberness. For the king knoweth of these things, before whom also I speak freely: for I am persuaded that none of these things are hidden from him; for this thing was not done in a corner. King Agrippa, believest thou the prophets? I know that thou believest."

11. Then Agrippa said unto Paul, "Almost thou persuadest me

to be a Christian." And Paul said, "I would to God, that not only thou, but also all that hear me this day, were both almost, and altogether such as I am, except these bonds."

12. And when he had thus spoken, the king rose up, and the governor, and Bernice, and they that sat with them: and when they were gone aside, they talked between themselves, saying, "This man doeth nothing worthy of death or of bonds." Then said Agrippa unto Festus, "This man might have been set at liberty, if he had not appealed unto Cæsar."

—*Bible—Acts 26.*

Exercise for Conversation and Study

By whom were the prophetic words at the beginning of this lesson uttered? Matt. 10: 16-20. How was the apostle Paul enabled to make this powerful defense before King Agrippa, if he had taken no thought as to what he should speak? Ex. 4: 10-12; Jer. 1: 6-9; John 14: 26. Was it foretold that Paul should be brought before kings to answer for his faith? Acts 9: 10-16. Who was Agrippa? Festus? Make an outline of Paul's speech. How did it affect Festus? Acts 26: 24. King Agrippa? Verses 27, 28. What style of expression did Paul use in making his defense? Read it as nearly as possible in the same style.

Figures of Speech

From the Bible select examples of antithesis and irony.

Word Study

1. Paul	4. authority	8. Gentiles
1. Agrippa	5. persecuted	9. Moses
2. religion	5. Damascus	10. Festus
2. Pharisee	6. Hebrew	11. persuadest
3. instantly	7. inheritance	12. governor
3. incredible	8. disobedient	12. liberty
4. Nazareth	8. Judea	12. Cæsar

APOSTROPHE TO THE OCEAN

"The sea is His, and He made it."

1. There is a pleasure in the pathless woods,
   There is a rapture on the lonely shore,
   There is a society where none intrudes,
   By the deep sea, and music in its roar.
   I love not man the less, but Nature more,
   From these our interviews, in which I steal
   From all I may be, or have been before,
   To mingle with the universe and feel
   What I can ne'er express, yet can not all conceal.

2. Roll on, thou deep and dark blue Ocean,—roll!
   Ten thousand fleets sweep over thee in vain;
   Man marks the earth with ruin,—his control
   Stops with the shore:—upon the watery plain
   The wrecks are all thy deed, nor doth remain
   A shadow of man's ravage, save his own,
   When for a moment, like a drop of rain,
   He sinks into the depths with bubbling groan,
   Without a grave, unknelled, uncoffined, and unknown.

   *　　*　　*　　*　　*　　*

3. The armaments which thunderstrike the walls
   Of rock-built cities, bidding nations quake,
   And monarchs tremble in their capitals;
   The oak leviathans, whose huge ribs make
   Their clay creator the vain title take
   Of lord of thee, and arbiter of war;
   These are thy toys, and, as the snowy flake,

NOTE.—From this point on, no drills are appended to the lessons; but the work should be continued, especially in modulation and figures of speech.

They melt into the yeast of waves, which mar
Alike the Armada's pride, or spoils of Trafalgar.

4. Thy shores are empires, changed in all save thee;
    Assyria, Greece, Rome, Carthage,—what are they?
Thy waters wasted them while they were free,
    And many a tyrant since; their shores obey
The stranger, slave, or savage; their decay
Has dried up realms to deserts; not so thou,
    Unchangeable save to thy wild waves' play;
Time writes no wrinkles on thine azure brow;
Such as creation's dawn beheld, thou rollest now.

5. Thou glorious mirror, where the Almighty's form
    Glasses itself in tempests; in all time,
Calm or convulsed; in breeze, or gale, or storm,
    Icing the pole, or in the torrid clime
    Dark heaving; boundless, endless, and sublime,
The image of Eternity, the throne
    Of the Invisible; even from out thy slime
The monsters of the deep are made; each zone
Obeys thee; thou goest forth, dread, fathomless, alone.

—*Lord Byron.*

DAILY PRAYER—MORNING

> *"My voice shalt Thou hear in the morning, O Lord; in the morning will I direct my prayer unto Thee, and will look up."*

1. The Scriptures of the Old Testament agree in enjoining prayer. Let no man call himself a Christian, who lives without giving a part of his life to this duty. We are not taught how often we must pray; but our Lord in teaching us to say, "Give us this day our daily bread," implies that we should pray daily. As to the particular hours to be given to this duty, every Christian may choose them for himself. Our religion is too liberal and spiritual to bind us to any place or hour of prayer. But there are parts of the day particularly favorable to this duty, and which, if possible, should be redeemed for it.

2. The first of these periods is the morning, which even nature seems to have pointed out to men of different religions as a fit time for offerings to the Divinity. In the morning our minds are not so much shaken by worldly cares and pleasures, as in other parts of the day. Retirement and sleep have helped to allay the violence of our feelings, to calm the feverish excitement so often produced by intercourse with men. The hour is a still one. The hurry and tumults of life are not begun, and we naturally share in the tranquillity around us. Having for so many hours lost hold on the world, we can banish it more easily from the mind, and worship with less divided attention. This, then, is a favorable time for approaching the invisible Author of our being, for strengthening the intimacy of our minds with Him, for thinking upon the future life, and for seeking those spiritual aids which we need in the labors and temptations of every day.

3. In the morning there is much to feed the spirit of devotion. It offers an abundance of thoughts, friendly to pious feeling. When we look on creation, what a happy and touching change do we wit-

ness! A few hours past, the earth was wrapt in gloom and silence. There seemed "a pause in nature." But now, a new flood of light has broken forth, and creation rises before us in fresher and brighter hues, and seems to rejoice as if it had just received birth from its Author.

4. The sun never sheds more cheerful beams, and never proclaims more loudly God's glory and goodness, than when he returns after the coldness and dampness of night, and awakens man and inferior animals to the various purposes of their being. A spirit of joy seems breathed over the earth through the sky. It requires little effort of imagination to read delight in the kindled clouds, or in the fields bright with dew. This is the time when we can best feel and bless the Power that said, "Let there be light," that "set a tabernacle for the sun" in the heavens, and made him the dispenser of fruitfulness and enjoyment through all regions.

5. If we next look at ourselves, what materials does the morning furnish for devout thought! At the close of the past day, we were exhausted by our labors, and unable to move without wearisome effort. Our minds were sluggish, and could not be held to the most interesting objects. From this state of exhaustion, we sank gradually into entire insensibility. Our limbs became motionless; our senses were shut as in death. Our thoughts were suspended, or only wandered confusedly and without aim. Our friends, and the universe, and God Himself were forgotten.

6. And what a change does the morning bring with it! On waking we find that sleep, the image of death, has silently infused into us a new life. The weary limbs are braced again. The dim eye has become bright and piercing. The mind is returned from the region of forgetfulness to its old possessions. Friends are met again with a new interest. We are again capable of devout sentiment, virtuous effort, and Christian hope. With what subjects of gratitude, then, does the morning furnish us! We can hardly recall the state of insensibility from which we have just

emerged, without a consciousness of our dependence, or think of the renovation of our powers and intellectual being, without feeling our obligation to God.

7. There is something very touching in the consideration, if we will fix our minds upon it, that God thought of us when we could not think; that He watched over us when we had no power to avert peril from ourselves; that He continued our vital motions, and in due time broke the chains of sleep, and set our imprisoned faculties free. How fit it is at this hour to raise to God the eyes that He has opened, and the arm that He has strengthened; to acknowledge His providence; to consecrate to Him the powers He has renewed! How fit that He should be the first object of the thoughts and affections that He has restored! How fit to employ in His praise the tongue He has loosed, and the breath that He has spared!

8. But the morning is a fit time for devotion, not only from its relation to the past night, but considered as the introduction of a new day. To a thinking mind, how natural at this hour are such reflections as the following: I am now to enter on a new period of my life, to start afresh in my course. I am to return to that world where I have often gone astray; to perform actions that will never be forgotten; to strengthen a character that will fit me for heaven or hell. I am this day to meet temptations that have often subdued me; I am to be entrusted again with opportunities of usefulness that I have often neglected. I am to influence the minds of others, to help in molding their characters, and in deciding the happiness of their present and future life. How uncertain is this day! What unseen dangers are before me! What unexpected changes may await me! It may be my last day! It will certainly bring me nearer to death and judgment!

9. Now, when entering on a period of life so important, yet so uncertain, how fit and natural is it, before we take the first step, to seek the favor of that Being on whom the lot of every day depends; to commit all our interests to His almighty and wise provi-

dence; to seek His blessing on our labors, and His succor in temptation, and to consecrate to His service the day that He raises upon us! This morning devotion not only agrees with the sentiments of the heart, but tends to make the day happy, useful, and virtuous. Having cast ourselves on the mercy and protection of the Almighty, we shall go forth with new confidence to the labors and duties that He imposes. Our early prayer will help to shed an odor of piety through the whole life. God, having first occupied, will more easily recur to our mind. Our first step will be in the right path, and we may hope a happy issue.

10. So fit and useful is morning devotion, it ought not to be omitted without necessity. If our circumstances will allow the privilege, it is a bad sign when no part of the morning is spent in prayer. If God find no place in our minds at that early and peaceful hour, He will hardly recur to us in the tumults of life. If the benefits of the morning do not soften us, we can hardly expect the heart to melt with gratitude through the day. If the world then rush in, and take possession of us, when we are at some distance and have had a respite from its cares, how can we hope to shake it off when we shall be in the midst of it, pressed and agitated by it on every side?

11. Let a part of the morning, if possible, be set apart to devotion; and to this end we should fix the hour of rising, so that we may have an early hour at our own disposal. Our piety is suspicious, if we can renounce, as too many do, the pleasures and benefits of early prayer, rather than forego the senseless indulgence of unnecessary sleep. What! we can rise early enough for business. We can anticipate the dawn, if a favorite pleasure or an uncommon gain requires the effort. But we can not rise, that we may bless our great Benefactor, that we may arm ourselves for the severe conflicts to which our principles are to be exposed. We are willing to rush into the world, without thanks offered, or a blessing sought. From a day thus begun, what ought we to expect but thoughtlessness and guilt! —*Channing.*

DAILY PRAYER—EVENING

> *"Evening, and morning, and at noon,
> will I pray, and cry aloud, and He
> shall hear my voice."*

1. Let us now consider another part of the day that is favorable to the duty of prayer; we mean the evening. This season, like the morning, is calm and quiet. Our labors are ended. The bustle of life is gone by. The distracting glare of the day has vanished. The darkness that surrounds us favors seriousness, composure, and solemnity. At night the earth fades from our sight, and nothing of creation is left us but the starry heavens, so vast, so magnificent, so serene, as if to guide our thoughts above all earthly things to God and immortality.

2. This period should in part be given to prayer, as it furnishes a variety of devotional topics and excitements. The evening is the close of an important division of time, and is therefore a fit and natural season for stopping and looking back on the day. And can we ever look back on a day that bears no witness to God, and lays no claim to our gratitude? Who is it that strengthens us for daily labor, gives us daily bread, continues our friends and common pleasures, and grants us the privilege of retiring, after the cares of the day, to a quiet and beloved home?

3. The review of the day will often suggest not only these ordinary benefits, but peculiar proofs of God's goodness, unlooked-for successes, singular concurrences of favorable events, singular blessings sent to our friends, or new and powerful aids to our own virtue, which call for peculiar thankfulness. And shall all these benefits pass away unnoticed? Shall we retire to repose as insensible as the wearied brute? How fit and natural is it to close with pious acknowledgment the day which has been filled with divine beneficence!

4. But the evening is the time to review, not only our blessings, but our actions. A reflecting mind will naturally remember at this hour that another day is gone, and to testify of us to our

Judge. How natural and useful to inquire what report it has carried to heaven! Perhaps we have the satisfaction of looking back on a day which in its general tenor has been innocent and pure, which, having begun with God's praise, has been spent in His presence; which has proved the reality of our principles in temptation; and shall such a day end without gratefully acknowledging Him in whose strength we have been strong, and to whom we owe the powers and opportunities of Christian improvement?

5. But no day will present to us recollections of purity unmixed with sin. Conscience, if suffered to inspect faithfully and speak plainly, will recount irregular desires, and defective motives, talents wasted and time misspent; and shall we let the day pass from us without penitently confessing our offenses to Him who has witnessed them, and who has promised pardon to true repentance? Shall we retire to rest with a burden of unlamented and unforgiven guilt upon our consciences? Shall we leave these stains to spread over and sink into the soul?

6. A religious recollection of our lives is one of the chief instruments of piety. If possible, no day should end without it. If we take no account of our sins on the day on which they are committed, can we hope that they will recur to us at a more distant period, that we shall watch against them to-morrow, or that we shall gain the strength to resist them, which we will not implore?

7. The evening is a fit time for prayer, not only as it ends the day, but as it immediately precedes the period of repose. The hour of activity having passed, we are soon to sink into insensibility and sleep. How fit that we resign ourselves to the care of that Being who never sleeps, to whom the darkness is as the light, and whose providence is our only safety! How fit to entreat Him that He would keep us to another day; or, if our bed should prove our grave, that He would give us a part in the resurrection of the just, and awake us to a purer and immortal life! Let our prayers, like the ancient sacrifices, ascend morning and evening. Let our days begin and end with God. —*Channing.*

HE CARETH

> *"Casting all your care upon Him,*
> *for He careth for you."*

1. What can it mean? Is it aught to Him
That the nights are long and the days are dim?
Can He be touched by the grief I bear,
Which saddens the heart and whitens the hair?
About His throne are eternal calms,
And the strong, glad music of happy psalms,
And bliss, unruffled by any strife.
How can He care for my little life?

2. And yet I want Him to care for me
While I live in this land where sorrows be.
When the lights die down from the paths I take,
When strength is feeble and friends forsake,
When love and music that once did bless
Have left me to silence and loneliness,
And my life-song changes to sobbing prayers—
Then my heart cries out for a God who cares.

3. When shadows hang over the whole day long,
And my spirit is bowed with shame and wrong,
When I am not good, and the deeper shade
Of conscious sin makes my heart afraid,
And this busy world has too much to do
To stay in its course to help me through,
And I long for a Saviour—can it be
That the God of the universe cares for me?

4. O, wonderful story of deathless love!
Each child is dear to that heart above.
He fights for me when I can not fight;
He comforts me in the gloom of night.

He lifts the burden, for He is strong;
He stills the sigh and awakes the song;
The sorrow that bows me down He bears,
And loves and pardons, because He cares.

5. Let all who are sad take heart again;
We are not alone in our hours of pain;
Our Father stoops from His throne above,
To soothe and quiet us with His love;
He leaves us not when the storm is high,
And we have safety, for He is nigh.
Can it be trouble which He doth share?
O, rest in peace, for the Lord will care!

—*Anonymous.*

THE HAPPINESS OF ANIMALS A PROOF OF THE DIVINE BENEVOLENCE

1. The air, the earth, the water, teem with delighted existence. In a spring noon or a summer evening, on whichever side we turn our eyes, myriads of happy beings crowd upon our view. "The insect youth are on the wing." Swarms of new-born flies are trying their pinions in the air. Their sportive motions, their gratuitous activity, their continual change of place without use or purpose, testify their joy, and the exultation which they feel in their lately discovered faculties.

2. A bee amongst the flowers in spring is one of the most cheerful objects that can be looked upon. Its life appears to be all enjoyment, so busy is it and so pleased; yet it is only a specimen of insect life, with which, by reason of the animal being half domesticated, we happen to be better acquainted than we are with that of others. The whole winged insect tribe, it is probable, are equally

intent upon their proper employments, and under every variety of constitution gratified, and perhaps equally gratified, by the offices which the Author of their nature has assigned to them.

3. But the atmosphere is not the only scene of their enjoyment. Plants are covered with little insects, greedily sucking their juices and constantly, as it should seem, in the act of sucking. It can not be doubted that this is a state of gratification. What else should fix them so closely to the operation, and so long? Other species are running about, with an alacrity in their motions that carries with it every mark of pleasure. Large patches of ground are sometimes half covered with these brisk and sprightly creatures.

4. If we look to what the waters produce, shoals of the fry of fish frequent the margins of rivers, of lakes, and of the sea itself. These are so happy that they know not what to do with themselves. Their attitudes, their vivacity, their leaps out of the water, their frolics in it, all conduce to show their excess of spirits, and are simply the effects of that excess. Walking by the seaside, in a calm evening, upon a sandy shore, and with an ebbing tide, I have frequently remarked the appearance of a dark cloud, or rather, very thick mist, hanging over the edge of the water, to the height, perhaps, of half a yard, and of the breadth of two or three yards, stretching along the coast as far as the eye could reach, and always retiring with the water.

5. When this cloud came to be examined, it proved to be so much space, filled with young shrimps, in the act of bounding into the air, from the shallow margin of the water, or from the wet sand. If any motion of a mute animal could express delight, it was this; if they had meant to make signs of their happiness, they could not have done it more intelligibly. Suppose, then, what there is no reason to doubt, each individual of this number to be in a state of positive enjoyment; what a sum, collectively, of gratification and pleasure have we here before our view!

6. The young of all animals appear to receive pleasure simply

from the exercise of their limbs and bodily faculties, without any reference to any end to be attained, or any use to be answered by the exertion. A child, without knowing anything of the use of language, is in a high degree delighted with being able to speak. Its incessant repetition of a few articulate sounds, or, perhaps, of a single word that it has learned to pronounce, proves this point clearly. Nor is it less pleased with its first successful endeavors to walk, or rather, to run (which precedes walking), although entirely ignorant of the importance of the attainment to its future life, and even without applying it to any present purpose. A child is delighted with speaking, without having anything to say; and with walking, without knowing whither to go. And, previously to both these, it is reasonable to believe that the waking hours of infancy are agreeably taken up with the exercise of vision, or, perhaps, more properly speaking, with learning to see.

7. But it is not for youth alone that the great Parent of creation has provided. Happiness is found with the purring cat, no less than with the playful kitten; in the armchair of dozing age, as well as in the animation of youth. To novelty, to acuteness of sensation, to hope, to ardor of pursuit, succeeds what is in no inconsiderable degree an equivalent for them all, "perception of ease." Herein is the exact difference between the young and the old. The young are not happy but when enjoying pleasure; the old are happy when free from pain. And this constitution suits with the degrees of animal power which they respectively possess. The vigor of youth was to be stimulated to action by impatience of rest; while to the imbecility of age, quietness and repose become positive gratifications. In one important respect the advantage is with the old. A state of ease is, generally speaking, more attainable than a state of pleasure. A constitution, therefore, that can enjoy ease, is preferable to that which can taste only pleasure.

8. This same perception of ease oftentimes renders old age a condition of great comfort; especially when riding at its anchor,

after a busy or tempestuous life. It is well described by Rousseau to be the interval of repose and enjoyment between the hurry and the end of life. How far the same cause extends to other animal natures can not be judged of with certainty. The appearance of satisfaction with which most animals, as their activity subsides, seek and enjoy rest, affords reason to believe that this source of gratification is appointed to advanced life under all, or most, of its various forms.

9. There is a great deal of truth in the following representation given by Dr. Percival, a very pious writer, as well as excellent man: "To the intelligent and virtuous, old age presents a scene of tranquil enjoyments, of obedient appetites, of well-regulated affections, of maturity in knowledge, and of calm preparation for immortality. In this serene and dignified state, placed, as it were, on the confines of two worlds, the mind of a good man reviews what is past with the complacency of an approving conscience; and looks forward with humble confidence in the mercy of God, and with devout aspirations toward His eternal and ever-increasing favor."

—*Parley.*

THE VANITY OF HUMAN PRIDE

*"Pride goeth before destruction, and
a haughty spirit before a fall."*

1. O, why should the spirit of mortal be proud?
Like a swift-fleeting meteor, a fast-flying cloud,
A flash of the lightning, a break of the wave,
Man passes from life to his rest in the grave.

2. The leaves of the oak and the willow shall fade,
Be scattered around and together be laid;
And the young and the old, and the low and the high,
Shall molder to dust and together shall die.

3. The child that a mother attended and loved,
   The mother, that infant's affection who proved,
   The husband, that mother and infant who blessed,
   Each, all, are away to their dwelling of rest.

4. The maid, on whose cheek, on whose brow, in whose eye,
   Shone beauty and pleasure—her triumphs are by;
   And the memories of those that beloved her and praised
   Are alike from the minds of the living erased.

5. The hand of the king that the scepter hath borne,
   The brow of the priest that the miter hath worn,
   The eye of the sage, and the heart of the brave,
   Are hidden and lost in the depth of the grave.

6. The peasant, whose lot was to sow and to reap,
   The herdsman, who climbed with his goats to the steep,
   The beggar, who wandered in search of his bread,
   Have faded away like the grass that we tread.

7. The saint, who enjoyed the communion of heaven,
   The sinner, who dared to remain unforgiven,
   The wise and the foolish, the guilty and just,
   Have quietly mingled their bones in the dust.

8. So the multitude goes, like the flower and the weed,
   That wither away to let others succeed;
   So the multitude comes, even those we behold,
   To repeat every tale that hath often been told.

9. For we are the same that our fathers have been;
   We see the same sights that our fathers have seen;
   We drink the same stream, and we view the same sun,
   And run the same course that our fathers have run.

10. The thoughts we are thinking, our fathers would think;
    From the death that we shrink from, our fathers would shrink;
    To the life that we cling to, they also would cling;
    But it speeds for us all, like a bird on the wing.

11. They loved, but their story we can not unfold;
    They scorned, but the heart of the haughty is cold;
    They grieved, but no wail from their slumbers will come;
    They joyed, but the tongue of their gladness is dumb.

12. They died—ay! they died—and we things that are now,
    Who walk on the turf that lies over their brow,
    Who make in their dwellings a transient abode,
    Meet the things that they met on their pilgrimage road.

13. Yea! hope and despondency, pleasure and pain,
    We mingle together like sunshine and rain;
    And the smile and the tear, the song and the dirge,
    Still follow each other like surge upon surge.

14. 'Tis the wink of an eye, 'tis the draught of a breath,
    From the blossom of health to the paleness of death,
    From the gilded saloon to the bier and the shroud;
    O, why should the spirit of mortal be proud?

—*William Knox.*

THE INSTABILITY OF TEMPORAL THINGS

> "*All flesh is as grass, and all the glory of man as the flower of grass. The grass withereth, and the flower thereof falleth away; But the word of the Lord endureth forever.*"

1. We receive such repeated intimations of decay in the world through which we are passing; decline and change and loss follow decline and change and loss in such rapid succession, that we can almost catch the sound of universal wasting, and hear the work of desolation going on busily around us. "The mountain falling, cometh to naught, and the rock is removed out of his place. The waters wear the stones," the things which grow out of the dust of the earth are washed away, and the hope of man is destroyed. Conscious of our instability, we look about for something to rest on, but we look in vain. The heavens and the earth had a beginning, and they will have an end. The face of the world is changing daily and hourly. All animated things grow old and die. The rocks crumble, the trees fall, the leaves fade, and the grass withers. The clouds are flying, and the waters are flowing away from us.

2. The firmest works of man, too, are gradually giving way, the ivy clings to the moldering tower, the brier hangs out from the shattered window, and the wallflower springs from the disjointed stones. The founders of these perishable works have shared the same fate long ago. If we look back to the days of our ancestors, to the men as well as the dwellings of former times, they become immediately associated in our imaginations, and only make the feeling of instability stronger and deeper than before. In the spacious domes which once held our fathers, the serpent hisses, and the wild bird screams. The halls which once were crowded with all that taste and science and labor could procure, which resounded with melody, and were lighted up with beauty, are buried by their own ruins,—mocked by their own desolation. The voice

of merriment, and of wailing, the steps of the busy and the idle, have ceased in the deserted courts, and the weeds choke the entrances, and the long grass waves upon the hearthstone. The works of art, the forming hand, the tombs, the very ashes they contained, are all gone.

3. While we thus walk among the ruins of the past, a sad feeling of insecurity comes over us; and that feeling is by no means diminished when we arrive at home. If we turn to our friends, we can hardly speak to them before they bid us farewell. We see them for a few moments, and in a few moments more their countenances are changed, and they are sent away. It matters not how near and dear they are. The ties that bind us together are never too close to be parted, or too strong to be broken. Tears were never known to move the king of terrors, neither is it enough that we are compelled to surrender one, or two, or many of those we love; for though the price is so great, we buy no favor with it, and our hold on those who remain is as slight as ever. The shadows all elude our grasp, and follow one another down the valley. We gain no confidence, then, no feeling of security, by turning to our contemporaries and kindred. We know that the forms, which are breathing around us, are as short-lived and fleeting as those were which have been dust for centuries. The sensation of vanity, uncertainty, and ruin is equally strong, whether we muse on what has long been prostrate, or gaze on what is falling now or will fall so soon.

4. If everything that comes under our notice has endured for so short a time, and in so short a time will be no more, we can not say that we receive the least assurance by thinking on ourselves. When they on whose fate we have been meditating were engaged in the active scenes of life, as full of health and hope as we are now, what were we? We had no knowledge, no consciousness, no being; there was not a single thing in the wide universe that knew us. And after the same interval shall have elapsed, that now

divides their days from ours, what shall we be?—What they are now. When a few more friends have left, a few more hopes deceived, and a few more changes mocked us, we shall be brought to the grave; "the clods of the valley shall be sweet" unto us, and every man shall follow us, as there are innumerable before us. All power will have forsaken the strongest, and the loftiest will be laid low, and every eye will be closed, and every voice hushed, and every heart will have ceased its beating. And when we have gone ourselves, even our memories will not stay behind us long. A few of the near and dear will bear our likeness in their bosoms, till they, too, have arrived at the end of their journey, and entered the dark dwelling of unconsciousness. In the thoughts of others we shall live only till the last sound of the bell which informs them of our departure has ceased to vibrate in their ears. A stone, perhaps, may tell some wanderer where we lie, and when we came here; but even that will soon refuse to bear us record. "Time's effacing fingers" will be busy on its surface, and at length will wear it smooth; and then the stone itself will sink or crumble, and the wanderer of another age will pass, without a single call upon his sympathy, over our unheeded graves.

—*Greenwood.*

"ALL THINGS ARE OF GOD"

"Thine is the kingdom, and the power, and the glory, forever."

1. Thou art, O God, the life and light
    Of all this wondrous world we see;
    Its glow by day, its smile by night,
    Are but reflections caught from Thee.
    Where'er we turn, Thy glories shine,
    And all things fair and bright are Thine.

2. When Day, with farewell beams, delays
    Among the opening clouds of even,
    And we can almost think we gaze
    Through opening vistas into heaven;
    Those hues that make the sun's decline
    So soft, so radiant, Lord. are Thine.

3. When Night, with wings of starry gloom,
    O'ershadows all the earth and skies,
    Like some dark, beauteous bird, whose plume
    Is sparkling with unnumbered eyes;—
    That sacred gloom, those fires divine,
    So grand, so countless, Lord, are Thine.

4. When youthful Spring around us breathes,
    Thy spirit warms her fragrant sigh;
    And every flower that Summer wreathes
    Is born beneath Thy kindling eye:
    Where'er we turn, Thy glories shine,
    And all things fair and bright are Thine.

—*Moore.*

ON THE PLEASURE OF ACQUIRING KNOWLEDGE

*"When wisdom entereth into thine heart,
And knowledge is pleasant unto thy soul;
Discretion shall preserve thee,
Understanding shall keep thee."*

1. In every period of life, the acquisition of knowledge is one of the most pleasing employments of the human mind. But in youth, there are circumstances which make it productive of higher enjoyment. It is then that everything has the charm of novelty; that curiosity and fancy are awake; and that the heart swells with the anticipations of future eminence and utility. Even in those lower branches of instruction which we call mere accomplishments, there is something always pleasing to the young in their acquisition. They seem to become every well-educated person; they adorn, if they do not dignify, humanity; and, what is far more, while they give an elegant employment to the hours of leisure and relaxation, they afford a means of contributing to the purity and innocence of domestic life.

2. But in the acquisition of knowledge of the higher kind,—in the hours when the young gradually begin the study of the laws of nature, and of the faculties of the human mind or of the magnificent revelations of the gospel,—there is a pleasure of a sublimer nature. The cloud, which, in their infant years, seemed to cover nature from their view, begins gradually to resolve. The world in which they are placed, opens with all its wonders upon their eye; their powers of attention and observation seem to expand with the scene before them; and while they see, for the first time, the immensity of the universe of God, and mark the majestic simplicity of those laws by which its operations are conducted, they feel as if they were awakened to a higher species of being and admitted into nearer intercourse with the Author of nature.

3. It is this period, accordingly, more than all others, that determines our hopes or fears of the future fate of the young. To feel no joy in such pursuits, to listen carelessly to the voice that

brings such magnificent instruction, to see the veil raised that conceals the counsels of the Deity and to show no emotion at the discovery, are symptoms of a weak and torpid spirit,—of a mind unworthy of the advantages it possesses, and fitted only for the humanity of sensual and ignoble pleasure. Of those, on the contrary, who distinguish themselves by the love of knowledge,—who follow with ardor the career that is open to them, we are apt to form the most honorable presages. It is the character which is natural to youth and which, therefore, promises well of their maturity. We foresee for them, at least, a life of pure and virtuous enjoyment, and we are willing to anticipate no common share of future usefulness and splendor.

4. In the second place, the pursuits of knowledge lead not only to happiness, but to honor. "Length of days is in her right hand, and in her left hand riches and honor." It is honorable to excel even in the most trifling species of knowledge, in those which can amuse only the passing hour. It is more honorable to excel in those different branches of science which are connected with the liberal professions of life, and which tend so much to the dignity and well-being of humanity. It is the means of raising the most obscure to esteem and attention; it opens to the just ambition of youth some of the most distinguished and respected situations in society; and it places them there, with the consoling reflection that it is to their own industry and labor, in the providence of God, that they are alone indebted for them. But to excel in the higher attainments of knowledge,—to be distinguished in those greater pursuits which have commanded the attention and exhausted the abilities of the wise in every former age, is, perhaps, of all the distinctions of human understanding, the most honorable and grateful.

5. When we look back upon the great men who have gone before us in every path of glory, we feel our eye turn from the career of war and ambition, and involuntarily rest upon those who have

displayed the great truths of religion, who have investigated the laws of social welfare, or extended the sphere of human knowledge. These are honors, we feel, which have been gained without a crime, and which can be enjoyed without remorse. They are honors also which can never die,—which can shed luster even upon the humblest head,—and to which the young of every succeeding age will look up, as their brightest incentives to the pursuit of virtuous fame. —*Alison.*

CHRIST IS RISEN

*"Ye seek Jesus of Nazareth, which was crucified;
He is risen; He is not here."*

1. The sound of shouting and the tumult ceased,
And pitying Night a melancholy pall
Let down o'er Palestine. The Christ of God
Was sleeping in the tomb of Joseph now
A dreamless sleep; and angry hosts had slunk
Away to reason with their consciences
Or drown them in the flow of ruddy wine.
Earth slumbered with her Maker sacrificed,
And held Him to her bosom—dead!

2.   The crown,
By mocking jesters pressed upon His brow,
Had left its cruel impress in the flesh
Condemned. The hands whose office work had been
To pour upon the head of youth and age
The kindliest blessings of a loving God;
The feet so often weary with the way
O'er mountain steep or by the rocky shore;
The lips that once had launched the moving spheres
And spoke to life the Adam of the race;—
Were lifeless all, and man in type was dead.

3. The night of sin—a dreary, cheerless night—
   Had here fulfillment manifest, and sin
   Itself, in type, triumphant sat enthroned.
   Old earth was tottering on the verge
   Of ruin absolute, while in the tomb,
   In bonds of death to satisfy the law
   By mortals broken, lay the Gift of God
   Enwrapped in Death's habiliments, that He
   Might work the purpose of Jehovah's mind,
   To conquer all that triumphed over men.

4. The ear of heaven was bowed to earth, but earth
   Was slumbering still, unconscious of the scale
   Jehovah held to weigh her destiny.
   The book of God was fair, the pages clean,
   And 'gainst the name of Jesus there appeared
   No sign of sin committed, or of thought
   To show that aught but fealty to God
   Inhabited the heart now held of Death.

5. "O Christ, come forth; the keepers of the dead
   Hold not dominion over You." The stone,
   By Roman order sealed, is powerless
   To hold whom God does not condemn.

6.   Roll back,
   Frail figment of the Roman realm, nor think
   To stifle with the hand of stone the life
   That paid sin's penalties from Adam down.
   Roll back, ye somber, silent gates of death;
   The conquering King comes through. Roll back, ye dark
   And threatening clouds of doom; the Sun comes forth
   To lighten with His gleam from pole to pole
   The sorrowing regions of a stricken world.

Roll back, roll back, ye hosts from heaven flung,
For man in type has conquered every foe,
And stands triumphant with the keys of death.

7. O grand, O glorious liberty is that
Which stepped with Christ from Joseph's open tomb,
And trimmed anew the fading, dimming flame
Of hope, and set a star to guide the race
From earth's long night to heaven's glorious day.
That tomb a cradle was; and pillowed there
Our freedom lay in natal robes, and harked
The velvet footfalls of the angel guard.

8. Down all the rolling years that since have passed,
A thorny way she threaded through the myths
Of pagan rites, and struggled hard to plant
A nobler tree whose leaves should heal the wounds
Oppression rained upon the hearts of men.
That tree is blooming yet whose seed was sown
Behind the stone a Roman law had sealed—
Within the tomb that shut a Saviour in.
His death our immortality insured—
His tomb the birthplace of our liberties.

9. Yes, Christ is risen and our souls are free—
Free in the liberty His life has given;
Free from the death that knows no waking hour;
Free from the sins that long have pressed us down;
And free to worship and obey His will.

10. We turn no tearful eyes to Joseph's tomb,
We bend no knee in mosque Mohammedan,
Nor slay in strife to win the vacant place
Where rested once the Saviour of mankind.

Go forth, go forth, and tell a waiting world
The Son of God is in His tomb no more.

11. Say not the heart, the head, the hand must yield
A servile homage to a human creed.
The life that burst the shackles of the tomb
Will burst this prison, too. The mind of God
Is broader, deeper than the wisest mind
His hand has fashioned from the clay of earth.
The strongest cord your puny hand may weave
Is rope of sand; and ne'er will anchor you
Within the veil. Ye can not build a tower
More stable than the pile that crumbles now
On Shinar's plain; and such is every creed.
But hollow tombs are all these instruments
By human mind conceived, and empty all;
They are but shells, and all are tenantless,
For Christ is risen—you'll not find Him there.

12. Nor is the presence of that Holy One
Enlinked with laws that seek by finite force
To scourge to God the unwilling wanderer.
The Son of God leans not on reed so frail
As human law, to work His holy will.
His law who made the spheres is not so weak
That laws of men must prop it or it fall.
We may not place against the ark of God,
Wherein His law abides, a steadying hand.
The lesson writ is ours to learn, and we
Are wiser when we heed. The fearful one
Who flees from laws oppressive to the shield
He finds in creed professed has buried deep
The love that would have won him to his God.

From such a tomb the Spirit flies. Our strength
Is weakness while we think to hold Him there.
Proclaim His truth in glorious ministry:—
Our Christ is risen and the soul is free!

—C. M. Snow.

AUTUMN

"*He reserveth unto us the appointed weeks of the harvest.*"

1. There is an "eventide" in the year,—a season, as we now witness, when the sun withdraws his propitious light,—when the winds rise, and the leaves fall, and nature around us seems to sink into decay. It is said, in general, to be the season of melancholy; and if by this word be meant that it is the time of solemn and of serious thought, it is undoubtedly the season of melancholy, —yet it is a melancholy so soothing, so gentle in its approach, and so prophetic in its influence, that they who have known it feel, as if instinctively, that it is the doing of God, and that the heart of man is not thus finely touched but to fine issues.

2. It is a season which tends to wean us from the passions of the world. Every passion, however base or unworthy, is yet eloquent. It speaks to us of present enjoyment,—it tells us of what men have done and what men may do, and it supports us everywhere by the example of many around us. When we go out into the fields in the evening of the year, a different voice approaches us. We regard, even in spite of ourselves, the still but steady advances of time.

3. A few days ago, and the summer of the year was grateful, and every element was filled with life, and the sun of heaven seemed to glory in his ascendant. He is now enfeebled in his power; the desert no more blossoms like a rose; the song of joy is no more heard among the branches; and the earth is strewed with that foliage which once bespoke the magnificence of summer. Whatever may be the passions that society has awakened, we

pause amid this apparent desolation of nature. We sit down in the lodge of the wayfaring man in the wilderness, and we feel that all we witness is the emblem of our own fate. Such also, in a few years, will be our own condition. The blossoms of our spring, the pride of our summer, will also fade into decay; and the pulse that now beats high with virtuous or with vicious desire, will gradually sink, and then must stop forever.

4. We rise from our meditations with hearts softened and subdued, and we return into life as into a shadowy scene, where we have disquieted ourselves in vain. Such is the first impression that the present scene of nature is fitted to make on us. It is the first impression that intimidates the thoughtless and the gay; and, indeed, if there were no other reflections that followed, I know not that it would be the business of wisdom to recommend such meditations. It is the consequences, however, of such previous thoughts that are chiefly valuable, and among these there are two that may well deserve our consideration.

5. It is the peculiar character of the melancholy which such seasons excite, that it is general. It is not an individual remonstrance; it is not the harsh language of human wisdom which too often insults while it instructs us. When the winds of autumn sigh around us, their voices speak not to us alone, but to our kind; and the lesson they teach us is not that we alone decay, but that such also is the fate of all the generations of man. "They are the green leaves of the tree of the desert, which perish and are renewed."

6. In such a sentiment there is a kind of sublimity mingled with its melancholy; our tears fall, but they fall not for ourselves; and although the train of our thoughts may have begun with the selfishness of our own concerns, we feel that by the ministry of some mysterious power they end in awaking our concern for every being that lives. Yet a few years, we think, and all that now bless or all that now convulse humanity will also have

perished. The mightiest pageantry of life will pass; the loudest notes of triumph or of conquest will be silent in the grave; the wicked, wherever active, will "cease from troubling," and the weary, wherever suffering, will "be at rest."

7. Under an impression so profound, we feel our own hearts better. The cares, the animosities, the hatreds that society may have engendered, sink unperceived from our bosoms. In the general desolation of nature, we feel the littleness of our own passions; we look forward to the kindred evening which time must bring to all; we anticipate the graves of those we hate as of those we love. Every unkind passion falls with the leaves that fall around us; and we return slowly to our homes, and to the society that surrounds us, with the wish only to enlighten or to bless them.

8. If there were no other effects of such appearances of nature upon our minds, they would still be valuable, they would teach us humility,—and with it they would teach us charity. In the same hour in which they taught us our own fragility, they would teach us commiseration for the whole family of man. But there is a further sentiment that such scenes inspire, more valuable than all; and we know little the designs of Providence when we do not yield ourselves in such hours to the beneficent instincts of our imagination.

9. It is the unvarying character of nature, amid all its scenes, to lead us at last to its Author; and it is for this final end that all its varieties have such dominion upon our minds. We are led by the appearances of spring to see His bounty, and we are led by the splendors of summer to see His greatness. In the present hours we are led to higher sentiments, and, what is most remarkable, the very circumstances of melancholy are those which guide us most securely to put our trust in Him.

10. We are witnessing the decay of the year. We go back in imagination and find that such, in every generation, has been the fate of man; we look forward and we see that to such ends all must

come at last; we lift our desponding eyes in search of comfort, and we see above us One who is ever the same, and to whose years there is no end. Amid the vicissitudes of nature, we discover that center Majesty in whom there is no variableness nor shadow of turning. We feel that there is a God; and from the tempestuous sea of life, we hail that Polar Star of nature, to which a sacred instinct had directed our eyes, and which burns with an undecaying ray to lighten us among all the darkness of the deep.

11. From the great conviction, there is another sentiment that succeeds. Nature, indeed, yearly perishes; but it is yearly renewed. Amid all its changes, the immortal spirit of Him that made it remains; and the same sun that now marks with his receding ray the autumn of the year, will again rise in his brightness, and bring along with him the promise of the spring and all the magnificence of summer.

12. Under such convictions, hope dawns upon the sadness of the heart. The melancholy of decay becomes the very herald of renewal; the magnificent circle of nature opens upon our view; we anticipate the analogous resurrection of our being; we see beyond the grave a greater spring, and we people it with those who have given joy to that which is passed. With such final impressions we submit ourselves gladly to the destiny of our being. While the sun of mortality sinks, we hail the rising of the Sun of Righteousness, and, in hours when all the honors of nature are perishing around us, we prostrate ourselves in deeper adoration before Him who sitteth upon its throne.

13. Let, then, the young go out in these hours under the descending sun of the year into the fields of nature. Their hearts are now ardent with hope,—with the hopes of fame, of honor, or of happiness; and in the long perspective which is before them, their imagination creates a world where all may be enjoyed. Let the scenes which they now may witness, moderate, but not extinguish their ambition. While they see the yearly desolation of

nature, let them see it as the emblem of mortal hope; while they feel the disproportion between the powers they possess and the time they are to be employed, let them carry their ambitious eye beyond the world; and while, in these sacred solitudes, a voice in their own bosom corresponds to the voice of decaying nature, let them take that high decision which becomes those who feel themselves inhabitants of a greater world, and who look to a Being incapable of decay. —*Alison*.

APOSTROPHE TO THE SUN

"Then shall the righteous shine forth as the sun in the kingdom of their Father."

1. Center of light and energy! thy way
 Is through the unknown void; thou hast thy throne,
 Morning, and evening, and at noon of day,
 Far in the blue, untended and alone;
 Ere the first-wakened airs of earth had blown,
 On didst thou march, triumphant in thy light;
 Then didst thou send thy glance, which still hath flown
 Wide through the never-ending worlds of night,
 And yet thy full orb burns with flash unquenched and bright.

2. Thy path is high in heaven;—we can not gaze
 On the intense of light that girds thy car;
 There is a crown of glory in thy rays,
 Which bears thy pure divinity afar
 To mingle with the equal light of star;
 For thou, so vast to us, art, in the whole,
 One of the sparks of night, that fire the air;
 And, as around thy center planets roll,
 So thou, too, hast thy path around the Central Soul.

3. Thou lookest on the earth, and then it smiles;
 Thy light is hid, and all things droop and mourn;

>   Laughs the wide sea around her budding isles,
>   When through their heaven thy changing car is borne;
>   Thou wheel'st away thy flight,—the woods are shorn
>   Of all their waving locks, and storms awake;
>   All that was once so beautiful is torn
>   By the wild winds which plow the lonely lake,
>   And in their maddening rush the crested mountains shake.

4. The earth lies buried in a shroud of snow;
       Life lingers, and would die, but thy return
   Gives to their gladdened hearts an overflow
       Of all the power that brooded in the urn
       Of their chilled frames, and then they proudly spurn
   All bands that would confine, and give to air
       Hues, fragrance, shapes of beauty, till they burn,
   When, on a dewy morn, thou dartest there
   Rich waves of gold to wreath with fairer light the fair.

5. The vales are thine:—and when the touch of Spring
       Thrills them, and gives them gladness, in thy light
   They flitter, as the glancing swallow's wing
       Dashes the water in his winding flight,
       And leaves behind a wave, that crinkles bright,
   And widens outward to the pebbled shore;—
       The vales are thine; and when they wake from night,
   The dews that bend the grass tips, twinkling o'er
   Their soft and oozy beds, look upward and adore.

6. The hills are thine:—they catch thy newest beam,
       And gladden in thy parting, where the wood
   Flames out in every leaf, and drinks the stream
       That flows from out thy fullness, as a flood
       Bursts from an unknown land, and rolls the food

Of nations in its waters; so thy rays
  Flow and give brighter tints than ever bud,
When a clear sheet of ice reflects a blaze
Of many twinkling gems, as every glossed bough plays.

7. Thine are the mountains,—where they purely lift
    Snows that have never wasted, in the sky;
  Which have no stain; below the storm may drift
    Its darkness, and the thunder-gust roar by;
  Aloft in thy eternal smile they lie
  Dazzling but cold,—thy farewell glance looks there,
    And when below thy hues of beauty die,
  Girt round them, as a rosy belt, they bear
  Into the high, dark vault, a brow that still is fair.

8. The clouds are thine; and all their magic hues
    Are penciled by thee; when thou bendest low,
  Or comest in thy strength, thy hand imbues
    Their waving folds with such a perfect glow
    Of all pure tints, the fairy pictures throw
  Shame on the proudest art.   .   .   .

9. These are thy trophies, and thou bend'st thy arch,
    The sign of triumph, in a seven-fold twine,
  Where the spent storm is hasting on its march;
    And where the glories of thy light combine,
    And form with perfect curve a lifted line
  Striding the earth and air;—man looks and tells
    How Peace and Mercy in its beauty shine,
  And how the heavenly messenger impels
  Her glad wings on the path, that thus in ether swells.

10. The ocean is thy vassal;—thou dost sway
    His waves to thy dominion, and they go

Where thou, in heaven, dost guide them on their way,
   Rising and falling in eternal flow.
Thou lookest on the waters, and they glow,
   And take them wings and spring aloft in air,
   And change to clouds, and then, dissolving, throw
Their treasures back to earth, and rushing, tear
The mountain and the vale, as proudly on they bear.

11. In thee, first light, the bounding ocean smiles,
      When quick winds uprear it in a swell
   That rolls in glittering green around the isles
      Where ever-springing fruits and blossoms dwell.
      O! with a joy no gifted tongue can tell,
   I hurry o'er the waters when the sail
      Swells tensely, and the light keel glances well
   Over the curling billow, and the gale
Comes off from the spicy groves to tell its winning tale.
                                            —J. G. Percival.

ON THE USE AND ABUSE OF AMUSEMENTS

"A merry heart doeth good like a medicine."

1. It were unjust and ungrateful to conceive that the amusements of life are altogether forbid by its beneficent Author. They serve, on the contrary, important purposes in the economy of human life, and are destined to produce important effects, both upon our happiness and character. They are, in the first place, . . . the wells of the desert; the kind resting-places in which toil may relax, in which the weary spirit may recover its tone, and where the desponding mind may resume its strength and its hopes.

2. They are, in another view, of some importance to the dignity of individual character. In everything we call amusement,

there is generally some display of taste and imagination,—some elevation of the mind from mere animal indulgence or the baseness of sensual desire. Even in the scenes of relaxation, therefore, they have a tendency to preserve the dignity of human character, and to fill up the vacant and unguarded hours of life with occupations innocent, at least, if not virtuous. But their principal effect, perhaps, is upon the social character of man. Whenever amusement is sought, it is in the society of our brethren; and whenever it is found, it is in our sympathy with the happiness of those around us. It bespeaks the disposition of benevolence, and it creates it.

3. When men assemble, accordingly, for the purpose of general happiness, or joy, they exhibit to the thoughtful eye one of the most pleasing appearances of their original characters. They leave behind them, for the time, the faults of their station and the asperities of their temper; they forget the secret views and selfish purposes of their ordinary life, and mingle with the crowd around them with no other view than to receive and to communicate happiness. It is a spectacle which it is impossible to observe without emotion; and, while the virtuous man rejoices at the evidence which it affords of the benevolent constitution of his nature, the pious man is apt to bless the benevolence of that God who thus makes the wilderness and the solitary place to be glad, and whose wisdom renders even the hours of amusement subservient to the cause of virtue.

4. It is not, therefore, the use of the innocent amusements of life which is dangerous, but the abuse of them. It is not when they are occasionally, but when they are constantly, pursued; when the love of amusement degenerates into a passion, and when, from being an occasional indulgence, it becomes a habitual desire. What the consequences of this inordinate love of amusement are, I shall now endeavor very briefly to show you.

5. When we look, in a moral view, to the consequences of hu-

man pursuits, we are not to stop at the precise and immediate effects which they may seem to have upon character. It is chiefly by the general frame of mind they produce, and the habitual dispositions they create, that we are to determine whether their influence is fortunate or unfortunate on those who are engaged in them. In every pursuit, whatever gives strength and energy to the mind of man, experience teaches to be favorable to the interests of piety, of knowledge, and of virtue; in every pursuit, on the contrary, whatever enfeebles or limits the powers of mind, the same experience everywhere shows to be hostile to the best interests of human nature.

6. If it is in this view we consider the effects of the habitual love even of the most innocent amusement, we shall find that it produces necessarily, for the hour in which it is indulged, an enfeebled and dependent frame of mind; that in such scenes energy resolves and resolution fades; that in the enjoyment of the present hour, the past and the future are alike forgotten; and that the heart learns to be satisfied with passive emotion and momentary pleasure.

7. It is to this single observation, my young friends, that I wish at present to direct your attention, and to entreat you to consider what may be expressed to be the effects of such a character of mind, at your age, upon the honor and happiness of future life.

8. First, it tends to degrade all the powers of the understanding. It is the eternal law of nature that truth and wisdom are the offspring of labor, of vigor, and perseverance in every worthy object of pursuit. The eminent stations of fame, accordingly, and the distinguished honors of knowledge, have in every age been the reward only of such early attainments, of that cherished elevation of mind which pursues only magnificent ends, and of that heroic fortitude which, whether in action or in speculation, pursues them by the means of undeviating exertion.

9. For the production of such a character, no discipline can be

so unfit as that of the habitual love of amusement. It kindles not the eye of ambition; it bids the heart beat with no throb of generous admiration; it lets the soul be calm, while all the rest of our fellows are passing us in the road of virtue and science. Satisfied with humble and momentary enjoyment, it aspires to no honor, no praise, no pre-eminence, and, contented with the idle gratification of the present hour, forgets alike what man has done and what man was born to do.

10. If such be the character of the youthful mind, if it be with such aim and such ambition that its natural elevation can be satisfied, am I to ask you what must be the appearances of riper years? what the effect of such habits of thought upon the understanding of manhood? Alas! a greater instructor, the mighty instructor experience, may show you in every rank of life what these effects are. It will show you men born with every capacity, and whose first years glowed with every honorable ambition, whom no vice even now degrades, and to whom no actual guilt is affixed, who yet live in the eye of the world only as the objects of pity or of scorn,—who in the idle career of habitual amusement have dissipated all their powers, and lost all their ambition, and who exist now for no purpose but to be the sad memorials of ignoble taste and degraded understanding.

11. The inordinate love of pleasure is, in the second place, equally hostile to the moral character. If the feeble and passive disposition of mind which it produces be unfavorable to the exertion of the understanding, it is in the same measure as unfavorable to the best employments of the heart. The great duties of life, the duties for which every man and woman is born, demand in all situations the mind of labor and perseverance. From the first hour of existence to the last,—from the cradle of the infant beside which the mother watches with unslumbering eye, to the grave of the aged where the son pours his last tears upon the bier of his father,—in all that intermediate time, every being can only be won by the steadfast magnanimity of pious duty.

12. If such be the laborious but animating destiny of man, is it in the enervating school of habitual amusement that the young are to fit themselves for its high discharges? Is it from hence that the legislator is to learn those lengthened toils which decide the happiness of nations; or the warrior that undaunted spirit which can scorn both danger and death in the defense of his country? Or is it here, my young friends, that experience tells you you can best learn to perform the common duties of your coming days,—those sacred duties of domestic life, which, far more than all others, open to you the solemn prospect of being either the blessings or the curses of society?

13. Alas! experience has here also decided. It tells you that the mind which exists only for pleasure, can not exist for duty; it tells you that the feeble and selfish spirit of amusement gradually corrodes all the benevolent emotions of the heart, and withers the most sacred ties of domestic affection; and it points its awful finger to the examples of those, alas! of both sexes, whom the unrestrained love of idle pleasure first led to error and folly, and whom, with sure but fatal progress, it has since conducted to be the objects of secret shame and public infamy.

14. In the last place, this unmanly disposition is equally fatal to happiness as to virtue. To the wise and virtuous, to those who use the pleasures of life only as a temporary relaxation, as a resting-place to animate them on the great journey on which they are traveling, the hours of amusement bring real pleasure; to them the well of joy is ever full, while to those who linger by its side, its waters are soon dried and exhausted.

15. I speak not now of those bitter waters which must mingle themselves with the well of unhallowed pleasure, of the secret reproaches of accusing conscience, of the sad sense of shame and dishonor, and of that degraded spirit which must bend itself beneath the scorn of the world; I speak only of the simple and natural effect of unwise indulgence; that it renders the mind cal-

lous to enjoyment; and that even though the fountain were full of water, the feverish lip is incapable of satiating its thirst. Alas! here, too, we may see the examples of human folly; we may see around us everywhere the fatal effects of unrestrained pleasure, the young sickening in the midst of every pure and genuine enjoyment; the mature hastening with hopeless step to fill up the hours of a vitiated being; and, what is still more wretched, the hoary head wandering in the way of folly, and with an unhallowed dotage returning again to the trifles and the amusements of childhood.

16. Such, then, my young friends, are the natural and experienced consequences of the inordinate love even of innocent amusement, and such the intellectual and moral degradation to which the paths of pleasure conduct. Let me entreat you to pause ere you begin your course, ere those habits are acquired which may never again be subdued, and ere ye permit the charms of pleasure to wind around your soul their fascinating powers.

17. Think, with the elevation and generosity of your age, whether this is the course that leads to honor or to fame; whether it was in this discipline that they were exercised who in every age have enlightened the world, whose shades are present to your midnight thoughts, and whose names you can not pronounce without the tear of gratitude or admiration. Think, still more, whether it was to the ends of unmanly pleasure that you were dedicated when the solemn service of religion first enrolled you in the number of the faithful, and when the ardent tears of your parents mingled with the waters of your baptism. If they live, is it in such paths that their anxious eyes delight to see you tread?

—*Alison.*

THE PLANETARY SYSTEM

"The heavens declare the glory of God, and the firmament showeth His handiwork."

1. Fair star of eve, thy lucid ray
    Directs my thoughts to realms on high;
   Great is the theme, though weak the lay,
    For my heart whispers, "God is nigh."

2. The sun, vicegerent of his power,
    Shall rend the veil of parting night,
   Salute the spheres at early hour,
    And pour a flood of life and light.

3. Seven circling planets I beheld,
    Their different orbits all describe;
   Copernicus these wonders told,
    And bade the laws of truth revive.

4. Mercury and Venus first appear,
    Nearest the dazzling source of day;
   Three months compose his hasty year,
    In seven she treads the heavenly way.

5. Next, Earth completes her yearly course;
    The moon as satellite attends;
   Attraction is the hidden force,
    On which creation's law depends.

6. Then Mars is seen of fiery hue;
    Jupiter's orb we next descry;
   His atmospheric belts we view,
    And four bright moons attract the eye.

7. Mars, soon his revolution makes,
    In twice twelve months the sun surrounds,
   Jupiter, greater limits takes,
    And twelve long years declare his bounds.

8. With rings of light, see Saturn slow,
    Pursue his path in endless space;
   By seven pale moons his course we know,
    And thirty years that round shall trace.

9. The Georgium Sidus next appears,
    By his amazing distance known;
   The lapse of more than eighty years,
    In his account makes one alone.

10. Six moons are his, by Herschel shown,—
     Herschel, of modern times the boast;
    Discovery here is all his own,
     Another planetary host!

11. And lo! by astronomic scan,
     Three stranger planets track the skies,
    Part of that high majestic plan,
     Whence those successive worlds arise.

12. Next Mars, Piazzi's orb is seen,
     Four years six months complete his round,
    Science shall renovated beam,
     And guild Palermo's favored ground.

13. Daughters of telescopic ray,
     Pallas and Juno, smaller spheres,
    Are seen near Jove's imperial way,
     Tracing the heavens in destined years.

14. Comets and fixed stars I see,
   With native luster ever shine;
   How great! how good! how dreadful! He
   In whom life, light, and truth combine.

15. O! may I better know His will,
   And more implicitly obey;
   Be God my Friend, my Father still,
   From finite to eternal day.

—*Mangnall.*

THE MUTUAL RELATION BETWEEN SLEEP AND NIGHT

"*Man goeth forth unto his work
. . . until the evening.*"

1. The relation of sleep to night appears to have been expressly intended by our benevolent Creator. Two points are manifest: first, that the animal frame requires sleep; second, that night brings with it a silence, and a cessation of activity, which allow of sleep being taken without interruption and without loss. Animal existence is made up of action and slumber; nature has provided a season for each. An animal which stood not in need of rest, would always live in daylight. An animal which, though made for action and delighting in action, must have its strength repaired by sleep, meets, by its constitution, the returns of day and night. In the human species, for instance, were the bustle, the labor, the motion of life, upheld by the constant presence of light, sleep could not be enjoyed without being disturbed by noise, and without expense of that time which the eagerness of private interest would not contentedly resign. It is happy, therefore, for this part of the creation, I mean that it is conformable to the frame and wants of their constitution, that nature, by the very disposition of her elements, has commanded, as it were, and imposed upon them at moderate intervals, a general intermission of their toils, their occupations, and their pursuits.

2. But it is not for man, either solely or principally, that night is made. Inferior, but less perverted natures, taste its solace, and expect its return, with greater exactness and advantage than he does. I have often observed, and never observed but to admire, the satisfaction, no less than the regularity, with which the greatest part of the irrational world yield to this soft necessity, this grateful vicissitude. How comfortably the birds of the air, for example, address themselves to the repose of the evening; and with what alertness they resume the activity of the day!

3. Nor does it disturb our argument to confess that certain species of animals are in motion during the night and at rest in the day. With respect to even them it is still true that there is a change of the condition in the animal, and an external change corresponding with it. There is still the relation, though inverted. The fact is, that the repose of other animals sets these at liberty, and invites them to their food or their sport.

4. If the relation of sleep to night, and in some instances its converse, be real, we can not reflect without amazement upon the extent to which it carries us. Day and night are things close to us; the change appeals immediately to our sensations. Of all the phenomena of nature, it is the most obvious and the most familiar to our experience; but, in its cause, it belongs to the great motions which are passing in the heavens. Whilst the earth glides round her axle, she ministers to the alternate necessities of the animals dwelling upon her surface at the same time that she obeys the influence of those attractions which regulate the order of many thousand worlds. The relation therefore of sleep to night, is the relation of the inhabitants of the earth to the rotation of their globe. Probably it is more; it is a relation to the system of which that globe is a part, and, still further, to the congregation of systems of which theirs is only one. If this account be true, it connects the meanest individual with the universe itself; a chicken, roosting upon its perch, with the spheres revolving in the firmament.

—*Paley.*

WHILE WE MAY

> "*Be ye kind one to another, tenderhearted, forgiving one another, even as God for Christ's sake hath forgiven you.*"

1. The hands are such dear hands;
   They are so full; they turn at our demands
   So often; they reach out,
   With trifles scarcely thought about.
   So many times; they do
   So many things for me, for you—
   If their fond wills mistake,
   We well may bend, not break.

2. They are such fond, frail lips
   That speak to us. Pray, if love strips
   Them of discretion many times,
   Or if they speak too slow or quick, such crimes
   We may pass by; for we may see
   Days not far off when those small words may be
   Held not as slow, or quick, or out of place, but dear
   Because the lips are no more here.

3. They are such dear, familiar feet that go
   Along the path with ours—feet fast or slow,
   And trying to keep pace—if they mistake
   Or tread upon some flower that we would take
   Upon our breast, or bruise some reed,
   Or crush poor hope until it bleed,
   We may be mute,
   Not turning quickly to impute
   Grave fault; for they and we
   Have such a little way to go—can be

Together such a little while along the way—
We will be patient while we may.

4. So many little faults we find,
We see them; for not blind
Is love. We see them, but if you and I
Perhaps remember them some by and by,
They will not be
Faults then—grave faults—to you and me,
But just odd ways, mistakes, or even less—
Remembrances to bless.
Days change so many things; yes, hours,
We see so differently in suns and showers—
Mistaken words to-night
May be cherished by to-morrow's light.
We may be patient; for we know
There's such a little way to go.

—*Selected.*

THE ADVANTAGES OF A TASTE FOR NATURAL HISTORY

> "*Ask now the beasts, and they shall teach thee;*
> *And the fowls of the air, and they shall tell thee;*
> *Or speak to the earth, and it shall teach thee;*
> *And the fishes of the sea shall declare unto thee.*"

1. When a young person who has enjoyed the benefit of a liberal education, instead of leading a life of indolence, dissipation, or vice, employs himself in studying the marks of infinite wisdom and goodness, which are manifested in every part of the visible creation, we know not which we ought most to congratulate, the public or the individual.

2. Self-taught naturalists are often found to make no little progress in knowledge, and to strike many new lights, by the mere aid of original genius and patient application. But the well-educated youth engages in these pursuits with peculiar advantage. He takes more comprehensive views, is able to consult a greater variety of authors, and from the early habits of his mind, is more accurate and more methodical in all his investigations.

3. The world at large, therefore, can not fail to be benefited by his labors; and the value of the enjoyments, which at the same time he secures to himself, is beyond all calculation. No tedious, vacant hour ever makes him wish for, he knows not what; complain, he knows not why. Never does a restless impatience at having nothing to do compel him to seek a momentary stimulus to his dormant powers in the tumultuous pleasures of the intoxicating cup, or the agitating suspense of the game of chance.

4. Whether he be at home or abroad, in every different clime, and in every season of the year, universal nature is before him, and invites him to a banquet richly replenished with whatever can invigorate his understanding, or gratify his mental taste. The earth on which he treads, the air in which he moves, the sea along the margin of which he walks, all teem with objects that keep his attention perpetually awake, excite him to healthy activity, and charm him with an ever-varying succession of the beautiful, the wonderful, the useful, and the new.

5. And if, in conformity with the direct tendency of such occupations, he rises from the creature to the Creator, and considers the duties which naturally result from his own situation and rank in this vast system of being, he will derive as much satisfaction from the anticipation of the future, as from the experience of the present, and the recollection of the past.

6. The mind of the pious naturalist is always cheerful, always animated with the noblest and most benign feelings. Every repeated observation, every unexpected discovery, directs his thoughts

to the great Source of all order and all good, and harmonizes all his faculties with the general voice of nature.

> "The men
> Whom nature's works can charm, with God Himself
> Hold converse; grow familiar, day by day,
> With His conceptions; act upon His plan,
> And form to His the relish of their souls."
>
> —*Wood.*

FROM "THE DESERTED VILLAGE"

"Chance and change are busy ever."

1. Sweet Auburn! loveliest village of the plain,
   Where health and plenty cheered the laboring swain,
   Where smiling spring its earliest visit paid,
   And parting summer's lingering blooms delayed;
   Dear, lovely bowers of innocence and ease,
   Seats of my youth, when every sport could please,
   How often have I loitered o'er thy green,
   Where humble happiness endeared each scene!
   How often have I paused on every charm,—
   The sheltered cot, the cultivated farm,
   The never-failing brook, the busy mill,
   The decent church that topped the neighboring hill,
   The hawthorne bush, with seats beneath the shade,
   For talking age and whispering lovers made!

2. Sweet was the sound, when oft, at evening's close,
   Up yonder hill the village murmur rose;
   There, as I passed with careless steps and slow,
   The mingling notes came softened from below,—
   The swain, responsive as the milkmaid sung;

The sober herd, that lowed to meet their young;
The noisy geese, that gabbled o'er the pool;
The playful children just let loose from school;
The watchdog's voice that bayed the whispering wind;
And the loud laugh that spoke the vacant mind;—

3. These all in sweet confusion sought the shade,
And filled each pause the nightingale had made.
But now the sounds of population fail,
No cheerful murmurs fluctuate in the gale,
No busy steps the grass-grown footway tread,
But all the bloomy flush of life is fled,—
All but yon widowed, solitary thing,
That feebly bends beside the plashy spring;
She, wretched matron, forced in age, for bread,
To strip the brook with mantling cresses spread,
To pick her wintry fagot from the thorn,
To seek her nightly shed, and weep till morn;—
She only, left of all the harmless train,
The sad historian of the pensive plain.

4. Near yonder copse, where once the garden smiled,
And still where many a garden flower grows wild;
There, where a few torn shrubs the place disclose,
The village preacher's modest mansion rose.
A man he was to all the country dear,
And passing rich with forty pounds a year.
Remote from towns he ran his godly race,
Nor e'er had changed, nor wished to change his place;
Unskillful he to fawn, or seek for power,
By doctrines fashioned to the varying hour;
Far other aims his heart had learned to prize,
More bent to raise the wretched than to rise.

5. His house was known to all the vagrant train;
   He chid their wanderings, but relieved their pain:
   The long-remembered beggar was his guest,
   Whose beard descending swept his aged breast;
   The ruined spendthrift, now no longer proud,
   Claimed kindred there, and had his claims allowed;
   The broken soldier, kindly bade to stay,
   Sat by his fire, and talked the night away;
   Wept o'er his wounds, or tales of sorrow done,
   Shouldered his crutch, and showed how fields were won.
   Pleased with his guests, the good man learned to glow,
   And quite forgot their vices in their woe,
   Careless their merits or their faults to scan,
   His pity gave ere charity began.

6. Thus to relieve the wretched was his pride,
   And e'en his failings leaned to virtue's side;
   But in his duty prompt at every call,
   He watched and wept, he prayed and felt for all:
   And, as a bird each fond endearment tries,
   To tempt its new-fledged offspring to the skies,
   He tried each art, reproved each dull delay,
   Allured to brighter worlds, and led the way.

7. Beside the bed where parting life was laid,
   And sorrow, guilt, and pain, by turns dismayed,
   The reverend champion stood. At his control,
   Despair and anguish fled the struggling soul;
   Comfort came down, the trembling wretch to raise,
   And his last faltering accents whispered praise.

8. At church with meek and unaffected grace,
   His looks adorned the venerable place;

Truth from his lips prevailed with double sway,
And fools, who came to scoff, remained to pray.
The service past, around the pious man,
With steady zeal, each honest rustic ran,
E'en children followed with endearing wile,
And plucked his gown, to share the good man's smile.
His ready smile a parent's warmth expressed;
Their welfare pleased him, and their care distressed;
To them his heart, his love, his griefs were given,
But all his serious thoughts had rest in heaven;—
As some tall cliff that lifts its awful form,
Swells from the vale, and midway leaves the storm,
Though round its breast the rolling clouds are spread,
Eternal sunshine settles on its head.

9. Beside yon straggling fence that skirts the way
With blossomed furze unprofitably gay,
There in his noisy mansion, skilled to rule,
The village master taught his little school.
A man severe he was, and stern to view;
I knew him well, and every truant knew;
Well had the boding tremblers learned to trace
The day's disasters in his morning face;
Full well they laughed with counterfeited glee
At all his jokes,—for many a joke had he;
Full well the busy whisper circling round,
Conveyed the dismal tidings when he frowned.

10. Yet he was kind, or if severe in aught,
The love he bore to learning was in fault;
The village all declared how much he knew,—
'Twas certain he could write, and cipher, too;
Lands he could measure, terms and tides presage,

And e'en the story ran that he could gauge.
In arguing, too, the parson owned his skill;
For e'en though vanquished, he could argue still;
While words of learned length, and thundering sound,
Amazed the gazing rustics ranged around,—
And still they gazed, and still the wonder grew,
That one small head could carry all he knew.
But past is all his fame. The very spot
Where many a time he triumphed is forgot.

11. Near yonder thorn that lifts its head on high,
Where once the signpost caught the passing eye,
Low lies that house where nut-brown draughts inspired,
Where gray-beard mirth and smiling toil retired,
Where village statesmen talked with looks profound,
And news much older than their ale went round.
Imagination fondly stoops to trace
The parlor splendors of that festive place,—
The whitewashed wall, the nicely sanded floor,
The varnished clock, that clicked behind the door;
The chest contrived a double debt to pay,—
A bed by night, a chest of drawers by day,
The pictures placed for ornament and use,
The twelve good rules, the royal game of goose;
The hearth—except when winter chilled the day
With aspen boughs, and flowers, and fennel gray;
While broken teacups, wisely kept for show,
Ranged o'er the chimney, glistened in a row.

12. Vain, transitory splendor! could not all
Reprieve the tottering mansion from its fall?
Obscure it sinks, nor shall it more impart
An hour's importance to the poor man's heart,

Thither no more the peasant shall repair,
To sweet oblivion of his daily care;
No more the farmer's news, the barber's tale,
No more the woodman's ballad shall prevail;
No more the smith his dusky brow shall clear,
Relax his ponderous strength, and lean to hear;
The host himself no longer shall be found
Careful to see the mantling bliss go round.
Nor the coy maid, half willing to be pressed,
Shall kiss the cup to pass it to the rest.

13. Yes! let the rich deride, the proud disdain,
These simple blessings of the lowly train;
To me more dear, congenial to my heart,
One native charm, than all the gloss of art:
Spontaneous joys, where nature has its play,
The soul adopts, and owns their first-born sway;
Lightly they frolic o'er the vacant mind,
Unenvied, unmolested, unconfined.
But the long pomp, the midnight masquerade,
With all the freaks of wanton wealth arrayed,—
In these, ere triflers half their wish obtain,
The toiling pleasure sickens into pain;
And e'en while fashion's brightest arts decoy,
The heart, distrusting, asks if this be joy.
Ye friends to truth, ye statesmen who survey
The rich man's joys increase, the poor's decay!
'Tis yours to judge how wide the limits stand
Between a splendid and a happy land.
—*Oliver Goldsmith.*

Figures and Expression

Give the standard formula of expression for this poem.
Select and classify the figures of speech.

"BLESSED ARE THEY THAT MOURN"

*"Blessed are they that mourn:
for they shall be comforted."*

1. O, deem not they are blest alone
   Whose lives a peaceful tenor keep;
   The Power who pities man, has shown
   A blessing for the eyes that weep.

2. The light of smiles shall fill again
   The lids that overflow with tears;
   And weary hours of woe and pain
   Are promises of happier years.

3. There is a day of sunny rest
   For every dark and troubled night;
   And grief may bide, an evening guest,
   But joy shall come with early light.

4. And thou, who, o'er thy friend's low bier
   Sheddest the bitter drops like rain,
   Hope that a brighter, happier sphere
   Will give him to thy arms again.

5. Nor let the good man's trust depart,
   Though life its common gifts deny,
   Though with a pierced and bleeding heart,
   And spurned of men, he goes to die.

6. For God has marked each sorrowing day,
   And numbered every secret tear,
   And heaven's long age of bliss shall pay
   For all His children suffer here.

—William Cullen Bryant.

A SUMMER MORNING

> *"In them hath He set a tabernacle for the sun, which is as a bridegroom coming out of his chamber, and rejoiceth as a strong man to run a race."*

1. The meek-eyed morn appears, mother of dews,
   At first faint gleaming in the dappled east:
   Till far o'er ether spreads the widening glow;
   And from before the luster of her face,
   White break the clouds away. With quickened step,
   Brown Night retires; young Day pours in space,
   And opens all the lawny prospect wide.

2. The dripping rock, the mountain's misty top,
   Swell on the sight, and brighten with the dawn.
   Blue, through the dusk, the smoking currents shine;
   And from the bladed field the fearful hare
   Limps awkward; while along the forest glade
   The wild deer trip, and often, turning, gaze
   At early passenger.

3.   Music awakes
   The native voice of undissembled joy,
   And thick around the woodland hymns arise.
   Roused by the cock, the soon-clad shepherd leaves
   His mossy cottage, where with Peace he dwells;
   And from the crowded fold, in order, drives
   His flock to taste the verdure of the morn.

4. Falsely luxurious, will not man awake,
   And springing from the bed of sloth, enjoy
   The cool, the fragrant, and the silent hour,
   To meditation due and sacred song?

For is there aught in sleep can charm the wise?
To be in dead oblivion, losing half
The fleeting moments of too short a life;
Total extinction of the enlightened soul!
Or else to feverish vanity alive,
Wildered, and tossing through distempered dreams?
Who would in such a gloomy state remain
Longer than nature craves; when every muse,
And every blooming pleasure wait without,
To bless the wildly devious morning walk?

5. But yonder comes the powerful king of day,
Rejoicing in the east, The lessening cloud,
The kindling azure, and the mountain's brow
Illumed with fluid gold, his near approach
Betoken glad. Lo, now, apparent all,
Aslant the dew-bright earth, and colored air,
He looks in boundless majesty abroad,
And sheds the shining day, that burnished plays
On rocks, and hills, and towers, and wandering streams,
High gleaming from afar.

6.   Prime cheerer, Light!
Of all material beings first, and best!
Efflux divine! Nature's resplendent robe!
Without whose vesting beauty all were wrapt
In unessential gloom. And thou, O Sun!
Soul of surrounding worlds! in whom best seen
Shines out thy Maker! may I sing of thee?
'Tis by thy secret, strong, attractive force,
As with a chain indissoluble bound,
Thy system rolls entire; from the far bourn
Of utmost Saturn, wheeling wide his round
Of thirty years, to Mercury, whose disk

Can scarce be caught by philosophic eye,
Lost in the near effulgence of thy blaze.

7. Informer of the planetary train!
Without whose quickening glance their cumbrous orbs
Were but unlovely mass, inert and dead,
And not, as now, the green abodes of life;
How many forms of being wait on thee,
Inhaling spirit, from the unfettered mind,
By thee sublimed, down to the daily race,
The mixing myriads of thy setting beam.

8. The vegetable world is also thine,
Parent of seasons! who the pomp precede
That waits thy throne, as through thy vast domain,
Annual, along the bright ecliptic road,
In world-rejoicing state, it moves sublime.
Meantime the expecting nations, circled gay
With all the various tribes of foodful earth,
Implore thy bounty, or send grateful up
A common hymn; while, round thy beaming ear,
High seen, the seasons lead, in sprightly dance
Harmonious knit, the rosy-fingered hours,
The zephyrs floating loose, the timely rains,
Of bloom ethereal, the light-footed dews,
And, softened into joy, the surly storms.
These, in successive turn, with lavish hand,
Shower every beauty, every fragrance shower,
Herbs, flowers, and fruits; till, kindling at thy touch,
From land to land is flushed the vernal year.
—*Thomson.*

Figures of Speech
Select and classify the figures in this poem.

GOD'S DOMINION AND MAN'S DEPENDENCE

1. The earth is the Lord's, and the fullness thereof;
The world and they that dwell therein.
For He hath founded it upon the seas,
And established it upon the floods.

2. Who shall ascend into the hill of the Lord?
Or who shall stand in His holy place?
He that hath clean hands and a pure heart;
Who hath not lifted up his soul unto vanity,
Nor sworn deceitfully.
He shall receive the blessing from the Lord,
And righteousness from the God of his salvation.
This is the generation of them that seek Him,
That seek Thy face, O Jacob.

3. Lift up your heads, O ye gates;
And be ye lift up, ye everlasting doors;
And the King of Glory shall come in.
Who is this King of Glory?
The Lord, strong and mighty,
The Lord, mighty in battle.

4. Lift up your heads, O ye gates;
Even lift them up, ye everlasting doors;
And the King of Glory shall come in.
Who is this King of Glory?
The Lord of hosts,
He is the King of Glory.

5. Lord, Thou hast been our dwelling place
In all generations.
Before the mountains were brought forth,

Or ever Thou hadst formed the earth and the world,
Even from everlasting to everlasting, Thou art God.

6. Thou turnest man to destruction,
   And sayest, "Return, ye children of men."
   For a thousand years in Thy sight
   Are but as yesterday when it is past,
   And as a watch in the night.

7. Thou carriest them away as with a flood; they are as a sleep:
   In the morning they are like grass which groweth up.
   In the morning it flourisheth, and groweth up;
   In the evening it is cut down, and withereth.

8. For we are consumed by Thine anger,
   And by Thy wrath are we troubled.
   Thou hast set our iniquities before Thee,
   Our secret sins in the light of Thy countenance.

9. For all our days are passed away in Thy wrath:
   We spend our years as a tale that is told.
   The days of our years are threescore years and ten;
   And if by reason of strength they be fourscore years,
   Yet is their strength labor and sorrow;
   For it is soon cut off and we fly away.

10. Who knoweth the power of Thine anger?
    Even according to Thy fear, so is Thy wrath.
    So teach us to number our days,
    That we may apply our hearts unto wisdom.

—*Psalms 24 and 90.*

GOD IS EVERYWHERE

> "'Do not I fill heaven and earth?'
> saith the Lord.''

1. O! show me where is He,
    The high and holy One,
    To whom thou bend'st the knee,
    And pray'st, "Thy will be done!"
    I hear thy song of praise,
    And lo! no *form* is near;
    Thine *eyes* I see thee raise,
    But where doth God appear?
O! teach me who is God, and where His glories shine,
That I may kneel and pray, and call *thy* Father *mine.*

2. "Gaze on that arch above;
    The glittering vault admire.
    Who taught those orbs to move?
    Who lit their ceaseless fire?
    Who guides the moon to run
    In silence through the skies?
    Who bids that dawning sun
    In strength and beauty rise?
There view immensity! behold! my God is there:
The sun, the moon, the stars, His majesty declare.

3. "See where the *mountains* rise;
    Where thundering *torrents* foam;
    Where, veil'd in towering skies,
    The *eagle* makes his home;
    Where savage nature dwells,
    My God is present, too;
    Through all His wildest dells
    His footsteps I pursue;

He reared those giant cliffs, supplies that dashing stream,
Provides the daily food which stills the wild bird's scream.

    4. "Look on that world of *waves,*
        Where finny nations glide;
        Within whose deep, dark caves
        The ocean monsters hide;
        His power is sovereign there,
        To raise, to quell the storm;
        The *depths* His bounty share,
        Where sport the scaly swarm;
Tempests and calms obey the same almighty voice
Which rules the earth and skies, and bids far worlds rejoice.

    5. "No human thoughts can soar
        Beyond His boundless might;
        He swells the thunder's roar,
        He spreads the wings of night.
        O! praise His works divine!
        Bow down thy soul in prayer;
        Nor ask for other sign
        That God is everywhere;
The viewless Spirit! He—immortal, holy, blest;
O, worship Him in faith, and find eternal rest!"

                                            —*Anonymous.*

WORK AWAY

"Work, for the night cometh when no man can work."

1. Work away!
   For the Master's eye is on us,
   Never off us, still upon us,
      Night and day.
      Work away!
   Keep the busy fingers plying,
   Keep the ceaseless shuttles flying;
      See that never thread lie wrong;
   Let not clash or clatter round us,
   Sound of whirring wheels confound us;
      Steady hand! let woof be strong
      And firm, that has to last so long!
      Work away!

2. Keep upon the anvil ringing
      Stroke of hammer; on the gloom
      Set 'twixt cradle and 'twixt tomb
   Shower of fiery sparkles flinging;
      Keep the mighty furnace glowing;
      Keep the red ore hissing, flowing
   Swift within the ready mold;
      See that each one than the old
   Still be fitter, still be fairer
   For the servant's use, and rarer
      For the Master to behold:
      Work away!

3. Work away!
   For the Leader's eye is on us,
   Never off us, still upon us,
      Night and day.

Wide the trackless prairies round us,
Dark and unsunned woods surround us,
Deep and savage mountains bound us;
    Far away
Smile the soft savannas green,
Rivers sweep and roll between:
    Work away!

4. Bring your axes, woodmen true;
Smite the forest till the blue
Of heaven's sunny eye looks through
Every wild and tangled glade;
Jungled swamp and thicket shade
    Give to-day!
O'er the torrents fling your bridges,
Pioneers! Upon the ridges
    Widen, smooth the rocky stair—
They that follow, far behind,
Coming after us, will find
    Surer, easier footing there;
Heart to heart, and hand to hand,
From the dawn to dusk of day,
    Work away!
Scouts upon the mountain peak—
Ye that see the promised land,
    Hearten us! for ye can speak
Of the country ye have scanned,
    Far away!

5.   Work away!
For the Father's eye is on us,
Never off us, still upon us,
    Night and day.

WORK AND PRAY!
Pray! and work will be completer;
Work! and prayer will be the sweeter;
Love! and prayer and work the fleeter
    Will ascend upon their way.
Fear not lest the busy finger
  Weave a net the soul to stay;
Give her wings—she will not linger;
  Soaring to the source of day;
Cleaving clouds that still divide us
  From the azure depths of rest,
She will come again! beside us,
  With the sunshine on her breast,
Sit, and sing to us, while quickest
  On their task the fingers move,
While the outward din wars thickest,
  Songs that she hath heard above.

6. Live in future as in present;
  Work for both while yet the day
Is our own! for lord and peasant,
  Long and bright as summer's day,
Cometh, yet more sure, more pleasant,
  Cometh soon our holiday;
    Work away!

—Selected.

ABSALOM

"Deal gently for my sake with the young man, even with Absalom."

1. The waters slept. Night's silvery veil hung low
On Jordan's bosom, and the eddies curled
Their glassy rings beneath it, like the still,
Unbroken beating of the sleeper's pulse.
The reeds bent down the stream; the willow leaves,
With a soft cheek upon the lulling tide,
Forgot the lifting winds; and the long stems,
Whose flowers the water, like a gentle nurse,
Bears on its bosom, quietly gave way,
And leaned, in graceful attitudes, to rest.

2. How strikingly the course of nature tells,
By its light heed of human suffering,
That it was fashioned for a happier world!

3. King David's limbs were weary. He had fled
From far Jerusalem; and now he stood,
With his faint people, for a little rest
Upon the shore of Jordan. The light wind
Of morn was stirring, and he bared his brow
To its refreshing breath; for he had worn
The mourner's covering, and had not felt
That he could see his people until now.
They gathered round him on the fresh, green bank,
And spoke their kindly words; and, as the sun
Rose up in heaven, he knelt among them there,
And bowed his head upon his hands to pray.

4. O! when the heart is full—when bitter thoughts
Come crowding thickly up for utterance,
And the poor, common words of courtesy

Are such a very mockery—how much
The bursting heart may pour itself in prayer!

5. He prayed for Israel; and his voice went up
Strongly and fervently. He prayed for those
Whose love had been his shield; and his deep tones
Grew tremulous. But O! for Absalom—
For his estranged, misguided Absalom—
The proud, bright being who had burst away,
In all his princely beauty, to defy
The heart that cherished him—for him he poured,
In agony that would not be controlled,
Strong supplication, and forgave him there,
Before his God, for his deep sinfulness.

6. The pall was settled. He who slept beneath
Was straightened for the grave; and as the folds
Sunk to the still proportions, they betrayed
The matchless symmetry of Absalom.
His hair was yet unshorn, and silken curls
Were floating round the tassels, as they swayed
To the admitted air, as glossy now
As when, in hours of gentle dalliance, bathing
The snowy fingers of Judea's girls.

7. His helm was at his feet; his banner, soiled
With trailing through Jerusalem, was laid,
Reversed, beside him; and the jeweled hilt,
Whose diamonds lit the passage of his blade,
Rested, like mockery, on his covered brow.

8. The soldiers of the king trod to and fro,
Clad in the garb of battle; and their chief,
The mighty Joab, stood beside the bier,

And gazed upon the dark pall steadfastly,
As if he feared the slumberer might stir.
A slow step startled him. He grasped his blade
As if the trumpet rang; but the bent form
Of David entered, and he gave command,
In a low tone, to his few followers,
And left him with his dead.

9. The king stood still
Till the last echo died; then, throwing off
The sackcloth from his brow, and laying back
The pall from the still features of his child,
He bowed his head upon him, and broke forth
In the resistless eloquence of woe:

10. "Alas! my noble boy, that thou should'st die!
Thou, who wert made so beautifully fair!
That death should settle in thy glorious eye,
And leave his stillness in this clustering hair.
How could he mark thee for the silent tomb—
My proud boy, Absalom!

11. "Cold is thy brow, my son! and I am chill,
As to my bosom I have tried to press thee!
How was I wont to feel my pulses thrill,
Like a rich harp-string, yearning to caress thee,
And hear thy sweet *'My father!'* from these dumb
And cold lips, Absalom!

12. "The grave hath won thee. I shall hear the gush
Of music, and the voices of the young;
And life shall pass me in the mantling blush,

And the dark tresses to the soft winds flung;
But thou no more, with thy sweet voice, shalt come
   To meet me, Absalom!

13. "And, O! when I am stricken, and my heart,
   Like a bruised reed, is waiting to be broken,
How will its love for thee, as I depart,
   Yearn for thine ear to drink its last deep token!
It were so sweet, amid death's gathering gloom,
   To see thee, Absalom!

14. "And now farewell! 'Tis hard to give thee up,
   With death so like a gentle slumber on thee—
And thy dark sin!—O, I could drink the cup,
   If from this woe its bitterness had won thee.
May God have called thee, like a wanderer, home,
   My erring Absalom!"

15. He covered up his face, and bowed himself
   A moment on his child; then, giving him
   A look of melting tenderness, he clasped
   His hands convulsively, as if in prayer;
   And, as if strength were given him of God,
   He rose up calmly, and composed the pall
   Firmly and decently, and left him there,
   As if his rest had been a breathing sleep.
             —*Nathaniel Parker Willis.*

THE BLIND PREACHER

"An eloquent man and mighty in the Scriptures."

1. It was one Sunday, as I traveled through the county of Orange, that my eye was caught by a cluster of horses tied near a ruinous old wooden house in the forest, not far from the roadside. Having frequently seen such objects before, in traveling through these States, I had no difficulty in understanding that this was a place of religious worship. Devotion alone should have stopped me, to join in the duties of the congregation; but I must confess that curiosity to hear the preacher of such a wilderness was not the least of my motives.

2. On entering, I was struck with his preternatural appearance. He was a tall and very spare old man; his head, which was covered with a white linen cap, his shriveled hands, and his voice, were all shaking under the influence of a palsy; and a few moments ascertained to me that he was totally blind.

3. The first emotions that touched my breast were those of mingled pity and veneration; but, ah! how soon were all my feelings changed! It was a day of the administration of the Sacrament; and his subject, of course, was the passion of our Saviour.

4. I had heard the subject handled a thousand times; I had thought it exhausted long ago. Little did I suppose that, in the wild woods of America, I was to meet with a man whose eloquence would give to this topic a new and more sublime pathos than I had ever before witnessed.

5. As he descended from the pulpit to distribute the mystic symbols, there was a peculiar, a more than human solemnity in his air and manner, which made my blood run cold and my whole frame shiver. He then drew a picture of the sufferings of our Saviour: His trial before Pilate, His ascent up Calvary, His crucifixion, and His death.

6. I knew the whole history; but never, until then, had I heard the circumstances so selected, so arranged, so colored! It was all new, and I seemed to have heard it for the first time in my life. His enunciation was so deliberate that his voice trembled on every syllable; and every heart in the assembly trembled in unison.

7. His peculiar phrases had that force of description that the original scene appeared to be at that moment acting before our eyes. We saw the upturned faces—the staring, frightful distortions of malice and rage; we saw the buffet. My soul kindled with a flame of indignation, and my hands were involuntarily and convulsively clinched.

8. But when he came to touch on the patience, the forgiving meekness of our Saviour; when he drew to the life His blessed eyes streaming in tears to heaven, His voice breathing to God a soft and gentle prayer of pardon on His enemies—"Father, forgive them, for they know not what they do!"—the voice of the preacher, which had all along faltered, grew fainter and fainter, until, his utterance being entirely obstructed by the force of his feelings, he raised his handkerchief to his eyes, and burst into a loud and irrepressible flood of grief.

9. The effect was inconceivable. The whole house resounded with the mingled groans, and sobs, and shrieks of the congregation. It was some time before the tumult had subsided so far as to permit him to proceed.

10. Indeed, judging by the usual but fallacious standard of my own weakness, I began to be very uneasy for the situation of the preacher. For I could not conceive how he would be able to let his audience down from the height to which he had wound them, without impairing the solemnity and dignity of his subject; or, perhaps, shocking them by the abruptness of the fall. But, no; the descent was as beautiful and sublime as the elevation had been rapid and enthusiastic.

11. The first sentence with which he broke the awful silence was a quotation from Rousseau: "Socrates died like a philosopher, but Jesus Christ like a God!" I despair of giving you any idea of the effect produced by this short sentence, unless you could perfectly conceive the whole manner of the man as well as the peculiar crisis in the discourse. Never before did I completely understand what Demosthenes meant by laying such stress on *delivery*.
—*William Wirt.*

TEACH Services, Inc.
P U B L I S H I N G

We invite you to view the complete
selection of titles we publish at:
www.TEACHServices.com

We encourage you to write us
with your thoughts about this,
or any other book we publish at:
info@TEACHServices.com

TEACH Services' titles may be purchased in
bulk quantities for educational, fund-raising,
business, or promotional use.
bulksales@TEACHServices.com

Finally, if you are interested in seeing
your own book in print, please contact us at:
publishing@TEACHServices.com

We are happy to review your manuscript at no charge.

www.ingramcontent.com/pod-product-compliance
Lightning Source LLC
Chambersburg PA
CBHW070932230426
43666CB00011B/2417